AF516613

PREHISTORY AND PROTOHISTORY OF EASTERN INDIA

(With Special Reference to Orissa)

PREHISTORY AND PROTOHISTORY OF EASTERN INDIA

(With Special Reference to Orissa)

Milan K. Chauley

AGAM KALA PRAKASHAN
NEW DELHI

First Published 2008

ISBN : 81-7320-065-3

Published by
Dr. Agam Prasad, M.A., Ph.D., Diploma in Museology
For **Agam Kala Prakashan**
34, Central Market, Ashok Vihar,
Delhi-110 052.
Ph. : 27212195, 65688806-7

Composed by
Elegant Printographics
319, IIIrd Floor, R. G. Complex,
Sector-14, Rohini, Delhi-110085

Printed by
Chawla Offset Printers
Delhi-110052.

Printed in India

Dedicated to my teachers :

Dr. V.N. Mishra
Dr. Amrandra Nath
Dr. D.K. Bhattacharya
&
Dr. K.K. Basa

FOREWORD

It gives me great pleasure to write the foreword to the labour of love of a person who had been a student of mine. Shree Milan K. Chauley has certainly shown extreme courage and deft expertise in bringing together various reports within a structural frame in order to develop what may be one of the rare attempts of regional archaeology in India.

Some time back Prof. Basudev Narain from Patna gave me the honour to write a foreword to his mammoth compilation titled *Archaeology of Bihar*. I remember having strongly advocated for regional archaeology at that time. Milan's work will show that my call did not go unheard.

If we allow ourselves to transcend from the level of a chronicler of events, we can at once see that every action of man is essentially aimed towards seeking adaptation within agiven environmental situation. Dichronically, therefore, one can demonstrate the constant effort of optimization of efficiency for successful adaptation. The choices made by a community are historically provided in the form of ingrained attributes of cognition. Thus, a specific form and technique of making a tool does not show any change for generations. Under the samelogic India should provide atleast eight different regional cultures because it maintains as many different ecozones. In Europe the countries are small and are situation in more or less similar environment. Yet one could successfully demonstrate that handane and cleavers are altogether rare in Central Europe. Thus, even the name of the earliest Lower Palaeolithic tradition viz., *Acheulian* is not used anywhere east of the Rhine.

Arguing along the same line one can certainly expect entirely different developments in different parts of India. Yet we seem to be too much in a hurry to create a monolithic macro pattern of succession for India as a whole. Certainly this would require the data to be trimmed at the edges to fit in a pre-determined slot. Developing regional archaeology, as such, would be the most important step we should undertake for understanding the complex and diverse nature of our prehistoric past. The present volume of Milan, therefore, fulfills a need of the hour. Even Prof. Sankhalia found it difficult to construct a clear- cut chapter called Neolithic India in his earlier book. This is because in the region lying south of the Godavari and north of Krishna we have Chalcolithic following a poorly developed Mesolithic. Ofcourse it is a different matter if some early layers within these Chalcolithic occurrences could be designed as pre-metal and hence Neolithic.

Consequently, if a region is taken as the universe of study then such and many other issues can be much more clearlyviewed. Indian archaeology shows numerous zones with distinctly different trends. Subbarao was the first among the earlier generation of archaeologyists who suggested some broad palaeo-cultural zones. One of the zones, which were identified by him as the most populous center of activity, was the Chattisgarh-Chhotanagpur region. Milan brings the adjoining region of Orissa into focus.

It is a very comprehensive work and records the details of almost all culturally significant occurrences. I am sure Milan will, some day in future, undertake a critical analysis to understand the differential character of the Coastal Orissa with Burhapahar and its extension in Srikakulam of Andhra Pradesh. May be Sulabdihi and Golbai Sasan at once will appear as two distinct varieties of imperatives operating broadly in two different ecosystems.

Prof. D. K. Bhattacharya
Retired Professor
Deptt. of Anthropology
University of Delhi
Delhi

PREFACE

Prehistory and Protohistory is a fascinating subject, which deals with the dawn of human cultures and its subsequent development through millions of year.

Prehistory as a subject has always been a hard nut to crack for me. Though, I had my masters from one of the most revered institutions in India and abroad i.e. Deccan college. I was a student of general Archaeology there. But in the first year as foundation course we were taught all the basics that an archaeologist needs to know, whether belonging to the field of Prehistory, Art, Architecture or Iconography. After joining the Institute of Archaeology, where we were taught all the branches of archaeology, here, I realized that all that I had learnt in Deccan College came handy, when in field. I always had an edge, when it came to field archaeology, especially when studying the artifacts and the ecofacts available at the site. Then in co-relating the past data with the present (ethnographical investigations) and interpreting the past, which became much easier.

As I had an aversion for Prehistory, especially remembering names of different tools and cultures while studying the European and African Prehistory, it gave me nightmares. This reminds me of the same feeling that I shared for mathematics when in school. My Director (Dr. Amrender Nath) was very much aware of this and one day suddenly, as if like a bolt from the blue I was assigned the topic of my dissertation "Pre and Proto

History of Orissa". I felt a numbness take over me. I went to the Director and pleaded, begged to get my topic changed but it was all like "singing to a deaf man" and I had to work on it.

As days passed by, I gradually started collecting materials. The saying from the book 'Alchemist' came true for me i.e. "If a man truly desires to achieve some thing then the whole universe conspires against him to get it for him", for help poured in from friends in the Institute of Archaeology in Deccan college, my uncles in ASI and my dad. As I kept gathering more and more informations, first to grasp the subject and then come to my topic. The subject, which was like bitter gourd for me started fascinating me and I was able to submit my dissertation in time.

After passing out from the institute when I was sitting unemployed. I got an offer to take classes in the Dept. of Archaeology, Utkal University and the topic assigned was "sciences in archaeology". As far as the topic was concerned, being a student of Deccan College it was cutting cheese but to teach was no trifles. But classes had to be taken and it was taken, not for one year but for two consecutive sessions. Besides this I had to teach Field archaeology and Prehistory to the first batch of master's students in the newly opened Dept. of Cultural Heritage and Conservation in Utkal University Culture, also located in Bhubaneswar.

It was a surprise to me, that the subject which I was so scared of, was the most talked, as more and more questions poured in the more interesting the subject became. I saw myself always going to the basics of Archaeology and Prehistory, whether I was talking on Geology, Zooarchaeology, Paleontology, Anthropology or any other sciences in archaeology.

But when I came to Prehistory of Orissa. I realized it was a subject, which has been very little written about, I remember the problems, I faced while collecting materials on it. For there is no comprehensive work on Prehistory of Orissa, what is available is a book written long back but the best till date is, by Dr. G. C. Mahapatra entitled "The Stone Age Cultures in Orissa" leaving this though a dozen or more scholars have done their Ph.D's and M.Phil's on this but they are lingering in the libraries of different Universities, unpublished. Many articles have been written but they are scattered in different journals, periodicals, commemorative and felicitation volumes etc.

In this book, I lay no claim on any direct or first hand research in the field of Pre and Proto History of Orissa. But it is a humble attempt to collect, not all but a few scattered materials on the said topic and bring it out in the form of a text book so as to give a skeletal idea on the subject at a place. An exhaustive bibliography has been made to help scholars and students to refer to detailed information if needed. This book is basically meant for the students of archaeology in particular and people interested in Pre and Proto History of Orissa in general. It shall be very satisfying to me, if this book in any way comes handy to any one in any way.

In compilation of this book I shall first of all like to thank my Director and Teacher Dr. Amrendera Nath for without his authoritarian diction of assigning me the topic, this work would never have seen the daylight.

I am equally thankful to my friends from the Institute of Archaeology and Deccan college especially to Dr. Balram Tripathy, Dr. Anup Mishra, Dr. Swamy Shrestra Panda, Varada Khaladkar, Kalyani Bhave, Piyush Kant Sharma, Subhash Khamari, Madan Lal Meena, Dhiren Sharma and others for their kind help and encouragement.

I am thankful to Sri J.P. Joshi, Dr. K. K. Basa, Sri S.B. Ota, Dr. J.K. Patnaik for their kind guidences in the work. Our Librarian in the Institute of Archaeology and Excavation Bo II for their kind help in getting the references and books.

I shall be failing in my duties if I forget to thank my friend Rupanjan Biswas, who always had been with me like a pillar while drafting work was going on and even in typing its first draft.

I shall be ever grateful to God for having given me such a supportive family, especially a Dad, who not only gave me moral support but being from the same field has always been an guiding force in my career and helped me in all possible way to bring out this book.

I beg apologise from those who have helped me at some point of time in some kind or the other in connection with this work and am unable to acknowledge it individually.

Last but not the least, I would like to thank "Chachu" that is what I call Dr. Agam Prasad of Agam Kala Prakashan for it was he who gave the assurance and took the initiative to see that the book come out to the public in its present form.

Milan Kumar Chauley

LIST OF ILLUSTRATIONS

PLATES

CONTENTS

CHAPTER 1

INTRODUCTION

Prehistory deals with the history of evolution of human being on earth over Millions of years. The Early men were hunter, food gatherer and user of stone artifacts or tools. In short it is the history of mankind in pre-literate stage devoid of any legend, tradition or literature.

As a discipline it seeks to study the culture and society of man before the dawn of history. The specific questions that an archaeologists study are:

(i) The sequence of prehistoric occupation in an area.
(ii) The origin and dispersion of a particular prehistoric population.
(iii) The life ways of the prehistoric people during a given period of time and
(iv) The laws of axioms which govern the socio-cultural evolution of a prehistoric population.

In terms of Geological time scale, the stone age falls in the Quarternary period, which in turn is a part of the Cenozoic Era. Of the total Five Billion years of Earth's history (approximately), Quaternary, period covers some three to four million years only. The period is divided into two epochs – Pleistocene (most recent) and Holocene (entirely new) or post glacial or post Pleistocene. The Pleistocene is of great importance in the study of Stone Age, for its contemporarity with the dawn of human beings.

The bulk of pre-historic materials that have survived the ravages of time are the stone tools (artifacts). The stone tools thus became prominent items (source material) for the reconstruction of the past history of mankind and this became an universal phenomena.

The Researches on Stone Age in India have advanced much beyond the stage of mere collection of artifacts. The main objective is to understand the history of pre-historic man and his behaviour. The study includes the environment in which he lived, his ways of living and the stages in his cultural advancement. Presently pre and proto historic studies has become an inter disciplinary field of investigation.

The initial beginning of the study of Prehistory of India began with discovery of a hand axe by Bruce foot on 30th May 1863 at Pallavaram near Madras and thereafter scholars (both English & Indian) took up the cause to study the history of ancient man in Indian sub-continent. It was only after 1930's that study of Stone Age Cultures began to be taken seriously. In 1930 Burkitt reported on Cammide's stone age tools collected from lower Krishna Valley in South India. He divided it into four series, Series I, Series II, Series III and Series IV, and also attempted to reconstruct the climatic succession for "Indian Pleistocene" period in terms of pluvial and inter-pluvial or wet and dry climatic conditions on the lines of those set for African Pleistocene period by Richardson. In 1939 De-terra and Paterson under the Yale Cambridge Expedition worked out the glacial and inter-glacial chronology for the Kashmir Valley corresponding to that in the Alps and then extended this study across the Pir Panjal Range and Poonch to the Stone Age tool-bearing terrace deposits in the Potwar region and further co-related the Himalayan evidences with that in the Central Narmada basin and as far south as Madras in Peninsular India.

F.E. Zeuner of the Institue of Archaeology, London, University made another landmark contribution to the Stone Age research by undertaking geo-chronological and environmental studies in Gujarat, in Maharashtra, in Uttar Pradesh, in Andhra Pradesh and the coastal region of Tamil Nadu. Many young Indians were trained during this expedition.

Then in 1944 after coming of Mortimer Wheeler Archaeology got a new lease of life. New methods, techniques and a new breed of archaeologists was bread. Even due to his encouragement, universities in the country entered the field. Dr. D. K. Bhattacharya very aptly summerizes his contribution in the following words "Weeler left the country in 1948, but the missionary zeal of the new converts, no matter how few they were was enough to develop a distinct variety of archaeologists in India to whome the time-frame space was the only goal an archaeologist was supposed to serve.

Till the 50's, leaving a few isolated areas, the Lower Palaeolithic culture was directly followed by Mesolithic for there was no clear evidence of any intervening cultural phase. This situation was changed in 1954 when H.D. Sankalia of Deccan College brought out cultural and statigraphical significance of the Middle Palaeolithic industry at Nevasa and this was subsequently established through regional studies.

Till 1972 there was debate over the existence of Upper Paleolithic between Middle Palaeolithic and Mesolithic in Indian context whereas Upper Palaeolithic was discovered by Michael Todd in stratigraphic context in 1939 from Khandivli near Bombay. Though this term was proposed by Sankalia in the International Symposium on Radiocarbon and Indian Archaeology in 1972 on the basis of the finds of blade and burin industry from Andhra Pradesh, Maharashtra, Gujarat and parts of Uttar Pradesh. But this was not accepted. The very next year on the basis of the finds at Patne in Maharashtra, enabled to clear the picture of existence of Upper Palaeolithic stage in the Indian stone age. During this period only a large number of books and journals were also released throwing new light on the subject i.e. 1950 – "Prehistoric India" by Stuart Piggot; "The Culture and Civilization of Ancient India an Historical outline" (1965). D.D. Kosambi, "The personality of India" (1958) Subbarao, "Radio Carbon and Indian Archaeology" (1972) Ghosh and Agarwal; Prehistory and Protohistory of India and Pakistan" (1974). Sankalia; "The Prehistory and Protohistory of the great Indian Desert (1978). Goudie & Hegde; "A Source Book of Indian Archaeology" (1979) Chakravarti; "Chopper –

Chopping Component of Palaeolithic India" (1982), Jaiswal; "The Archaeology of India" (1982) Agarwal, are only a few to name and the important journals were "Puratattva" (1967); "Indian Society for Prehistoric and Quarternary Studies" (1977); "Man and Environment" (1977) and every year the recent researches in the field of Excavation and Exploration are reported in the "Indian Archaeology – A Review", broughtout by the Archaeological Survey of India every year.

Besides this it is seen that the earlier studies in this field were those of Col. Medows Tylor, who in the early 19th century showed interest in South Indian Megaliths. Then in 1863-1885. A.C. Corlleyle discovered Microlithic in the rock-shelters at Mirzapur along with Mesolithic cave paintings. This was the earlier reported cave paintings in the world.

The results of such a move by the doyns on Indian Pre-historic studies and their research are highly fascinating and thus in almost all the States of India, pre-historic remains have been brought to light. The studies and researches are ongoing process and much attention is now-a-days given on micro studies, which generally deals with subjects like climate, environment, flora and fauna, raw materials, their beliefs, rites and rituals etc.

The Discovery of Rock Art, Rock paintings have added another interesting aspects to pre-historic studies, Rock-art has been reported from has been Panchmari, Mirazapur, Adamgarh, Bhimbetka and thereafter Scholars untiring efforts have brought to light the remains of large number of paintings and associated artifacts from throughout the length and breadth of the country covering almost all the states.

Orissa – North Lat 17° 49'/22 ° 54', East Long. – 81 ° 23' and 87 ° 29' has an area of 155845 Sq. k.m. It has 480 km long coastline. The State forms a part of Eastern Ghat hills. Valleys, river plains, plains, rivers, lakes, beaches and tidal flats belonging to different ages and of different dimensions and orientations forms the to pographical features of the state. The nature of the topographical features controls the land use, for example flood plains are suitable for agriculture, high and inaccessible area are suitable for forest development, rivers and lakes are for water resources etc.

In Orissa the cultural succession is primarily based on chronology, so far the absolute dates for Pre-historic cultures in Orissa are not satisfactory, though recent researches have come out with valuable data on different periods of Prehistory and Protohistory to bridge the gap or heat us, still deserves fresh review to bring it at par with national level.

Most parts of Orissa, excepting the coastal strip are covered with hills and forests, which had provided suitable environment for the habitation of primitive man, as primary necessities like food, water and shelter were available in plenty on these hills. Forests of western Orissa, Chattisgarh, South East Bihar formed a single unit in pre-historic period, these areas have been exploited almost similarly by primitive man at different point of times resulting in great akin-ness and similarity in the pre-historic implements that have been reported from Chakradharpur, Chaibasa, Ranchi and Manbhum, with those that are discovered in the hilly regions of Orissa and presently Orissa in the field of prehistory is figuring as one of the most rich States within the union of India. So far Archaeological heritage is concerned it is available right from the appearance of early man and its subsequent development in chronological order from Palaeolithic to Mesolithic to Neolithic to Iron age and then to historical period in a unbroken sequences.

Right from its beginning in the 19th century till to date many scholars and researchers are engaged in unveiling more and more Pre-historic remains from the length and breadth of the state and thus series of artifacts like hand axe, clever, scraper, points, discoid, irregularly flaked pebbles, irregularly flaked biface of the pre historic period, probably used for cutting, chopping, digging and killing of animals etc. are reported on regular basis.

The Old Stone age culture i.e. Palaeolithic period in Orissa is well defined, highlighting the successive stages of stone age culture viz. Lower Palaeolithic, Middle Palaeolithic and Upper Palaeolithic which are at par with rest of the country stratigraphically and typologically.

Mesolithic period too has achieved satisfactory progress and has yielded varieties of micoliths and rock shelters which have been reported from throughout the length and breadth of the State Efforts are going on to highlight and corelate them in proper context with other regions of India.

The Neolithic phase of Orissa is also rich and well established in chronological sequences. The technology of fabrication, especially the Neolithic celts varies from one specific type to another. Again technology being constant, its variation cannot be ruled out. The factors working as parameters depend on the raw materials, the perception and skill of the tool maker and at the same time the dimensions of the raw materials. (Behera – 1989).

The next phase of development is chalcolithic but in Orissa pure chalcolithic assemblage is rare like at Chirand, Pandu-Rajar-Dhibi, Maski etc. till date. Researchers have coined a new terminology for the cultures Neo-Chaleolithic phase, since neoliths and metal were found together both at Golabai, Sankarjung and Kuchai in the excavations.

The Megalithic phase in Orissa is not well defined as it is distinct in Kerala, Karnataka, Maharashtra, Madhya Pradesh etc. Thus, this period deserves more serious review and research through scientific excavation and exploration, classification, analysis of cultural material, interpretation etc.

The historical period of Orissa needs no elaboration as it is well established since long back, its History (6th Century B.C. onwards) Art, Architecture, Religion and Culture is well known to the world..

Due to the adoption of more radical and explicit models by a new generation of archaeologists, the second half of the 20th century witnessed revolutionary changes within archaeological studies and researches. This new breed of archaeologists have defined themselves by arguing in favour of the development of "a science of archaeology". Their research effort intend to go beyond mere cataloging, excavation and historical reconstruction of the past cultures. The study of the past is viewed in terms of socio-cultural processes. Further the adoption of new technologies by these archaeologists affected the methodological realm, as dating technique refined chronologies, spectrographic probes characterised the elemental composition of the material, new methods facilitated innovative research designs and data analysis and field archaeology became increasingly sophisticated, incorporating even more complicated research designs and technologies in Orissa.

However, despite the all round development in the field of research and increase in the number of sites discovered yet enormous gap exists in our knowledge pertaining to the Archaeological record in Orissa. The archaeological record of Orissa is one of immense diversity i.e. formal, temporal and spatial, adding to them is ecological variability and the inter playoff both of indigenous and outside influence in the origin and development of cultures. All this makes Orissa one of the most attractive area for archaeological investigation and much more has to be done especially in the Pre and Protohistoric phase, for it is full of potentialities.

However, painstaking researches of a few scholars in certain isolated areas at different points of time, throw light on the early activities of the pre-historic men here. At present Orissa empitomizes to a great extent the various stages of mans cultural evolution in India.

Herein, and effort has been made to bring together the material on Pre and Proto-historic researches done till date in Orissa, basing on published works of scholars and an attempt made to present a comprehensive picture on the Pre and Proto history of Orissa.

Only a few decades after the pioneering declaration of Bouches-de-perthes in France, Bruce foot made the discovery of a cleaver in a laterift pit at Pallavaram near Madras in the year 1863. While Foot was busy in peninsular India, (V. Jayasal 1978) it was Valintine Ball who laid the foundation of Prehistoric research in Orissa by discovering four stone implements from Dhenkanal, Kaliakata in Angul district, Harichandanpur in Talcher sub-division and Bursapali in the Sambalpur district. He published about his findings in the "Proceedings of the Asiatic Society of Bengal" in the year 1880. He surveyed altogether an area of 240 KM (Mohanty, 1992).

Then after a long gap, in 1923-24, Padmasri Paramanand Acharya, a reputed archaeologist of Orissa, discovered polished stone Celts at Baidipur in Mayurbhanj district (Chand 1923-24). Subsequently R.D. Banerji in 1930 made systematic survey of the Baidipur area and writes "the most important feature of the Baidipur find is association of the Paleolithic with Neolithic and the occurrence of the pottery as well".

In 1939 E.C. Worman (A Harward University Research Scholar) and Acharya explored other Paleolithic and Neolithic sites. At Kuliana they discovered tools occurring in the Laterite bed (Mahapatra 1962, Panigrahi 1981).

A new scientific orientation of Prehistoric research in this region was started by Calcutta University in the year 1939 under the direction of N.K. Bose and Dharani Sen of Anthropology Deptt. Extensive investigation were carried out in Kuliana area, excavation was carried on at places and report was published in 1948 (Sen & Bose 1948). This work broke fresh ground among Indian Prehistorians by studying a Palaeolithic assemblage in the context of geostratigraphic background. All the sites located within a radius of ten miles from Kuliana and spread along both the banks of the Burhabalanga River were studied. It won't be out of the way, here to mention that Kuliana is the first excavated lower Palaeolithic site in India.

Prehistoric investigation was carried on extensively in other parts sof the stale also, leaving aside parts of South Orissa. G.C. Mohapatra's work "The stone age cultures of Orissa" published in the year 1962, stands out prominently. The significance of his work is that, for the first time it has brought to light a succession of Stone Age cultures in Orissa. He demonstrated that the Paleolithic industry extends beyond the frontiers of Mayurbhanj district and flourished over a much larger area. In all he discovered 24 Early stone age sites, 25 Middle stone age and 8 Late stone age sites. His investigations extends over an area of 38,560 Sq. Km. Comprising the district of Mayurbhanj, Keonjher, Sundergarh, Sambalpur and Dhenkanal. His work is pioneering in this field.

During the late 50's and 60's quite a few isolated discovereies of stone age sites have been reported, Microliths from Kanika in talcher sub-division by Ghosh (1958-59), Baramandar, Bonaikala, Danguposi in Keonjher Distt. by Mitra (1961-62), from Tel and its tributaries and from the districts of Bolangir, Ganjam, Kalahandi by Raghunath in 1963 and from Bolangir by Mukherjee in 1968-69.

B.K. Thaper under took excavations at Kuchai to study the Neolithic Cultural sequence and other details. In his report in 1976 he has depicted the two stages of the Neolithic culture viz. a ceramic and the ceramic phases. Kuchai excavation has also divulged the transition of the early man from food gatherer to food producer stage in the region. The evidence relating to the use of rice has also been traced (Thaper 1976, Mohanty,

1992). D. K. Bhattacharya carried out further research in the area where V. Ball undertook research work and Bhattacharya collected more than 1000 Lower Palaeolithic tools from at least 3 more sites proceeding from Balasore to Bangriposi (Bhattachraya, 1996).

S.B. Ota's research in the Phulbani district has revealed thirty open air Mesolithic sites. All these sites have produced a typical Microlithic industry, essentially made of quartz (Ota 1986).

S.K. Mishra's survey in and around Joshipur and Baripada in Mayurbhanj district has brought to light several stone age sites pertaining to Lower Paleolithic to Neolithic phases (Mohanty-Unpublished).

Chakraborty in 1990 discovered many Stone Age sites from the Lower Palaeolithic to the Mesolithic in secondary context, from the area around Kiching in Mayurbhanj district.

S. C. Nanda's exploration between 1975-80 along river Indravati and its tributaries in the eastern part of Koraput district has brought to light 17 Upper Palaeolithic sites and 85 Mesolithic sites. He has tried to explain the occurrence of these sites with the help of ecological and ethnographical models (Mohanty-Unpublished).

The work of Tripathy in the early 70's in southwest Orissa has brought to light several stone age sites from Tel river basin. He discovered three sites of pebble tool industry, sixteen sites giving flake tool industry of Middle Paleolithic culture and 27 sites of flake blade industry covering the district of Phulbani, Bolangir, Kalahandi and Sambalpur.

P.K. Singh's intensive exploration in the 80's brought to light 53 Lower Paleolithic, 6 Mesolithic and 19 Neolithic sites in the Dhenkanal district of central Orissa.

Ratha and Bhattacharya (1988) reported Lower Palaeolithic artifacts are plates from Kuchinda in Wester Orissa. (Rath and Bhattacharya 1988).

H.C. Prusty in Dharamgarh sub-division of Kalahandi district discovered several Lower Paleolithic and Mesolithic sites from the Moter and Behra river basin. Most of the sites occur in the foothill regions.

In the late 80's and 90's systematic survey was carried out by P.K. Behra. He has brought to light many sites of Lower, Middle and Upper Palaeolithic, Mesolithic and Neolithic cultures in the Upper Brahmani

Valley and its tributaries in the district of Sundergarh. His survey in Bonaigarh sub-division has brought to light an important habitation-cum-workshop site called Sulabhdhi belonging to the Neolithic phase.

An important development in prehistoric studies in the 80's was use of ethnographic studies for archaeological inferences (Basa, 1992).

Pradeep Mohanty's archaeological and ethno-archaeological field work for seven seasons between 1983 to 89 in Keonjher district has resulted in the discovery of 58 Mesolithic sites.

R. N. Dash surveyed the evidences of Neolithic Culture in various regions of Orissa (Dash R.N. 1987).

B. K. Sinha of ASI excarated the site of Golabai in Khurda Dist. (Sinha B.K., 1993 – Excavation of Golbai Season, Dist., Puri, Orissa, Puratatva 23 : 48-50).

B. Tripathi's survey in 1996 the area along the Mahanadi and the Saulnki rivers in Boudh district has brought to light 9 Mesolithic sites. All of them are open-air sites and located on alluvial deposits.

Pre-historic relics were also land around Burla in Western orissa (Behera, P.K. 1996).

Extensive exploration in the Baripada, Bisoi, Rairangpur and Karanji tehsils, resulted in the discovery of four Lower Palaeolithic and 9 Mesolithic sites in the Mayurbhanj district. Mostly they are primary in nature and have preserved habitation deposits (Mohanty, Basa and Tripathy 1997).

B.K. Khilar (1998) in the course of his investigation in Panjang region of Dhenkanal district has brought to light several stone age sites belonging to the Lower Palaeolithic, Mesolithic and Neolithic periods (Mohanty Unpublished).

S.Biswal (1998) has brought to light 25 Lower Palaeolithic, 11 Mesolithic and 5 Neolithic sites in Kamakshyanagar region of Dhenkanal district. Many of these sites are primary in nature and have preserved habitational deposits.

Recent researches by the Department of Anthropology, Utkal University has resulted in the discovery of an Iron Age site around Sankerjang, Central Orissa.

During the last two decades a vast number of Stone Age sites are being regularly reported, and these are mostly brought to light in the course of fieldwork carried out by the post graduate student of the Anthropology Department of Utkal University and the History Department of Sambalpur University.

CHAPTER II

GEOGRAPHY AND GEOLOGY

The geographical features have always played an important role in the land use pattern from time immemorial. Human occupation and landuse pattern has always been influenced by the geographical features. Riverbanks, coastal plains, lateritic flat lands have been generally preferred by humans for occupation and settlement. Whereas, it is seen that the sandy areas, hilly areas, shallow region, flood prone low areas etc. were not generally preferred. Generally areas' which provide easy accessibility, flat lands, easy access to water resources, fertile lands were preferred by men for settlement purpose. This is evident from the large number of sites found throughout the world along the fertile bank of mighty rivers and other water bodies.

The state of Orissa lies between 17° 49′ and 22° 34′ North latitude and 81° 23′ and 87° 29′ East longitude on the eastern coast of India. It has 30 districts and occupies an area of 1,55,845 sq kms, out of this 75,125 sq km is covered by the hills and forests. It has a long coastline of 480 km. The state forms part of the eastern gemorphic province of India. On the north it is bounded by the districts of Maidanapur of West Bengal and Singhbhum of Bihar, on the north-west by Ranchi, on the west by the Raipur district of Chattisgarh and on the south by Srikakulam of Andhra Pradesh.

Its gemorpholigical features are the result of 3500 million years of geological history that has affected the rock types and the land forms here. It consits of rocks of Granite, Iron formations, Volconic sediments, protozoic metasediments in north Orissa; coal bearing Gondwanas in central Orissa, high grade granulites, migmatites and geneisses in south Orissa; extensive granites, least distributed Vindhyan sedimntary rocks in west Orissa and the laterites and Quaternary sediments forming the much younger and present plains and plains in the coastal Orissa. The Pre-Cambrian formations have been affected by numerous tectonic movements resulting in folding, faulting and vertical movements of rock masses. Leaving this for centuries the weathering agents have been working to cut, erode and fill the elevations and depressions in the landforms resulting the present land form pattern seen. The geomorphology of Orissa characterizes a NE-SW oriented central axial highland on its either sides and a lowlying coastal plain on the east. (Fig. 1) the rivers originate from the central axial highlands and of these several rivers flows across the central highlands i.e. Mahanadi, Brahmani, Baitaranie from west to east; a few others flows either to the east (Burhabalanga, Salandi, Rushikulya, Nagavallie, Vansdhara) or to the west (Indravati, Kolab river) (Fig. 2). The three mightiest rivers i.e. Mahanadi, Brahmani and Baitarani form a compound delta along the coast (Fig. 3). The largest brackist water lake of Asia, Chilka has developed from the Bay of Bengal.

Geographically, this region is divided into two broad divisions, namely the hills known as the mehals or Garjats and the plain deltaic land (Mahapatra 1962, Thapar 1974) Morphologically it can be divided further into five parts, (a) the coast plains, (b) the middle mountainous country, (c) the rolling uplands, (d) the river valleys and (e) the subdued Plateau.

The Hills

The hill region on the hinterland is a part of Eastern ghat, Vindhya and Chotanagpur hill system in geological formation. The area is thickly forested. It lies between 22° and 34′ and 19° and 2′ North latitude and 82° and 32' and 87° and 11′ East longitude and has an area of 28,125 sq. miles. It is dotted with hill ranges of Bankasamo, Karlapat plateau, Malayagiri, Meghasani, Tikriguri, Mankadnacha, Baplaimali, Badamgarh,

Gandhamardan, Chhelitoka, Thakurani, Tomak, Panchara, Goaldes, Suliya and Kapilas.

The whole region can be divided into three watersheds. The valley of Mahanadi between the two steep peaks like one at Satkasia near Barmula. From the north bank of Mahanadi a hill range runs in north-west to south-east direction forming the boundary between the former states of Baramba and Narasingpur. The watershed formed by the valley of Brahmani is in the middle. On its north is the watershed of Baitarni and on the south is that of the Mahanadi. A range of hills starts from the north bank of the river Brahmani and reaches at Keonjhar. The peaks of this range are 2500 to 3500 feet high. Malayagiri is regarded as the highest peak. The watershed of the Brahmani gradually slopes down to that of Baitarni and it formed the third water shed of the series. The hills of Mayurbhanj rises from the eastern bank of Baitarni and measures 3000 to 4000 feet in height.

The Plains

Orissa has an extensive plain which includes the coast area. The plains lies between the Bay of Bengal and the hilly tracts on the west i.e. from Chilka in the south to Subarnarekha river in the north covering a distance of about 350 km. It is widest around Bhadrak and Cuttack with a thickness of about 75 km and it narrows down towards North East and South West. It roughtly comprises of the coastal districts.

The plains are generally formed by the Tertiary and Quaternary sediments deposited under pluvial, sea marginal morine and Aeolian environments. The various features that can be observed in the plains are Paleo-channels, active channels, recent and Paleo-beaches, beach ridges, tidal flats, spits, mangrove swamps, lakes, extensive alluvial flood palins etc. The eastern portion of this plain, bordering the sea, is mostly plain, but while advancing to the west and along the foothills the surface is almost irrgular and undulating and is covered with the patches of wood here and there.

The alluvial palin is formed due to the silt deposited by the rivers such as the Mahanadi, Suvernarekha, Burhabalanga, Baitarni, Brahmni. Through out the northern part of Orissa there is much similar older alluvium, but to the south of the river Brahmani this is not seen. However the plain can be divided into three divisions : (1) the swampy jungle on the sea face, (2) the fourty miles wide alluvial land and (3) the laterite shelves on the irregular upland margin in the extreme west, bordering the hills.

Sand hills cover a considerable area of the coast. These sand hills are indicative of the gradual recession of the sea and the rising of land. P.N. Bose found the evidences of a marine deposit as old as Miocene in the Oyster fossils and other Tertiary deposits discovered near Baripada. The terraces of recent alluvial in the lower reaches of the Suvarnerkha bear indication of the very recent uplift of the area. The famous Konark temple in Puri district was once situated on the fluvial deposit near the mouth of Suvarnarekha in the northern part of Balasore district, during a period not later than the Upper Jurassic time. But whatever might have been its recent character and behaviour, the east coast as a whole took shape only during the Upper Jurassic time.

River System

Rivers are the most important geomorphic feature of any region. They are like ateries of a state or country. It is seen that all the ancient civilizations flourished on the banks of rivers. Of the rivers in Orissa Mahandi, Suvarnarekha and Brahmani are inter state rivers i.e. have originated in Madhya Pradesh and Bihar cutting across the central axial highlands. Baitarini and Burahabalang have originated in Mayurbhanj and Keonjhar districts (North Orissa Plateu) whereas the rest of the river system have originated from the southern Orissa highlands. Of the river in Orissa Indravati, Kolab and Machhkund are tributaries of the Godavari river system. Leaving the above rivers which empty themselves directly into Godavari river, rest of them empty themselves directly into the Bay of Bengal.

Mahanadi

The Mahanadi (literary meaning – a great river) rises near Sihawa, 25 miles south of Raipur in Madhya Pradesh and flows after collecting the rainfall of 45,000 sq miles, pour down on the delta through a narrow george just above the city of Cuttack. Its total average length is 550 miles and has a catchment area of 130,000 sq. km.. It is a large river, below Sambalpur the channel becomes constricted due to the enormous hills of the Eastern Ghats. It meets the Bay of Bengal near Cuttack.

It is joined by rivers like Seonath, Haselu, Mand, Kelu, Ib and Tel (Mahapatra 1962).

Brahmani

This river is formed by the meeting of Sankh and Koel at Panposh near Raurkela. It passes through Bonai, Bamra, Talcher, Dhenkanal, Cuttack and then joins Baitarini and meets the sea at Dhamra. Its length is 362 miles and has a catchment area of 38,060 sq. km. E.H. Pascoe is of the opinion that Brahmani at one time joined the Mahanadi before the latter joined the Bay of Bengal.

Baitarini

It rises from Gandhamardhana peak in the south west of Keonghar. It formed the boundary between keonjhar and Mayurbhanj districts. It reaches the Orissan delta at Jaipur and again forms the boundary between Cuttack and Balasore districts. A branch of Brahmani meets with it at Chandbali and finally falls into the sea at Dhamra.

The Baitarini is approximately 150 miles in length and has a catchment area of 13,000 sq. km. Its main affulated is the Salandi, which rises from Mayurbhanj district and meets Baitarini at Bhadrakh in Balasore district.

Burhbalang

It starts from Simlipal hill in the district of Mayurbhanj. After receiving the waters of Palpala and Chipat it passes close to Baripada town; near Balasore it receives son and Gangahar and falls into the sea at Chandipur. Its average length is 100 miles and has a catchment area of 4,837 sq. km.

Suvarnarekha

It starts from the South-West of Ranchi and flows through Singhbhum, Mayurbhanj, Maidnapur and Balasore district. Roughly it forms the boundary between Orissa-Bihar and Orissa-Bengal. It reaches the Bay of Bengal at the extreme north of the Balasore district. Its total length is 300 miles and has a catchment area of 19,000 sq. km.

Other Tributary Rivers

Tel : The Tel rises from the Kalahndi district and flowing northeast meets the Mahandi close to Sonepur town. Its chief affluent is Hati, Sunder, Raul and Suktel.

Ang : It rises in the hills of Borasamber in Sambalpur district. After a northward journey and afterwards eastwards it meets Mahanadi between the Binki and Sonepur town in Bolangir district.

IB : It rises in Jaspur in Madhya Pradesh and passes through Sundergarh district of Orissa and meets the Mahanadi near Hirakund. It is 90 miles long and its tributaries are Jeha, Baisunder and Sopai. Its riverbank is very rich in Prehistoric relics.

Rushikulya : It has a catchment area of 7300 sq. km and is a interstate river.

Nagavalli : It has a catchment area of 9980 sq. km. and is a interstate river.

Indravati : It has a catchment area of 4201 sq. km. and is a interstate river.

Kolab-Sabri : It has a catchment area of 2405 sq. km. and is a interstate river.

Chilka Lake

Chilka is located on the Southwest corner of Mahanadi delta along the coast of Orissa. It is the largest coastal lagoon in Asia. It is about 64 km.

long and its width is variable i.e. it is widest on the north about 20 km. and tappers towards the south.

It is believed that the Chilka lake came into existence in the Upper Pleistocence period, when there was transgression of the sea much inland followed by regression and during this regression period, when Mahanadi delta was actively building, formation of beach ridges and spits enclosed a body of sea water resulting in the formation of Chilka lake. Its western and southern borders are the Eastern ghat hills where as on the East 8 km. wide sandy beach ridge and barrier splits separate this from the Bay of Bengal and is connected to it through a tidal inlet. At present the lake faces a grave environmental problem which is threatening its very existence.

Geology

As noted earlier Orissa has two main geological formations viz. the coastal plain land and the western hilly region. This plain level is formed out of river deposits in Pleistocene and recent times and falls into 3 parts i.e. (1) swampy jungles and sand dunes on the sea face, (2) a zone of some 40 miles wide of firm alluvium, (3) the laterite shelves on the irregular upland margin. The river deposits either belong to the old or newer alluvium is mixed up with laterite gavels. As a result of this mixing of organic constituents they are fertile. The soil becomes muddy and pasty during the rainy season.

Soils are also formed out of weathering of older rocks. These belong to the ancient Metamorphic, Chuddapah, Vindhyan, Gondawana groups on the eastern coast of Indian peninsular, there are fluvial and lacusterine Upper Gondowana beds which are thought to be of Upper Jurassic to lower Createaceous in age. As these deposits are the earliest strata on this coast after the Pre-Cambrian period, it is thought that the Eastern coast of India took shape only during the upper Jurassic Period. Further the Upper Gondawana rocks are seen in the series of detached out crops along the Eastern coast of Orissa, between Cuttack and Cape Coromin. Apart from these Oligocene and the Lower Miocene marine deposits are found at Puri and Mahulia respectively.

The inland areas on the other hand is chiefly composed of the rock of very ancient date, they are so completely altered and crystallined by Metamorphic action that all the traces of their original structure are lost and their original organic remains are completely obliterated.

Rocks are of later date than the Metamorphics formations that occurs in the tracks known as the Talcher coalfields and Dhenkanal and other places like Angul, Bomra, Athmalik and Rairakhal. High up the Brahmani a series of very slightly altered and unaltered rocks, comprising of Jasper, Quartzite and Schistose beds are known to occur. They also occur in some places of Keonjhar and Bonai.

Rock System

Dr. G. C. Mahapatra in the following table gives a list, in the descending order of the rock formation in orissa.

Table showing the geological formations in Orissa.

Rock System	*Age*
11-Blown Sand	
10-Raised Beaches	
9-Aluvium	
b-River valley and delta alluvium	Pleistocene and Recent.
(a) Older alluvium of the Coastal Plain	
8-River gravels	
7-Laterite – b – High level	
a – Low level	
6-Miocene	Tersiary
5-Cuttack group Sand stone	Jurassic
4-Mahadev Sandstone and grit	Triassic
3-Damud Sandstone, shales, Grit and coal	Permian
2-Talcher Sandstone, Shales, Boulder bed	Upper carboniferous
1-Metamorphic and crystalline rocks	Archacan
c-Vindhyan	
b-Cuddapah	
a-Dharwarian	

The table cited above gives a brief idea about the Pre-Pleistocene geology of Orissa. Pebbles occur within the formation of middle Gondawana series off Trassic times has been the most popular raw material for the Early Stone Age industries.

The quartz pebbles scatterd all over the Talcher area also provided a suitable raw material to the people of the Stone Age for their tools and implements. Apart from Talcher they occur near Intosona in Rairakhal and towards its west. Granite and early Sehists of Early Archieon age as well as Sehists, Limestone and Quartzite of Late Archieon (Dharwar) times are found else where.

The Pleistocene Formation

The Pleistocene formation occurs in Orissa in the following order :

(a) Laterites
(b) River Gravels
(c) Alluvium
(d) Raised beaches
(e) Blown sand

Laterites

It is well distributed in the hilly region of Orissa. The rock is dark reddish-brown in colour and is found on the surface of the hilltops. Mainly two types of laterites are found (1) the high level laterite (found in the hilltops above 2000 feet) and (2) the low level laterite-usually found on the plains at the base of the hills.

The high level laterite might be formed during Pliocene time or even earlier. It is being formed even at present. Being of a later formation the lower level coastal laterite must obviously be still younger. The Early Stone Age implements are found in the low level laterite.

River Gravel

Two types of gravel formation are seen in the river cliff sections at many places in Orissa. Dr. G.C. Mohapatra has given the section of river gravels as, the first and lowest gravel layers in almost all places, is over lained by a thick deposit of silt on alluvium (red, slightly red, or yellow in colour), ranging from two to thirty-five feet in thickness. The gravel layer ranges from 2 feet to 15 feet in thickness. The gravel is well cemented either by calcium carbonate or red ferruginous material where it is over lained by the silts, where the silt above is thin or absent the gravels are to be comparatively loose and reddish in color in the upper part and firm and blackish at the bottom. These gravels occur at several places from Pratappur to Bangriposhi in Burhabalanga. They also occur in the rivers like Son, Suvarnarekha, Khairi, Mankara, Netanad, Baitarini. The lower gravel yields lots of Early Stone Age artifacts. The second layer is thin and small and contains the tools of Middle stone age.

Patches of loose gravel occur at several places in the bed of almost all the rivers. They occur at Huma and Tikripara in the Mahanadi delta; Banor, Bonai, Panposh and Talcher in the Brahmani delta; Baripada, Kamarpala, Bangriposhi, Domuhani in the Burhabalanga and Sirsa in the Suvarnarekha delta.

Alluvium

The alluvium deposit can be divided into two parts :

(a) Older Alluvium of coastal plain and
(b) River valley and delta Alluvium.

(a) Older Alluvium of coastal plain

The alluvium of the coastal area is old and stretches over 125 miles, extending from Balashwar to Chilka Lake and from here it stretches for about 50 miles till it merges into the Bay of Bengal. It is composed of clay, sand, usually more or less mixed and in most of the places contains Calcareous Concretions (Kankar) and Ferruginous nodules. It is well distinguished by the occurrence of more sand and nodule.

River Valley and Delta Alluvium

The river valleys generally are deposited by river soil every year due to the river floods. The alluvial deposits are highly fertile. The morum alluvium deposition can be distinguished by the flatness of its surface and is also less sandy than older alluvium. The kankar does not occur frequently.

The valley of Mahanadi from Sambalpur to Tikarapur has alluvium, which is much mixed with local rock debris and laterite. In the valley of the Tel there is a kankar bearing alluvium of a very wide extend. Dr. G.C. Mohaptra at several places on river Brahmani has observed a thick deposit of river born yellowish alluvium of nearly 30 to 40 feet. At Mahulia the Burhabalang shows twenty feet of silt. Nearly thirty to fourty feet of silt accumulation has been observed by Dr. Mahaptra on the river Suvernarekha at Sirsa (Mayurbhanj) where it overlies an accumulation of gravel of nearly two and half feet.

Blow Sand

This covers a considerable area from Balasore to Puri. They are blown inland from the beach. There are several ranges of sand hills of sixty to eighty feet high. On the innermost range there is almost always vegetation and it seems to serve as a boundary between the barren sandy seashore and the fertile alluvial plain. It has been proved that each range of sand hills marks an old seacoast and the sea has retired gradually and that the land has been raised at intervals by interrupted movements.

Raised Beaches

Raised beaches, some of them are elevated to as much as fifty to hundred feet above the present sea level, it occur at several places along the eastern coast of India. They contain the shell of recent day species. Such deposits are common along the coast of Orissa. The Chilka Lake on the Ganjam coast dates back to the Pleistocene. Near the southwestern end are the sandpits which separates the lake from the sea, is a deposit of the shells 20 to 30 feet above high tide level which can be said to have been an older beach of the Bay of Bengal.

The above study gives an idea of the diverse geomorphology of Orissa. Study of geomorphology is an important part of archaeological studies for a better understanding of the man-land relationships. Thus geoarchaeology has emerged as an important branch of archaeology since it is important to understand the formation processes of a site before taking-up any behavioural interpretation of archaeological data. Such geo-archeological applications have been hardly applied in Orissa. Hence we see that there is ample scope for the geologists and the archaeologists to join hands for a comprehensive understanding and interpretation of Orissa's archaeology.

CHAPTER III

ECOLOGICAL BACKGROUND

The contribution of ecology to the evolution of man and his culture was stupendous in Pre-historic times as well as in the modern times. In the stoneage, man's very subsistence was depending upon the environment and ecosystem. The term ecology means the study of animals and plants in relation to their habitat and habits. Cultural economy concerns man alone among a marid of animals, obviously for his singular capacity to create cultures in the material sense. (Mahapatra 1983).

Influence of ecology and environment on economic, social and agricultural life of man is no less. Exploration of natural resources such as soil, water, flora, fauna changed mans subsistence pattern and a mixed economy of agriculture, animal husbandry later on developed. With the change in the economic system, social setup also changed. Thus ecology has a great bearing in evolution of human culture and civilization.

Soil

It has been stated above that the coastal districts of Orissa are made of silt deposits of rivers. The alluvials are mixed with the laterites and other calcarious nodules known as kankars. Thus the land is loose and fertile due to the rich organic constituents. It is muddy and pasty during the rainy season and powder like when dry. The soil is meant for jute, paddy and pulse cultivation. In the hilly districts the alluvium appears in the big river valleys and they are more or less like the newly deposited alluvium of the coastal areas. Besides alluvium, soil formed out of the weathering of the older rocks belonging to ancient crystalline metamorphic, Chuddapa and Vindian and Gondwana groups occur at many places.

Climate

Orissa enjoys a tropical monsoon type of climate as the tropic of cancer passes through Orissa. Metrologically four seaons are identified here, they are : the Southwest monsoon season (June-Sept.), the retreating Southwest monsoon season (Oct.-Nov.), Northeast monsoon season (Dec.-Mar.) and the hot season (Mar-May). But practically only 3 climatic conditions prevails i.e. the cold, hot and the monsoon season.

The cold season generally starts from November and it is the coldest in December, when the cold dry winds flow from the north. It is in December that the rice harvest starts. It continues up to February end and the month of February and March are pleasant. Generally the rains are felt in this season except in some pockets in the hilly region.

The hot season starts from the end of March and generally continues up to July. This period at times becomes very intolerable. During this period due to the creation of low pressure on land, this period experiences showers and the atmosphere during this period is generally dusty but gets cleared after the showers. The air is at times very dusty and the atmosphere very humid. In the mid-summer days, the day temperature rises up to 48°C and at night it goes down by 10 to 11°C.

The rainy season generally onsets in June and continues up to September-October. It comes with the Southwest monsoon current. The annual rainfall that Orissa receives is about 1600 mm. During the monsoon floods are common and if rains fail any year, there is drought and failure of crops, for here agriculture is mainly dependent on monsoon. Rainfall is variable in different areas i.e. hilly areas receive less rain then the delataic regions and the coastal plains.

Flora

Essentially the natural vegetation of Orissa is arboreal. As discussed above, half of its total area is under forest cover and the topography of Orissa is divided mainly into two parts i.e. the hills and the plains. The forest vegetation of the state differs from place to place according to the distance of the land mass from the sea and the distribution of rainfall. On a broader basis the forests of Orissa come under the tropical forest division. It is further divided into :

(1) Tropical wet evergreen and semi-evergreen forests, there areas basically receives more then 120 inches of rainfall and have a relatively short dry season. This type of forest cover does not exist in Orissa now. But in places, which still receives rainfall of about 60 to 80 inches, trees like bamboo, neem, tamarind, jamun, teak, ebony etc. grow. Along the coast coconut palms grow abundantly.

(2) Tropical Deciduous vegetation. The areas which receives annual rainfall of about 40-80 inches have Tropical Deciduous vegetation. Tees like gamhar, tendu or ebony, mahua, osona, bandhan, karam, sisoo, paisal are the common types available here. Mango and tamarind are the most common trees found here. These trees are commercially very viable.

(3) Littoral forests. The Littoral forests are generally found in the deltas of the Mahanadi, the Brahmani and the Baitarani and the areas that are washed by the high tides and salt waters. Mangroves or tidal forests are the most common types of littoral forest, canes and palms grow wild. The forest products are commercially exploited.

As Orissa has abundant of water bodies in the form of rivers, lakes, ponds, marshy fields etc. in these water bodies water plants thrive in plenty, some of the important ones among them are red and white lotuses, red blue, white lilies and many other water plants.

The plains and the hilly areas are equally fertile and yield good harvest. In the hilly areas shifting cultivation is practiced. Rice is the stample food of the people, so it is the main cereal grown here. Rice is supplemented by millets, maize and pulses (such as birhi, mug, kurthi, arhar and gram). Commercially, fiber crops like linseed and jute, oilseeds like mustard, seasum, castor etc., sugarcane (is grown exclusively); tobacco; turmeric; various types of vegetables are grown.

In the hilly area various types of tubers and edible roots grow. This constitutes the main diet of the aboriginals living there. There is lot of land that are fallow and these act as pastures for the cattle's.

Fauna

Of the total area of 60,136 sq. miles that Orissa enjoys, 28,125 sq. miles are under hills and forests. These hilly and forested parts of Orissa have preserved many old wild species of animals, birds and reptiles.

Among the primates that are found now a days only two types are found in Orissa. They are 'Langur' or 'Hanuman' and the 'Bandar'.

Among the carnivores, we have animals belonging to 3 groups i.e. cats, dogs and bear. In the cat group are the tiger, panther, chitah, small cats, the civets and the mongoose. In the dog group are the wolves, jackals, foxes, hyena and wild dogs.

In the bear family the sloth-bear is the only variety found among the big bears, which is very common among the small bear are the weasels, the honey-badger, these are generally found near the rivers, tanks or backwaters, feeding largely on fish.

The rodentia group consits of squirrels, rats, mice, porcupine and hares. Besides the above elephants, horses, cattle, deer and pig are also found. Elephants are found in abundance in the Simplipal ranges in Mayhurbhanj district. wild horses and bison were found earlier in the former state of Gangpur. Wild buffalo are found in western Orissan forests. Nilgai are found in the less heavily wooded forests.

Orissan forests have a number of varieties of deers and they are found throughout the state. Sambar deer, hog deer, mouse deer and the chital or spotted deer are the common tyres.

Birds like crows, sparrows, ravens, parrots etc. are found throughout the state. In the forests there are a variety of birds of these only few are seen and known. Peacock, quails, jungle fowl, peafowl, patridge and megapodes are the available game birds. The birds of prey are vulture, hawks, kites, falcons etc. Cuckow and lark are music birds; cranes kingfishers and water crow are fishing birds; cocks, pigeons, parrots, duck, swans, dove and peacock are domesticated. During the winters in the lakes and water reservoirs of Orissa birds like ducks, teals, geese come from the north.

The most frequently found reptiles are the snakes, lizards, crocodiles, alligators, tortoise etc. Alligators are found in may of the rivers, crocodiles are found in the fresh water swamps, lakes and rivers. Among the snakes that are found all over the state are, carpet snake, ratsnake, the harass and water snakes, the whip snake, the cobra, the krait, russels viper, python and the king cobra.

There are many varities of toads and frogs found in Orissa. They spread the most during the monsoon.

Orissa has a very rich fish fauna. They are both of the fresh water and the sea water variety. They are generally fished for food. Crabs and tortoise are found both in the fresh and sea waters.

hawks, Kites, falcons etc. Cuckoo, and lark are music birds. Cranes, kingfishers and water crow are fishing birds; cocks, pigeons, parrots, ducks, swans, dove and peacock are domesticated. During the winters in the lakes and water reservoirs of Orissa birds like ducks, teals, geese come from the north.

The most frequently found reptiles are the snakes, lizards, crocodiles, alligators, tortoise etc. Alligators are found in many of the rivers; crocodiles are found in the fresh water swamps, lakes and rivers. Among the snakes that are found all over the state are, carpet snake, rat snake, the kraits and water snakes, the whip snake, the cobra, the krait, russels viper, python and the king cobra.

There are many varieties of toads and frogs found in Orissa. They spread the most during the monsoon.

Orissa has a very rich fish fauna. They are both of the fresh water and the sea water variety. They are generally fished for food. Crabs and tortoise are found both in the fresh and sea waters.

CHAPTER IV

PALEOCLIMATE AND STRATIGRAPH

Climate always has a direct bearing on the cultural pattern of man and his environment. To understand the evolution of the Stone Age cultures it is needed to know the climatic phases under which the Prehistoric man lived. Pleistocene period was marked with several climatic fluctuations throughout the world. In the colder regions (temperate region) we had the glacial and interglacial periods. Where as in the tropical region we had pluvial and inter-pluvial phases i.e. wet and dry phases. These climatic fluctuations in the Pleistocene period have left enough evidences on the surface of the earth and has shaped the human life also to a great extent. Orissa being situated in the semi-tropical zone, experienced during this phase three wet and three dry phases (Thaper 1976). During this phase the rivers aggraded and eroded their valleys. Now we find the cultural relics of the pre-historic man in these deposits. These deposits are found on the secondary laterite layers.

CLIMATIC FLUCTUATIONS

Ist Wet Phase

In this phase the primary laterite of Orissa are formed and they are found distributed over a wide area in Orissa. They occur just over the bed-rock.

According to G.C. Mohapatra. "There is no doubt that at least a part of the primary laterite were formed during the first wet phase of the Pleistocene period. They have been covered by clay, gravel and silt (Mahapatra 1962). No evidence of man has been traced on the primary laterite. Same type of laterite deposit are even seen at Sabarmati area in Gujarat where it is termed as "P" horizon (zeuner-1950) and in the Narmada valley and South East Coast (De Terra and H.D. Paterson T.T., 1955).

Ist Dry Phase

Above the primary laterite, alluvium is deposited. The rivers surveyed and observed by Mahapatra indicate that the silt on the surface and the mettled clay, clay and sand in the sections are the results of the climatic change. But G.C. Mohpatra believes that the evidences of silt on the surface, mottled clay and sands in the sections speaks of climatic condition that was less humid than that which led to the formation of the primary laterites. The silt deposit which are rarely seen in the sections have a greater thickness in the plains but in the hills they are only a few feet thick. In these silt pisolitic ferruginaus nodules are reported. No evidence of man is found in this phase as well. Zeuner has identified this Horizon as "Q" Horizon in the Sabarmati area, where as in the Narmada Valley the occurance or this type of deposit is absent. But the Orissan type of climatic phase is found in the phase Southeast coast where during this time the evidence of early man is found living on the laterite of Southeast coast.

IInd Wet Phase

On the clay and calcified sand a layer of coarse gravel occurs which varies from ten to twelve feet in thickness. They are big and well cemented. The lower part is black in color due to the water action and the top portion is red and are basically lateritic soils. As observed at Mahulia and Banspal, the matrix is either yellowish silt or calcified sands. During this wet phase the deposit is basically gravels with little of silt and sand in it. The secondary laterite seems to have been formed in this phase. In the preceding dry phase, the primary laterite on the hill top and the high land have weathered and later on brought by the rivers and deposited on the low land. This redeposited primary laterite of the Ist wet phase is known as the Secondary laterite. The First evidence of man in Orissa comes from these coarse gravel and secondary laterite deposits. He might have lived in the end of the Ist dry phase and beginning of the of the IInd wet phase. Stratigraphic cultural sequence and the climatic context of this gravel is somewhat similar to that found at Narmada and the Southeast Coast. In the Narmada valley the lower gravels in its climatic context and cultural contents roughtly correspond to that of Orissa. Where as in the Southeast coast this phase is phase 3. As seen earlier Early man appears in the phase 2. So it is presumed by Burkitt and Cammiade that the cultural relics of the people living on the surface during the Ist dry phase must have been washed away during the IInd wet phase and deposited in the deposit of the IInd wet phase in the valleys of the rivers or low lying areas.

At the same time the gravel deposit identified by Zeauner as 'R' horizon resembles our coarse gravels.

IInd Dry Phase

On the coarse gravel, a red silt deposit, ranging in the thickness, from 30 to 45 feet is seen. This silt deposit over the gravel gives the indication of the dry period, sand and kankar also occur here probably due to river gradation. A layer of small gravels occurs over it, which indicates another wet phase. Unlike the Sabarmati valley and Narmada valley, in Orissa, in this red silt deposit no Palaeoliths have been found. It is believed that this deposit may have contained tools but because of no systematic effort and research, tools could not be discovered here. It is believed that people in early times lived on the surface of the secondary laterites as is evident from the finds of tools in the Bonai region in the murram deposit. The Murram deposit is the product of weathered secondary laterite which in the subsequent IIIrd wet phase were carried away along with the tools of the people living on it and deposited in the near by low lying areas. Tools belonging to the Middle stone age are found in this layer. This red silt phase of Orissa corresponds with the 'S' horizon of Zeuner in Gujarat where similar silt deposit is reported and from this silt deposit Sankalia found Palaeoliths. In the Narmada valley in the lower clay in which red silt with Kankar and bands of moral and lamination occur are similar to the fine red silt deposit. But unlike in Orissa, they have yielded acheulian tools and flakes where as in the Southeast coast this phase is called the phase IV and during this phase

Southeast coast this phase is called the phase IV and during this phase people of Series II started living on the secondary laterite of Southeast coast.

IIIrd Wet Phase

Above the red silt, a small layer of fine gravel is found. Humidity in this phase is less than the previous one. It is evident from the deposits of the finer gravels over the cemented coarse gravel. Due to less rainfall, bigger pebbles couldn't be carried and deposited. This gravel deposit is also 2 to 3 feet in thickness. In the large rivers small rolled gravels are seen in this layer, where as in the layers of the tributaries the percentage of angular rocks are more than the rolled gravels. These tributaries must have accumulated these rocks during heavy seasonal floods but due to lack of load of the river they were not carried to a long distance. So are confined to the tributaries. Tools belonging to the Mesolithic culture are found in this layer. The deposited murram as noticed in Bonai and other regions might have been deposited in this wet phase. Murram is weathered secondary laterite off the IInd dry phase. At places this deposit is 5 to 10 feet thick. Secondary deposit of laterite yields tools of Palaeolithic Age and the murram deposits yields tools of Mesolithic period. In the Gujarath area instead of fine gravel found in Orissa, buried red soil is found and Zuener calls it 'T' horizon. Here in this horizon no tools are reported either. In Southeast coast the rivers deposited silts containing Series II tools and this phase has been named as phase '5' by Burkitt & Cammiade. In the Narmada Valley the upper gravel which is a redeposited deposit are similar to the Orissa deposit and this deposit in Narmada has yielded rolled Abbevillio-Acheulian and Late Sohan tools.

IIIrd Dry Phase

Above the layer of fine gravel and angular rocks we find a thick deposit of red silt. Upper portion's at places is less red. Kankar is found with this deposit. At places, local variations are seen i.e. instead of Red silt the color of the silt is yellow, at other place rock debris are seen overlying this silt layer. This dry phase does not seem to have been so sever in Orissa so as to form blow sand dunes like in Gujarat.

The IIIrd Dry Phase of Orissa corresponds to take 'U' horizon of Zenuer in Gujarat. But this phase in Gujarat was damper, which was not the case in Orissa.

This period corresponds to phase 6 and 7 in the Southeast Coast and from this were found Series III and IV tools. In the Narmada Valley the upper clay deposit corresponds to the silt deposit of Orissa and they have yielded tools of Late Sohan type. Unlike the other places no stone tool of any type has been reported from Orissa from this silt deposit.

The Present Scenerio

At present the aridity is gradually increasing which is believed to give rise to climatic conditions, like is seen in Gujarat at present. The river basins of all the big rivers are filled up and their mouths are practically closed for the rainfall at present is not adequate to carry all the loads of debris coming down to the bed of the rivers. This load gets accumulated on the slopes of the hills, in the forest area and on the plains. Thus it is observed that now a days even a slight heavy rain causes floods. This phenomenon of aggradation by all the rivers in the plains and erosion in the hills is believed by G.C. Mohapatra to have started from the last dry phase i.e. IIIrd dry phase, which is represented by the red silt deposit seen as top layers of the sections in Orissa.

Critical Review

Now a days, increasing aridity is observed in Orissa. It perhaps started in the living memory of man. Till about 50 year's back the main rivers were navigable and forests were thick due to much more rainfall. Thus in the Pleistocene and Holocene, a trend towards aridity is observed. The sequence of deposits during this period starts with coarser gravel and ends with finer ones. The Ist wet phase is true pluvial and the rest can be called humid phase (Mahapatra 1962). The coarse gravel yielding Palaeolithic tools is Middle Pleistocene deposit. The Mesolithic culture could be assigned to the Upper Pleistocene period and Neolitic cultural deposits to the Holocene or recent deposits. This hypothetical dating of the lithic cultures in Orissa, go well with modern theory of dating of Prehistoric cultures of India. Following is the stratigraphic sequence in this region:

(1) Bedrock
(2) Gravel I
(3) Alluvium
(4) Gravel II
(5) Silt

CHAPTER V

PREHISTORY OF ORISSA

Orrisa is very rich in Pre-histoic remains. In Orrisa the sites yielding the cultural relics of the prehistoric period have been grouped under four zones North, South, East and West respectively on the basis of reported sites and their concentration. Thus it is generalized that the Lower Palaeolithic sites are more in the northern zone consisting of earlier district of Dhenkanal, Mayurbhanj, Keonjhar and Sundergarh. The Middle Palaeolithic sites are concentrated both in the northern and western zones i.e. Sambalpur, Bolangir and Kalahandi. The Eastern zone comprises of Cuttack, Balasore and Puri districts and the southern zone comprises of the earlier districts of Ganjam, Koraput and Phulbani, these districts account for less number of Middle Palaeolothic sites. Mesolithic and flakes blade industry predominate the western zone. This type of concentration may be related to the ecology, resources, raw material, economic subsistence and technological ability and they can be better understood on the basis of their geomorphologic locations.

The different lithic industries of this period are (1) Lôwer Palaeolithic (2) Middle Palaeolithic (3) Upper Palaeolithic (4) Mesolithic and (5) Neolithic

PALAEOLITHIC CULTURES

(a) Lower Palaeolithic

The Lower Palaeolithic is characterized by its tool type i.e. "Handaxe – cleaver and chopper – chopping tool industries". It is stratigraphically found in the coarse gravel deposit over lying on the bed rock. Tools of this culture have been found in Sambalpur, Sundargarh, Bolangir Mayurbhanj, Keonjhar, Dhenkanal and Koraput district.

Mahapatra's studies show that Early Stone Age tools occur in the gravels of the river sections over the bedrock. They also occur loose in the gravel beds of the river, on the surface in the forests, slopes of the hills and in the secondary laterites. The raw material used for making these tools is generally the coarsed grained quartzite and the majority of them are on pebbles. Only in Central Orissa i.e. in Dhenkanal district they are found made of sand stone and grits. Quartzite of various shades such as red, pink, white, greenish, brown, blackish are used. Patination of any kind is not found on any of the tools.

Stratigraphically and technologically the evolution cannot be marked, for both crude and developed ones occur together. Dr. G.C. Mahapatra has classed them into three stages on the basis of their technique. (Mahapatra 1962). D. K. Bhatacharya states that "Mahapatra formed a kind of typo-technological succession which lays more stress on showing an internal evolution and this is still being the basis of any research in this direction." (Bhattacharya, 1996)

Stage I

Technologically the tool of this stage represents the beginning of the Early Stone Age cultures of Orissa. The technique adopted is basically block-on-block, which is marked with deep, big and irregular flake scars, which are few and mainly struck from the top region. Therefore the resulting tools are crude in appearance, asymmetrical body, rought and crude working edge, irregular profile and the shapes are far from being standardized. These are the characteristics feature of these tools, which clearly distinguish them from those of the latter stage. Mostly half of the tool comprises of cortex. Their size are mostly big with a heavy un-worked butt end. Following are the main tool types of this stage :

(1) Handaxes
(2) Irregular flaked bi-faces
(3) Flakes
(4) Scrapers
(5) Irregularly flaked pebbles

Stage II

This stage is marked by the introduction of the cylindrical hammer technique. The flake scars becomes small, shallow and uniform. Though a fairly good amount of control over the flaking technique was obtained, still bold flake scars occur on many of the specimens, which could have been the result of the block-on-block technique. Probably in this phase tools were primarily flaked by the block-on block technique and the final finish was given by the cylinder hammer technique. The shape of the tools obtains symmetry and the size tends to be smaller and handy. The working edge was thin and sharp which ran around the periphery. Flakes are removed from all parts unlike that seen in the Ist stage. There was increase in the tool types i.e. cleavers, cores and a large number of miniature variety tools (the miniature variety shows more controlled and careful flaking). The nondescript tools of the previous stage, like the regularly flaked bifaces completely disappear and the number of irregularly flaked pebbles get reduced. As a whole the tools show a tendency towards full bifacial working. The following are the different tool types of this stage :

(1) Hand axes
(2) Cleavers
(3) Scrapers
(4) Cores
(5) Flakes
(6) Irregularly flaked pebbles.

Stage III

The tools of this stage show complete mastery over the cylinder hammer technique. The tool types become more varied by the addition of the large number of miniature variety tools like the points and a number of side and round scrapers. Cores and flakes are also found in considerable quantity. They can be called the *Achulian* flake tools of Orissa (Mahapatra 1962 pp82). The tools belonging to this stage may be considered as representing the stage of the technical development of the early stone age industries. Following are the different tooltypes of this stage.

(1) Handaxes
(2) Cleavers
(3) Points
(4) Scrapers
(5) Flakes
(6) Cores
(7) Irregularly flaked pebbles
(8) Discoids

So we see that the Early Stone Age industries of Orissa show a gradual development in technique. They range from the crudest to the developed ones. The tools of the middle phase are predominant. The preparation of the smaller flake tools in the IIIrd stage might have contributed to the birth of the full flake-tool culture of the Middle Palaeolithic. G. C. Mohapatra (Mahapatra 1962) observes that the Levallious technique was not used for making flakes. But subsequent researches show that both Levallions and Clactonian technique were used for making flakes. Where as, it has been seen that there is no distinction between flakes and the core industries as such.

The tools of the Lower Palaeolithic culture in Orissa, technologically and typologically correspond with the Abbevillian and early Achulian Industries of Europe. So we can say that the Early Stone Age of Orissa is a culture of the Abbevillio-Achulian tradition of India.

Some of the researchs done in lower Palaeolithic in Orissa are discussed in belief from the earliest times, to give an insight into the regional variations observed in the different areas of the state.

The pioneer in the field of prehistoric research in Orissa was Valentine Ball. He in 1875 for the first time picked up four stone implements from four different places in Orissa namely Dhenkanal, Angul (Kaliakata), Talcher (Harichandanpur) and Sambalpur (Bursaoali). He reported about his finds in the "Proceedings of the Asiatic society of Bengal" in 1876 and his book entitled "Jungle life in India", 1880. (Mahapatra, 1962)

V.Ball remarks on the tool type" On comparison with a series of Madras implements, the resemblance to some of the forms is very striking, and the conclusion that a connection existed between the people who manufactured these implements, respectively, seems a legitimate one to draw.

Mahapatra hails this finds as important for he states, "firstly, it speaks about the wide area of its distribution. Secondly, the tools were found from different stratigraphic horizons. Thirdly, it gives us an idea of the varied shapes and sizes i.e. tool from Dhenkanal is a handaxe broken at the point, from Kaliakata is a broad, ovate biface and the one from Bursapali is painted wedge-shaped and lastly, it speaks about the raw material used. All the four tools have been made out of different varities of quartzite.

In 1930 Prof. R.D. Banerjee undertook exploration to find some prehistoric sites in Mayurbhanj. A brief account of his finds and sites get mention in his book “History of Orissa”.

Mayurbhanj District

Kuliana : It is situated about 16 km to the Northwest of Baripada, on the Baripada Bangiriposi road, Kuliana is the headquarters of Mayurbhanj District. The site is located on the bank of river Burhabalanga. The earliest reported Palaeoliths from here was in 1939 by Paramananda Acharya, an State Archaeologist in the erstwhile princly state of Mayurbhanj and E.C. Worman (jr.) a research fellow of the Harward University. On the basis of this reporting further research was taken up by N.K.Bose and D. Sen of the University of Calcutta in between 1939 to

1942. Their work was confined to Kuliana and the surrounding villages (Kalabaria, Kailisuta, Nuaberi, Pralappur, Kendudiha, Sandim, Brahmangaon, Buramara, Patinja, Mundaboni, Bhuasuni, Pariakoli and Kamta) and along the bank of river Burhabalanga, within a radius of 16-18 Km. They not only undertook exploration work but also took up excavation on the margins of some of the tanks and on a quarry around Kuliana. The stratigraphy that was revealed here consisted of yellowish earth and below it was the laterite that is of detrital origin and was not very compact. It was on this latter laterite deposit that Palaeolithic tools were tound.

In all 663 tools were unearthed from the excavation here, the tools found here were mainly found from the secondary laterite. According to Bose, Sen and Ray (Bose, Sen and Ray. 1954, p-7) typologically these tools are more advanced that those found in the boulder conglomerate at Kamarpal. In the lower levels it starts with crude handaxes and choppers and end in finer bifaces and a few flake tools.

The raw material used for making the tools was quartzite. The industry is mainly core industry but pebbles and flake tools are also reported. The flakes were made by using Clactonian technique, which is evident from the high flaking angle and unprepared or unfacetted striking platform. Where as, there are others (flakes) that show evidence of Levalloisian technique.

Among the assemblage choppers dominate, other tools in the assemblage are handaxes, cleavers, knives and scrapers. The excavators have described the assemblage as a whole as crude and have divided the whole assemblage in to three techno-typological evolutionary stages. But these stages cannot be proved stratigraphically. Choppers with straight or convex edge at one side and a thick margin on the opposite represent the earliest tools. The next stage is represented by bifaces of irregular form and flake tools with high-angled unprepared striking platform. The third stage includes much more neatly worked bifaces of regular form and a few rather crude cleavers. The choppers show improvement in technique. They become smaller, often indistinguishable from sidescrapers, and also resemble some form of bifaces.

Bose and Sen had further classified the tools on the basis of their imagined function. They are:

A. Cutting or hacking by means of heavy blows.
B. Scraping.
C. Piercing.
D. Doubtful use.

Typologically they have divided the tools under three categories namely pebble tools, core tools and flake tools (their percentage of occurrence are Pebble tools-12.21 % which includes choppers, chopping tools, cleavers, handaxes; Core tools-81.29% which include handaxes and cleavers; and lastely Flake tools-6.48%) and further they have been divided into numerous groups and sub-groups i.e choppers, chopping tools, scrapers, handaxes, cleavers and flake tools. Of these the largest number of tools comprised of choppers, handaxes and cleavers. Discoid choppers constitute 10.56% and side choppers 13.72%. If the rostroid handaxes, handaxes and cleavers are taken together then their total reaches 63.3% whereas scrapers and points together form just 4% of the total assemblage.

Dani (Dani, 198l, p. 32) sums up the finds of Kuliana and its neighbouring areas in the following words "The Kuliana industry shows varying traditions of stone working. The typological description given above makes it clear that the artifacts are a mix of crude forms with well-made tools. It appears to be solely on this account that Bose and Sen have tried to make a chronological distinction between cruder and better forms. But there is no other evidence available to support this distinction. A calculation on the percentage basis may throw further light on this question, if and when comparable material is available".

A lot of similarity has been found between the tools at Kuliana and those found at Singrauli basin in Mirzapur district of Gujrat and of South India. The pebble tools are similar to the pebble tools reported ftom Punjab and are described in De-Terra and Petersons book "Studies in Ice Age in India and associated Human Cultures". Mahapatra Mahapatra (Mahapatra, 1962) compared the different tool types with the following sites in Europe and Africa. The discoids and side choppers are similar to those of Wayland's Early Kufuan and Leakey's Oldowan industries of east Africa. The narrow long pick-like handaxes found insitu with a roughly rhomboidal section, is similar to a tool described and illustrated by

Sandford in his "Palaeolithic Man and the Nile Valley in upper and middle Egypt", (Sandford 1934, pp-111). Some of the cleavers show a rhomboidal section as in one form Pinel, illustrated by Burkitt. But at the same time Mahapatra states "That the industry of Kuliana was not necessarily homotaxial with similar industries in other parts of India or Africa".

The excavations undertaken at two quarry pits at Kuliana and Kamarpara on the ancient Burhabalanga river valley by N.K. Bose and D.Sen in 1939-42 did not give a satisfactory stratigraphy but yielded a rich tool assemblage belonging to the Lower Palaeolithic culture from a gravel bed which was extremely stained with laterite. (Bose, N.K and Sen. D. 1949) To solve this problem N.K.Bose and others took fresh expedition in the Burhabalanga area. Here they took up some sections with a view to throw some more light on the problem of chronology. With this objective three sections were taken up and reported. (N.K.Bose and Others 1951)

Section No. I is within half a mile upstream of Churguniaghat near the confluence of Burhabalanga with a small nullah. Of the six beds distinguished, the lowest is said to be of yellow white clay of unknown depth. The next bed is described as compact Laterite having a typical ferruginous lateritic appearance with characteristic vermicular structure. Mottled in color red, yellow and dark brown in patches. Then follow boulder conglomerates, separated in to upper and lower beds by a thin layer of sandy clay containing gravels of various sizes. The matrix of the conglomerates shows some concentration of ferruginous material. The upper most bed is called "Top soil" said to be formed by a thick deposit of alluvium. One core tool was dug out from the upper boulder conglomerate.

Section. No. II was located further down stream. Here the yellow clay bed and a portion of the compact laterite are said to lie under water. This section is very much similar to section No. I, except that the lower boulder is said to have a peletty lateritic structure, in which pebbles are embedded. Here in the lower boulder bed a pebble tool was found and in the upper a crude handaxe both showing the sign of rolling.

Section No. III was located between section No. I and II and was nearly identical with the previous two in character.

Besides this stratigraphic sequence another was established by Prof. F.E.Zeuner in the same locality in 1953. (Dani, 1981, pp.2l) Here the lower most layer is of limestone over which lies the bluish-white clayey silt. Over it lies the mottled clay which is the same as the compact laterite of Bose and others. Then followed by a bed of cemented gravels i.e. the boulder conglomerate beds of Bose and others have been integrated into one, the thin sandy layer being possibly considered as insufficient to demarcate the bed into two divisions. Prof. Zeuner divides the topsoil of Bose and others into two beds, Ist of red and brown and over it brown and red silt.

On the basis of the stratigraphy obtained so far and its correlation with the finds. It can be said with certainty that below the topsoil has been found deposits of Microliths and Neoliths, which are definitely known to be post-pleistocene on the basis of the associated skull and teeth of a modern wild horse and ass. In the gravel bed of the Burhabalanga River have been found Palaeolithic tools. So far no human remains have been found in the lower beds. (Dani, 198l, pp. 22)

Kamarpal : This site was also excavated by Bose and Sen of Calcutta University in 1942 (Bose and others, 1951, pp 6-7). Here in the excavation over the hard calcareous bed was found grayish blue clay, over it was a continuous bed of boulder conglomerate, below this bed at places deposits of compact laterite is found but its exact stratigraphic position/relation could not be established and on top over the boulder conglomerate is a thick deposit of alluvium. The excavators believe that this stratigraphy is not a proper indicative of a true cycle of dry and wet phases. Here the tools were found in the river cliff section from the boulder conglomerate deposit. The tools recovered here insitu from the upper and lower boulder conglomerates are all rolled and weathered and show a yellowish brown stain. The workmanship is crude. The assemblage contains both core and pebble and flake tools, the flake tools being very less in number. The core and pebble tools mainly comprise of handaxes of Early Abbevillian type and show crude form and workmanship. It is seen that the butt is pebbly and much of the cortex remains intact. Among these, a few crude pearform and oval or Ovaloid handaxes can be roughly distinguished. The flake tools comprise a few large and small specimens, with a little cortex remaining intact over it. The striking platform being plain and unfacetted and very little secondary retouching is observed. The working edges are rather irregular. Some crude scrapers and knives with irregular outlines have been reported. The flakes type found can be compared with the Cromerian and Pre-Sohan types. The pebbles used for the purpose are large elongated river rolled pebbles of quartzite. The excavator have compared the tools technologically to the pebble-tool industry of Africa. (Mahapatra, 1962) and the tool assemblage found here made on cores according to Sen has resemblance with the tools found from the boulder conglomerate at Vadamadurai near Madras. On the basis of this he has tentatively dated the tools to the Lower middle Pleistocene. (D. Sen, 1954).

Kalapathara : Is an open air site on the isolated hillock with fairly wide area for habitation, here trial excavation was taken in a grid of 1x1 m and an area of 3 m non-grid. A total of 135 artifacts were collected from both the areas. The raw material used was mostly ryolite, besides this dolerite, dyke, quartzite, milky quartzite, chert and basalt were used. The tools found were classed into two groups i.e. shaped tools (comprising of scrapers, burins, borers, points, knives, notch) and simple artifacts (core and flakes). It is seen that the number of simple artifacts out numbered the shaped tools in both the areas.

Baripada complex : This complex extends to the south and north of Baripada. The principal sites are Raghunathpur, Bijoy Ramchandrapur to the south of Baripada and to its north lies a large number of sites. Kalabaria, Sandim, Kakapathara, Kamta, etc. These sites at the macro level are situated in the same geological unit but at the micro level are located in different geomorphological settings. The Lower Palaeolithic tools have been reported from eight sites of which four are single cultural sites, two have yielded Lower and Middle Palaeolithic and one Lower, Middle Palaeolithicand Mesolithic tools. In all 174 tools from these sites. The tools were divided into two groups; shaped tools (totaling 65 tools and comprising of handaxes, cleavers, knives, choppers, picks, scrapers, chisels, points and a non-descriptive flake tool) and simple artifacts (totaling 109 tools and consisting of flakes, cores and other wastes).

The tools recovered, from here on the basis of techno-morphological features have been designated as belonging to the Lower and Upper Acheulian phases. Among the tools belonging to the Lower Acheulian phase show minimum of chipping and no attempt at retouching is seen, this makes them appear much cruder than the tools reported from other Lower Acheulian sites in India, refers to its higher antiquity on this basis. Chakarbati (Chakarbati, 2000) says "Typology is no surer ground for dating but where there are occurrences in geological context, it assumes chronological significance and therefore, to push back the date of the Lower Acheulian here to the Lower Pleistocene would not be too far fetched".

Bangiriposi : Bangiriposi is at a distance of about 16 Km to the north-west of Kuliana. It is on the left bank of Burhaba langa river. The river flows at a distance of 2 Km south of the Bangiriposi railway station. Here in 1948 during exploration work by D. Sen and G.S. Ray (Sen, Ray & Beteille, 1956 pp-233-246) from two laterite quarries 13 tools were reported. Here at the bottom is the layer of schist, over the schist is a layer of laterite, which is detrital in origin. They are soft on the top and comparatively hard at the bottom. Over this layer of laterite is a thin over burden of about one and half feet.

Of the total 13 tools, eight are handaxes of different types. Other are, one pebble-chopper, a cleaver and three flakes. The workmanship of all the tools is basically crude and they are massive in size. They are mostly asymmetrical and no secondary working is observed. On the core and the flakes original cortex is seen over a large part. All the tools are made of light coloured fine grained quartzite, leaving one which is made on quartz. Except one tool which looks much worked out due to rolling, all others look fresh and new but all of them have ferruginous red laterite staining in varying % on them.

Khiching : Explorations undertaken by Subrata Chakrabarti in and around this area (Chakrabarti S. 1990, 92,93,2000) have thrown new light on Palaeolithic culture in Mayurbhanj district. For these areas were believed to be devoid of Palaeolothic sites. The area towards the east of Khiching consisting of the Simlipal massif is the area where most of the file sites are located. The area is watered by the river Baitarani and its tributaries. The sites in the Khiching plateau occurs in a radious of 5 Km square. The sites are single culture as well as multicultural and they are of various types i.e. open air sites, channel bed sites and cliff-section sites. The Lower Palaeolithic tools according to Chakarbati are reported from only 4 sites (of these two are single-culture) from the pebbly cobbly gravel having contact with laterite. Amongst this one is open air site and the other is a channel-bed site. The other two sites are cliff section sites. They have mixed deposit, that yielded both Lower Palaeolithic and Middle Palaeolithic tools. The tools are mostly made on quartzite of various shades. The 30 tools reported consist of choppers, handaxes, scrapers, flakes, core and wastes.

Angul and Dhenkanal Districts (Central Orissa)

These areas lies between 20°29′ and 21°42′ N lat and 84°16′E and 86°02′E long covering an area of 10,826 sq.km. The area is divided into 2 halves by the river Brahmani and it flows for 160 Km in this region. 58% of the area in central Orissa is covered by mountain ranges and forests. P.K.Singh undertook extensive exploration works in this area for a period of 6 years between 1980 to 1985 and reported 53 Lower Palaeolithic sites. From these sites he collected 1599 tools. These included choppers, handaxes, cleavers, disc, scrapers, flakes and points, of these handakes and cleavers forms the main tool assembly. Most of the tools are recovered from the surface so it is difficult to assigen them to any stratigraphic period. But in some cases they have been reported from the lower pebbly gravel and in the kankarised soil and they have laterite encrustations on them. Nodules and pebbles of quartzite and quartz were the chief raw material used during the Lower Palaeolithic period.

SAMBALPUR DISTRICT

The exploration undertaken by the members of Anthropology Dept of Gauhati University and Dept of Ancient Indian History Culture and Archaeology Sambalpur university, Orissa, in the river valleys of

Mahanadi and Kharla lead to discovery of a good number of tools belonging to various cultural stages of the stone age periods.

Mahanadi River Valley : Here at Daridungri which is a small hillock, located on the left bank in front of the Barapahar there lies a swampy area, which the explorers believe was a palaeochannel of Mahanadi. Here on either side of the Palaeochannel a few scrappy and thin deposits of lateritic implementiferious gravel conglomerates in eroded form were come across. Form these deposits lower Palaeolithic tools were reported.

Kharla River Valley : Kharla is a tributary of river Mahanadi and the area of research was confined to 4 sq Km to the south of the Kuchinda town which is 100 km from Burla. On the river bank two terraces have been observed. The lowest terrace (T2) is composed of loose subrounded and rounded gravels. The height of this terrace is partially covered by sandy silt, which forms a talus. Here in a tunnel which is cutting across the terrace, can be seen the gravels that were deposited unconformably over a fissured clay. On this loose gravel in the tunnel, handaxes, cleavers and cores were found scattered on the surface. Over the Terrace II is the Terrace 1, which has a height of 104 m. Here a big channel was found which passes towards the river by cutting across both the terraces. The upper part of the terrace is covered by concretized implementiferrous laterite and it is highly eroded. The Kuchinda town is at present located on it.

The upper part of the terrace is further cut by gulleys. In these galleys a glimpse of the stratigraphy could be seen. At the bottom fissured or molted clay is partly exposed over which a thin layer measuring 15cm to 15 cm, quartz grits has been deposited. The laterite layer was deposited over this quartz layer and was implementiferrous. From this laterite layer choppers, handaxes, cleavers were found insitu and also on the surface. These tools are believed to be belonging to the Lower Palaeolithic phase. (IA-1983-84 - A Review)

Kuchinda : The site is located in Sambalpur district. D.K. Bhattacharya along with S.N. Rath discovered at Kuchinda which is on the bank of one of the tributaries of river Mahanadi a huge Lower Paleolithic assemblage.

Here the industry is mainly pebble dominated but handaxes and cleavers were also reported. The technique adopted according to Bhattacharya was cylinder hammer technique and Levalloise flakes were also made. (Rath S.N. and Bhattacharya D.K. 1988, pp. 23-27).

SUNDERGARH DISTRICT

In the upper Brahmani Valley in this district, exploration work was carried out by P.K.Behera of BHU (Behera P.K. 1989). Tools of the lower Paleolithic phase were collected from the valley of the Brahmani, the Sankh and the Deo nullah, a tributary of the river koel. Majority of the tools were found in the gravel beds. The tools are mostly rolled and thickly patinated.

At Garjan which is located on the right bank of the Brahmani, about 4 km south of the Panposh railway station stratified deposits were noticed. The section is 2.40 m thick and is composed of compact yellowish sandy-gravel, sandy-coble deposit, coarse sand of reddish color, sandy-cobble deposit and lastly, kankary reddish-brown sandy-silt from bottom upwards. From the middle sandy-cobble deposit two choppers were found. (I.A. 1983-84 - A Review)

DHENKANAL DISTRICT

Explorations was conducted here in the year 1984-85 by a team consisting of members from the Archaeological Survey of India and the Dept of Archaeology, Govt of Orissa. At the foot of Jiminia hillock, which is an open air site located in the upper valley of the Kumaria Lower Palaeolithic tools were discovered. The tools were collected from the red soil deposit, which was lying in patches on the foothill area as well as along the banks of Kumaria. This deposit appeared to be of colluvial origin. The raw material used for making the tools was quartzite. The tools comprised of cores, flakes, ovates and Acheulean handaxes. The team observed an interesting feature here that some of these tools were embedded on the heaps of oval or circular quartzite stones, in some instances laterite stones were also seen fixed to these heaps of quartzite stones. They believe these structures to be burials. (I.A. 1984-85. A Review).

Middle Palaeolithic Culture

The appearance of the highly advanced upper Acheulian phase is generally taken as the end of the Lower Palaeolithic. During this period there was an appreciable change in the environment that is stratigraphically represented by erosional activities. The change in the environment is also reflected in the change in the choice of tools and the raw material to make this tools. In the initial stages the handaxes and cleavers continue with other tools but their number is comparatively less and they are relatively smaller in size. But gradually they were left out of the tool kit and used only the new types of tools that were much smaller in size than those used by the people in the Lower Palaeolithic period.

The main tool types of this period are the scrapers, points, borers, handaxes, choppers, blades, knives and burins, which are also known as 'light duty' tools. These were mainly made on flakes and so this industry is also called the flake industry. But it has been seen from the data published from different places that flakes were not a necessity, flat natural chips or nodules or even smaller tabular pebbles were directly turned into desired tools by simple retouching or step-trimming thus saving time and labor, Then the raw material used was basically silicious variety of fine-grained basalt, as the silicious materials gave smooth surface and conchoidal fracture.

The techniques that were applied for making tools was Clactonian technique, Musterian technique, stone hammer technique, step technique for controlled flaking and Levallois technique, cylinder hammer technique, punch technique, etc.

It was in the beginning of the ZOth C. i.e. 1930's that a distinct flake industry was identified in at least 4 regions of India, namely, Sohan, Narmada, Kumnool and Khandivli near Bombay, by De-Terra and Peterson (1939), Lammiade and Burkitt (1939), and Todd (1939).

In 1954 H.D. Sankalia (Sali, 1990, pp-164) found this culture in the gravels at Nevasa, which is located on river Pravera in Ahmadnagar district of Maharastra and was the first person to establish its stratigraphical and cultural significance. Here over the bedrock of basalt in a basal cemented coarse gravel he found Lower Palaeolithic tools and termed them as Series I. Over this cemented coarse gravel bed lay another layer of gravel that was finer in composition and less cemented than the basal. From this deposit he found tools that were very different technologically and also in the material used to make them, than that which were used for making the Lower Palaeolithic tools. He christened it first as series II and later termed it as the Middle Palaeolithic.

The data collected since then, from other excavations and explorations from other parts of the country have established Sankalia's observations at Nevasa. Stratigraphically, now it has been established that the Middle Palaeolithic occupies an intermediatary position and is found in the gravel deposit which succeeds that containing the Lower Palaeolithic tools and underlies that yielding the Upper Palaeolithic tools. This chrono cultural phase is other wise also known as 'Nevasian'; 'Series II'; 'Flake industry'; 'Flake-Blade-Scraper industry and 'Middle Stone Age'.

The Middle Palaeolithic sites are well distributed and are mostly found in those areas where Lower Palaeolithic sites were found. The middle Palaeolithic sites are found in the various districts of Kashmir valley, Rajasthan, Gujrat, Madhyapradesh, Meghalaya, West Bengal, Orissa, Maharastra, Karnataka, Tamilnadu, Andhra Pradesh and Kerala.

This period on the basis of the C14 dates obtained from Middle Palaeolithic sites in Gujrat, Uttar Pradesh, Maharashtra, Andhra Pradesh and Madhya Pradesh has been dated between 37000 to 11000 B.P. It is about 100,000 years later than that found in Europe and Africa (Bhattacharya, 1996, pp 115.)

In Orissa, stratigraphically the tools of the Middle Palaeolithic occurs above those of the Lower Palaeolithic tools which are found in the coarse gravel. Generally it has been observed that the Middle Palaeolithic sites are found little away from the Lower Palaeolitic sites. This is because of the non-availability of suitable raw material. The raw materials used in this phase are different from those used in Lower Palaeolithic Age. Most of the tools are made up of fine grained rocks, such as chert, jasper, opal, chalcedony and fine grained quartizite. At Bijatala, a very advanced type, fresh and beautiful handaxe was found in the layer yielding Middle Palaeolithic tools. This shows that the people of this culture had a complete mastery over the technique of making handaxes.

Majority of the tools are made on small flakes. The flakes have been detached by the soft cylinder-hammer technique. In many cases they are detached directly from the core without removing the cortext, as a result the platform shows a portion of it. Prepared multifaceted platform flakes are very few. Majority of the specimens are diffused bulb.

Retouching are always marginal. Very few specimen show secondary flaking on both the surfaces. In majority of the cases the upper surface is flaked and the flake surface is seen clean. Retouching are mainly done from the upper surface. On the whole it can be said that the authors of this culture had no complete mastery over the technique of retouching.

Very few are well finished in the group of regular tool types. Majority of them are roughly finished. The regular tool types constitute of scrapers, borers, burin, point and scraper-borer. Nodules cores and blades occur but in very limited quantity and they have been mostly used as side scrapers.

No fossils are reported with the association of the flake tools, though a large number of sites have been discovered. The Middle reaches of Mahanadi, Brahmani, Baitarni and the Burhabalanga valley are the areas of the distribution of this culture.

In this period scrapers predominate with its sub type i.e. side scraper, end scraper, hollow scrapers, round scrapers and point scraper. Points followed next, they are the simple point variety. They show marginal retouching. Majority of them are made on flakes. Their two sub types are points on flake and point on nodules.

Borers are very few in number, their types are borers on cores, borers on flakes, borers on nodules. Burins are also few in number.

Nodules are usually small in size and the cortex is seen to be covering more than half of the area. Like the cores they are also classed in two groups : (1) Nodules in the regular tool type, (2) Nodules as Nodules.

G. C. Mahapatra during his survey (1957-59) has mentioned about discovery of 29 Middle Palaeolithic sites. As in the pan Indian context no fossil or any other solid evidence for dating was come across. In all 404 specimens of this period were collected of these the regular tools. (Scrapers, points, borer, burin and scraper-borer) were 210; flakes were 101; cores were 38; nodules were 27; blades and blade-like flakes were-22; and rejects were 6.

These tools are stratigraphically found in the fine gravel, which rests over a layer of red silty clay and below the red silt layer is the coarse gravel from which the Lower Palaeolithic tools were found. In some cases the tools of the Lower Palaeolithic are found along with Middle Palaeolithic tools on the surface, which Mahapatra believes, are factory sites. He differentiates the tools mainly on the basis of raw material. The raw material used are mainly fine grained rocks like chert, jasper, opal, a few chalcedony and fine grain grained quartizite. Then majority of the tools were made on small flakes, so are smaller in size than the Lower Palaeolithic tools and retouchings are observedon them. Mahapatra observes "but the re-touchings were marginal due to which the tools are not well-finished". The technique used for making the tools was mainly cylinder hammer technique. The flakes were detached directly from the cores, leaving a major part of the cortex on it or at times the cortex are removed by further flaking for flake scars are seen on the flakes which were remade by soft cylinder-hammer. Very few flakes are reported which are made on prepared cores. Some of the tools found show weathering but majority are intact and those found from the different sections look completely new and fresh.

SAMBALPUR DISTRICT

In between the hillocks called Daridungiri (on which Sambal Unviersity is located) and Barapahar range lies a swampy area, which is believed to be a Palaeochannel of Mahandi. (IA-1983-84-A Review) On either side of the Palaeo channel at the foot of Daridengri and Barapahar a few Scrappy and thin deposits of lateritic implementiferous grand conglomerates in ordered form were observed. From these deposits S.N. Rath had collected Middle Palaeolithic tools like scrappers, points, flakes, cores, chunks etc.

In the Kharla river valley, a tributary of Mahanadi, two terraces were identified. Here in these terraces in the tunnels were found Lower, Middle and Upper Palaeolithic tools. The Middle Palaeolithic tools comprised of scrapers, cores, points, flakes and chunks.

SUNDARGARH DISTRICT

Near Jhirpani town at a distance of half a k.m., on the left bank of river Koel a tributary of River Brahmani, a cliff section was studied (IA – 1983-84-A Review). The lower part of the section is composed of alternative bands of fine gravels and coarse sand, which also yielded a few yellow patinated Middle Palaeolithic artifacts. Middle Palaeolithic tools were also collected from the gravel beds and surface at Kentaposh and Rill, and also from a rain gully near Garjan.

KHICHING AREA

Explorations undertaken by Subrata Chakrabarti in and around this area (Chakrabarti. S. 1990, 92, 93, 2000) have thrown new light on Palaeolitic Culture in Mayurbanj district. For these areas were believed to be devoid of palaeolithic sites. The area towards the east of Kiching consisting of the Simlipal Massif is the area where most of the sites are located. The area is watered by the river Baitarani and its tributaries. The Sites in the Khiching Plateau occurs in a radius of 5 sq. km The sites are single culture as well as multi cultural and they are of various types i.e. open air sites. channel bed sites and fliff-section sites.

The Middle Palaeolithic artifacts were found at six sites, the single-culture unit sites numbered only two. The multi culture occurrences aer represented by two sites of Lower and middle Palaeolithic, one site of Middle+Upper Palaeolithic+Mesolithic. The Middle Palaeolithic sites, wether single culture unit or otherwise, are divisible into channel bed sites and cliff section sites. Randomly 70 tools of this period were discovered, made mostly of crypto crystalline silica of various kinds. The types of tools collected were scrappers, flakes, borers, cores, points, notches and wastes of these tools scrapers predominated followed by blades, cores and borers. But of the 70 specimens largest were wastes forming about 31% of the collection.

Baripada Area

The sites in this area extend to the south and north of Baripada. The sites here at the macro level are situated in the same geological unit but at the micro level are located in different geomorphological settings. The Lower Pamaeolitic tools have been reported from 8 sites of which 4 are single cultural sites, 2 have yielded Lower and Middle Palaeolitic and one Lower, Middle and Mesolitic tools. In all 174 Palaeolithic tools were reported from these sites. The tools were divided into two groups; shaped tools (total 65) and simple tools and artifacts (total 109).

The middle Palaeolithic tools here have been collected from 3 sites, namely Bijay Ramchandrapur, Sandim and a site close to it on the right bank of the Ghuntru. There is however, no single culture unit Middle – Palaeolithic site from the area nor are they found from primary sites. Total 35 artifacts were collected. The assemblace consisted of scrapers, borers, points, notche, cores and flakes and included various types of scrapers borers and scraper-combination tools. F these the flakes were the largest followed by scrapers. The raw material used are fine graine stones like chert, chalcedony, jasper etc.

Upper Paleolithic Culture

The last cultural phase of the Palaeolithic is termed as the Upper Palaeolithic. This phase was unknown in India till the 60's. It was only in the 70's that a flake-blade industry, sometimes in association with burin were reported from various parts of the country (Till 1972 it was believed that no Upper Palaeolithic Cultural Stage at all existed in Indian Prehistory). Chittoor and Kurnool in Andhra Pradesh (Murty 1970), Sharanpur Doab in Karnataka (Paddaya 1970) Visadi in Gujrat (B.Allchin et al 1969, 70, 71, 72), Patne in Maharashtra (Sankalai 1974) and Belan river in Uttar Pradesh (G.R. Sharma 1973). It was seen that this industry was well defined and was stratigraphically placed between the Middle Palaeolithic and the Mesolithic. But Bhattacharya states (Bhattacharya 1996, pp. 116) "Upper Palaeolithic as a distinctive cultural stage in India is still not comparable to what we would understand by this term in southwest France, or for that matter Ukraine. It is essentially a typologically identified stage for most part of India. That is to say that except for the leaf points of Europe and Africa we have all the Upper Palaeolithic types of both Europe and Africa known from India". The other thing that is observed is the bone tools and art objects that start appearing and form a major characteristic of European Upper Palaeolithic is absent in India. But use of bone, ivory and antler for making various types of tools, weapon-heads and ornaments are reported. Bone tools were found in the Excavations at Billa Surgam cave in Kurnool district, at

Muchatla Chintamani Gavi cave also bone tools have been found. At Patne beads of Ostrich egg-shells and shells along with engraved Ostrich eggshell pieces have been reported. From this period onwards we start getting rock paintings also in the naturally formed rock shelters and caves. For executing these the roofs and walls were used. The colours used were organic and mineral colours in the shades of green, purple, red and white. The subject varied from hunting, ceremonial dancing, representations of animals and imaginative images. etc.

In India the industry of this period shows more stress on blade production, in this the principal tool-types being the blunted back knife, scraper, burin, lunate, point, awl, etc. generally the chief raw material used in this phase is fine to medium grained quartzite, quartz, porcelintic rocks, black lydianite, chalcedony, agate and blood stone and locally available raw material like jasper and chert of various shades. But as a whole variation is observed from region to region, in the frequency of occurrences of various tool types and their size and raw material i.e. at Muchchatla Chintamani Gavi in the Kurnool caves over 90% of the tools were of bone comprising of scrapers, chisels, perforators, scrapers, spatulas etc. (Thapar – 1985, pp. 12) (Murty-1974) where as at Renigunta in Dist. Chittoor the tools are largely dominated by blades and burins (Murty 1968, 1970).

The blade cores used in this period were also different from those used in the Upper Palaeolithic period. They were irregular, ovaloid, circular and discoidal in the Middle Palaeolithic but in the Upper Palaeolithic period they were made cylindrical, prismatic and conical.

In term of absolute years this period has been dated between 40,000 and 12,000 years B.P. and in geological time scale it belongs to the late part of the Pleistocene. In India this phase is also referred to as "Series III", "Blade and Burin", "Blade – Tool" and "Flake – Blade" industries.

The people in this period occupied the area on the river banks, foothills, rock shelters, caves and the plains and the tools of this culture have been found both on the surface and in stratified deposits.

Sites of this period are reported in the states of Rajasthan, Maharashtra, Madhya Pradesh, Bihar, Andhra Pradesh, Uttar Pradesh and Karnataka.

The technique used for making the blades were mainly indirect percussion or punch technique, chest-pressure technique, direct percussion technique, besides these methods various types of retouching were done on the blades i.e. steep retouch, abrupt retouch, blunting and backing.

Scholars also believe on the basis of the excavation at Patne in Maharashtra that man for the first time in this period started living a life of sedentism. For he started consumption of consumable foodgrains, construction of structures to live in, learnt the art of weaving, decorated his body with beads, decorated his living space with paintings, use of bow and arrow for hunting and sickle for harvesting and it is believed that with all these traits religious beliefs must have also evolved (Sali 1990, pp. 202) for a mother goddess figurine made of bone datable to 26, 100 B.P. is reported from Son (Bagor) (Thapar 1985, pp. 14).

Till the beginning of the 80's this phase was unknown in Orissa to the archaeologists. In the Pan Indian Context also the evidence of Upper Palaeolithic Culture was very scanty until a few decades ago. It is only in the last 4-5 decades that many Upper Palaeolithic Sites have been reported. (Sarkalia, 1956, Soundara Rajan 1958, Issac 1960, Seshadri 1962, Reddy 1968, Paddayya 1968-70, Murty 1974, Mishra 1974 and Sali 1990). In Orissa context after the Middle Palaeolithic, the Late Stone Age (Mesolithic) used to follow, for in Orissa the terminology used were the Early stone age for Early Palaeolithic, Middle stone age for Middle Palaeolithic and there was no Upper Palaeolithic. So the Late stone age was used for the Mesolithic. Even G.C. Mahapatra had said that, there is no Upper Palaeolithic culture in Orissa (Mahapatra 1962). However, now this does not hold true, for Upper Paleolithic cultures in Orissa is quite distinct by the distribution of the tool type of this epoch i.e. Blade and Burin.

It was due to the untiring efforts of S.C. Nanda who, in course of his 6 seasons of explorations for a period of 12 months spread from 1975 to 1980 for the first time explored the Indravati river basin along with its tributaries in the former Koraput Dist. He identified 17 sites belonging to this phase. According to Nanda, all the sites are open air sites located on the top, slope and foot of hills, on the plain lands and elevated coaste land covered with wild bushes and trees. Many Blade and Burin industry from Sundergarh, Mayurbhanj, Sambalpur and Kalahandi districts have been reported in the district gazetteer. At the present state of knowledge it is difficult to fix this culture in a definite stratigraphic horizon, unless systematic excavations are carried out at the identified Upper Paleolithic sites. The caracteristic features of the tool types of this period is "Blade and Burin". The chisel edge burins were probably used for engraving. In Orissa we don't find engravings on the bones, for they might have perished. There might have been engravings on them as evident from cave paintings and engravings etc., as noticed at Vikramkhol in Sambalpur district.

The Upper Paleolithic industry is divided into two groups on the basis of typo-technology. These are shaped artifacts and simple artifacts. The first group indicates delicate deliberate retouching on one or more edges with the exception of the Knife and includes scrapers, denticulates, notches, knives, borers, burins, backed blades and micro cresents. The second group of tools are the by products of the shaped tools, been used as tools with exception of utilized blades and flakes. They are cores, flakes, blades, chips and worked nodules. Chert was the principal raw material used for making artifacts. For making the tools the nodules were first made to required shape and size with a stone hammer. This is proved by the find of primary flakes with major portion of cortex, intact, existing on the dorsal surface. After this the blades were removed from it. Then it is observed that the percentage of blade core found is less than the percentage of blades reported. It is beleieved and proposed that the blade cores were further exploited for the removal of microblades. On the basis of the found specimens it is believed that for preparing blades no elaborate platform was made and they were generally made by indirect percussion technique, resulting in mostly irregular or some what parallel and comparatively thicker blades.

The flakes that are found are thick, irregular and large with prominent positive or negative bulbs. They were probably removed by stone hammers. They were then given final shape by chipping, Punching and retouching by soft and hollow hammers. As a whole the industry represents a very cruade craftsmanship.

The characteristic of the Upper Palaeolithic in Orissa on the basis of field work in defferent parts of the state is discussed briefly below.

MAYURBHANJ DISTRICT

Khiching Platue : The sites belonging to this period found in this area are mostly multi-culture sites, they are divisible into open air sites, channel-bed sites and cliff section sites. The occurrence of flake-blade and blade elements in two of the cliff sections suggest that the Middle Palaeolithic here was evolving into Upper Palaeolithic (Basa 2000, pp. 80).

Baripada – Kuliana – Kalabaria Complex : In this area of Mayurbhanj Dist. Upper Palaeolithic was unknown to the archaeologists till 1992, for before this period only Lower Palaeolithic, Middle Palaeolithic and Mesolithic was known. (Bose and Sen 1948, Mahapatra 1962, Thapar 1976). Chakrabarti in 1993 in course of his exploration in this area (Chakarbarti S. 1993) found the only Upper Palaeolithic from the site Kalapathara from 1m grid and about 3m non-grid area, Kalapathara is an ope-air site on an isolated hillock ata height of 70M contour with fairly wide area for habitation. In all about 135 artifacts were collected of thse 64 were collected from the 1x1 m grid and the rest 71 from the 3 m non-grid area. The raw material used for making the tools were ryolite, dolerite, dyke, quartzite, milky quartzite, cherty quartizite and basalt. Of these 110 tools were shaped tools consisting of burins, borers, beaks, points, knives, scrappers and notches and 92 were simple artifacts consisting of blades, flakes, cores, unfinished tools and waste products.

UNDIVIDED KORAPUT DISTRICT

It was S.C. Nanda who for the first time reported Upper Palaeolithic sites in Orissa during the course of his exploration work along the banks of the river Indravati and its tributaries. In all he discovered 17 sites belonging to this period. All these sites are open air sites located on the top, slope and foot of the hills, on the plains and waste lands. The area lies between 20m and 250m contour. The sites are distributed in between 1 and 7 km from the main river course as well as its tributaries.

In all 1281 tools were collected. The tools were divided into two groups. (1) Shaped artifacts consisting of scrapers, denticulates, notches, knives,Borers, burins, backed microblades and micro-crescents and (2)

Simple artifacts consisting of cores, flakes, nlades, chips and worked nodules. Of the total only 129 are shaped artifacts and the rest 1153 are simple artifacts. All the artifacts were collected from the surface and in association with them no other fossils or organic materials were found. The proportion of simple tools out number the shaped tools in the ratio 9:1 so the site must have been a workshop site. The raw material used is mainly chert. The technique was a combination of techniques i.e. stone hammer, soft hammer, indirect percussion or punch technique, and pressure chipping. No evidence of elaborate preparation of the platform is seen.

SAMBALPUR DISTRICT

Daridungri is small hillock located on the left bank of the newly dried up river Mahanadi in front of the Barapahar range. A swampy area lies between the Daridungri and Barapahar, which the explorers* believes is an palaeochannel of Mahanadi. On either side of the palaeochannel at the foot of Daridungri and Barapahar a few scrappy and thin deposit of lateritic implementifereous gravel congolomerates in eroded form were observed. From these deposit Upper Palaeolithic tools were collected. The tools collected mainly consisted of blade flakes and burins. (IA-1983-84-A Review. Pp. 64-66).

SUNDERGARH DISTRICT

In this area Behera (Behera P.K., 1989) for the first time discovered a full fledged blade industry at Brahmanimara, south of Jangla. In total 494 artifacts were collected, of these 139 were blades, 66 were bladelets, 206 are flakes and 83 are blade and bladelet cores. The finished tools comprised of retouched blades and flakes, few burins, backed bladelets, lunates, 2 awls and a triangle. As the tools were found on the surface their stratigraphical horizon could not be determined. So to ascertain the stratigraphy and the potentialities of the Upper Palaeolithic cultures in the region trial excavations at 2 different sites were carried out.

---

* (team from Guwahati University and Sambalpur University)

The first site selected was Birsa, a eroded cliff section located on the right bank of Birsa nullah which is a small tributary of river Koel and the site is located at a distrance of 18 Km Northeast of Roulkela. Here two trenches were taken for excavation measuring 3×2 m and 3.25 m sq. at two different sites. At both the places the upper cliff surface has been completely eroded. Below the upper deposit is a massive deposit of red silt, in this deposit Upper Palaeolithic artifacts were found in a very thin horizon of 5 cm thickness. The tool bearing horizon appeared at a depth of 96 cm. In Trench I and 40 cm in Trench II. The tools found were divided into finished and unfinished artifacts. The finished artifacts comprised of retouched and backed blades and bladelets, besides, lunates, points and scrapers. The unfinished ones comprised of croes, flakes, blades, bladelets and chips. The unfinished artifacts outnumbered the finished artifacts. The main raw material used for making the tools was milky quartz but tools made on black cherty, red jasper and hematite have also been found.

The second excavation was carried out at Bamanmara village that is located at a distance of 3 km from Jangra. Here also two trenches were taken, measuring 3x2 m and 2×2 m. In trench I a deposit of 1.30 m was come across above the bed rock. The deposit was divisible into 3 layers. The upper most layer was that of yellowish sandy silt and measured 30 cm. From the lower most part of this deposit were found highly patinated flaked nodules and chips of dolerite. This horizon is associated with the Neolithic industry of the region. The second layer was composed of reddish silty sand, from the lowermost part of this was found Upper Palaeolithic tools i.e. five blades and 3 flakes of chert. The lowest layer consisted of pale whitish brown silty clay with homogenous distribution of leached murram and no implements were found in it.

The second trench revealed only a deposit of 33 cm and only two layers were identified in it. The top one being of light brown fine sandy loam and the below one being of reddish coarse sandy loam. Upper Palaeolithic artifacts were encountered at the base of the second layer laying just above the undulating bedrock.

The tool assembly that was found from both the trenches were those of retouched blades, bladelets, flakes, lunates, backed-bladelets and a few triangles. The main raw material used for making these tools being chert. It is observed that the tools reported from Birsa and Bamanmara differ from each other in techno-typological details. (IA, 1984-85, A Review, pp. 60-61).

Thus we see that Upper Palaeolithic sites though not many in number yet their occurrences are significant as their presence suggests an unbroken continuity in stone age tradition in Orissa. But with more discovery of Upper Palaeolithic sites and their proper identification in the stratified layers of the riverine sections or in the excavations and after having a better insight into their distribution pattern we can have a much clearer picture of this phase of the prehistoric culture in Orissa.

MESOLITHIC CULTURE

Mesolithic period is the earliest post-pleistocene human culture i.e. Holocene, that occurs before the advent of agriculture. It is a period that bridges the Palaeolithic with Neolithic. The people in this period made very small tools of stone so they are referred to as microliths. But one should always remember that not all microliths belong to the Mesolithic phase. Microliths are found from the later Upper Palaeolithic phase and continues in the Chalcolithic and at places even in the historical period. So according to Sali "those microlithic industries which belong to the post Pleistocene times prior to those of Neolithic are only regarded as Mesolithic". (Sai 1990, pp. 229).

The Mesolithic phase in India can be dated approximately between 10,000 to 5,000 B.C. As agriculture does not begin at the same time in all the areas, hence Mesolithic period also shrinks or expands in India, depending on how late or early agriculture begins. The upper limit for Mesolithic is a tentative date and is an assumed one, for there is no C14 dates for the earliest Mesolithic phase till date. But this date of 10,000 is given on the basis of the evidence being found in succession after the Upper Palaeolithic with out any break from throughout the country. Where as the lowest level date of 5000 has been procured from Adamgarh and Bagor.

The tools of this phase are mainly blades, crescents or lunates, triangles or lunates, triangles, trapezes, rhombs, points, arrowheads, burins, scrapers and occasionally small choppers. The Mesolithic tools are grouped into two broad categories (1) geometric and (2) non-geometric.

Lunates are groupd in the non-geometric category and are believed to be of earlier date and the triangles and trapezes are geometric and are of later date. The other important aspect of the Mesolithic tool types is that almost each class of tool is further sub-divided into various subtypes i.e.blades are further divided into blunted or edge blade, pen-knife blades, crescentric blades etc.

Microliths normally range from 1cm to 6 cm in length and as they are detached by pressure flaking they measure not more than .5 to 1.5 cm in breadth. But evidences of much smaller specimens are reported from Baghor in Rajasthan. On the basis of the size and the technology Sali observes "thus in the progressive reduction in the size of stone tools the microlihs cultures represent the final stage of the technological evolution." (Sali 1990, pp. 229).

The raw material used by the people of this phase for making tool were mainly the locally available fine grained varieties of rocks like quartz, chert, agate, carnelian, chalcedony, jasper and crystal. At times silcified woods were also used.

On the basis of the finds of Mesolithic sites it is presumed that the Mesolithic people settled wherever they found favorable condition Mesolithic settlement have been found from almost all over the country, on the hills and plateaus, their foot and slopes, in the plains whether sandy, alluvial or rocky, in the rock shelters and caves, on the banks of the rivers, lakes, sea side and in the forests.

In this period some advanced traits were also noticed from all over the country which speak of their advancement towards sedentism and religious and spiritual beliefs. (For circular huts have been reported from Chopanimando, rubble structures are found at Karhegha and Baghor II, postholes at Patne; hearths, charcoal bits, burnt clay bits, red patches of land surface from Baghor II and Birbhanpur; stone flooring of a hut at Baghor; pottery, bones of domesticated animals, saddle querns and mullers, pestles and digging sticks from Patne, Baghor II, Adamgarh; burials were exposed at Langhnaj and Baghor).

In Orissa The Upper Paleolithic culture is followed by the Mesolithic culture. This culture is chiefly characterized by the Microliths and the regular tool types are scrapers, borers, burins, points, lunates, blade and burin both of single and backed variety. Flute, ordinary cores and flakes also occur in suitable number. No traces of fire or potsherds are found in this period. Economy of man was hunting and fishing. Use of ornaments and some type of burial practices were perhaps known to them (Sankalia 1979).

A large number of sites of Mesolithic cultural phase with Microlithic or flake blade industry have been found in many parts of Orissa, there by showing its wide spread distribution. The main features of this industry are as follows : (1) chert is the main material, (2) high percentage of blades occur in this assemblage, (3) backed blades is found to be the predominate type, (4) among the cores fluted core is found to be dominant and (5) there is high percentage of scrapers. The Microlithic collection also includes scrapers, denticulates, knives etc. made on large flakes of more than 6cm in length.

The Microliths are generally found in the same site along with the Middle Paleolithic tools or in the neighbouring areas. The inter-relation between the tool industries of two different cultural periods has been explained due to the use of the same type of raw material. At times the Microliths are found situated in red silt deposits and is collected from the surface (it is observed in case of Mesolithic sites of south-western Orissa).

The Microlithic industry in Orissa is mainly non-geometric in nature and no were are they found in association with pottery. The large number of Microlithic tools found at Udaygiri hills and other sites in Bhubaneswar, sites in Mayurbhanj, Keonjhar, Sundergarh basically show non-geometric form and includes core and blade in abundance. The other tool types are blades, points, scrapers, burin and flakes. These tools are generally found loose on the surface or in the dry bed of the river. Technically the industry appears to be crude and in some cases the tools specimen are found rolled and weathered. Same is the case with the Microlithic finds of southwestern Orissa, where the industry shows a high percentage of blades. The tool types include parallel sided blades, fluted cores, scrapers, flakes, obliquely retouched blade and lunates. This industry also presents a technically crude appearance.

The raw material used for the preparation of the Microlithic tools are similar to that of the Middle Palaeolithic industry. Apart from cherty-quartzite, chalcedony, jasper, opal and quartzite are the main rock types used in this industry. The Mesolithic sites of Keonjher, interestingly, have yielded heavy duty implements along with Mesolithic artifacts in the same assemblage. The lithic types comprises choppers, core-scrapers, picks, knives and large flake tools. Some times celts fashioned by means of flaking, pecking, grinding and polishing are also found in the assemblage, P. Mohanty suggests a culture of Mesolithic hunter-gatherers who exploited extensively the forest environment including forest clearance of extensive areas. The raw material for the heavy duty implements and Micrlithic tools are found to be completely different.

Kuchai, where systematic excavation in small scale was carried out by A.S.I. in 1961-66, does not give any clear-cut picture either of its age or the environmental condition at the time of the Microlithic industry (Thapar 1976). However, Mahapatra believes that this industry in Orissa begun in the Early Holocene period (Mahapatra 1964). Stratigraphically they occur before the advent of the polished stone celt and above the Upper Paleolithic and can be well compared with that of Sangankallu Phase I. Certain amount of similarity is also noticed in the tool type of Mirzapur (M.P.), Birbhanpur (W. Bengal) and Nagarjunakonda. (Andhra Padesh). At Nagarjunakonda Microliths have been reported from lower deposit and from the surface as well, like that seen in case of Orissa. This distribution pattern of the Mesolithic industry of Orissa has close similarity with other parts of India.

MAYURBHANJ DISTRICT

Khiching Area : The sites discovered here by Subrat Chakraborti (Chakraborti, S. 1990) are both single culture sites and multi-culture sites occurring within a radius of 5 km in the Khiching plateau. The sites can be categorized into open-air sites, channel bed sites and different section sites. Here Mesolithic has been reported from a channel bed, situated about half a kilometer donstream from Khiching inspection bungalow. The total collection exceeds 100 but they were collected randomly. The industry consists of backed blade-lets of various kinds. The tool types found are blades, points, scrapers, flakes, cores and wastes; of these the blades dominate the assemblage. Majority of tools are made on chert.

Kuchai : Excavation at the site of Kuchai was undertaken in 1961, by B.K. Thapar (Sali 1990, pp. 249). The Mesolithic remains were found in a deposit composed of gravels mixed with grayish earth and loose laterite, the tools reported are points, lunates, scrapers etc. (I A. 1961-62, A Review, p. 36, Fig. 11). Here a microlithic horizon without any ceramics was reported from the levels below a Neolithic horizon and both these are not very far from areas where Lower Palaeolithic was found (Bhattacharya 1996, pp. 129). The tools found were largely non-gemetric and was not found in association with pottery.

Damodarpur and Sandim : Here microliths are found on the surface. The tools collected are small and consisted of points, borers, scrapers, thumbnail scrapers, small chopper, blades and cores. As can be seen from the tool assembly the industry is purely non-geometric. Though the tools collected are in negligible number yet their occurrences are significant as the presence of these cultures suggests an unbroken continum in stone age tradition in Mayurbhanj.

PHULBANI DISTRICT

Khomananta : At Khomananta near the village Kalarajhuli a trial excavation was taken up by Ota (Ota S.B. 1986) at an open-air site to ascertain the undisturbed cultural horizon and the stratigraphical context of the microliths. (1A. 1982-83. a Review) The site is located on an oval shaped, flat ridge, lying 10m high and 2km south of the river. A seasonal stream, Adapatharjura flows on the eastern side of the ridge. The artifacts were found scatterd in an area of 30,000 sqm.

The trial pits were dug on the eroded surface of the rain gully and exposed a 1.35 thick deposit of red soil resting on laterite. The upper 80cm portion of the sidement was sterile, the cultural material was found in the bottom portion measuring 55cm in thickness. The principal raw material used was quartz, chert, chalcedony and quartzite.

The assemblage consisted of simple artifacts and retouched tools were small in number. The latter consisted of traiangles, backed blades; retouched tools were small in number. The later consisted of triangles, backed blades, retouched blades and crescents. Heavy tools were found along with the assemblage, consisting of unifacial pebble tools, large flakes, ring stones, retouches, anvils and hammer stones. Surface exploration yielded a few polished stone celts of dolerite.

Trial pits dug at this site showed that the Mesolithic occupation at this site was a prolonged one and that even the heavy tools from a part of the Mesolithic industry.

BOLANGIR AND PHULBANI DISTRICT

Exploration were undertaken in this two districts, covering the left banks of the Tel and the Mahanadi, both banks of the rivers Bagh and Gudguda and Meherani, both affluents of Mahanadi.

The Mesolithic sites on the left bank of river Tel were located in the reserve forest near Dhababahali, Kustapli, Lakarma, Ramai and Tithipali, one site has been found at Paikapal on the left bank of the Bagh. Mesolithic sites were discovered at Jamtangi, Saupara, North right bank of Jomghati, west of Chhelibahal, South west of Talupali and west of Karadapara. Gudguda nullah has yielded altogether four Mesolithic sites. (localities of which are distributed on both the banks) Near the bridge on the nullah, west of Jomtangi, west of Jampali and south of the Talpadar-Burhikan road. The upper reaches of Meherani has yielded eleven Mesolithic sites. (localities of which are distributed on both the banks) located at Santipali, Rabiri, Boulsingha, Sadanandapur road, Boulsingha, Tunimunda, Dhourakul, Gahirapali, Pachkhandi road, Badtharamunda, Selamal and Dolabali. Most of these Mesolithic sites are located close to the banks except in few cases, like the reserve forest sites on the left bank of the Tel, Paikapali on the left bank of the Mahanadi and Bad jharamunda on the left bank of the Meherani nullah, which lies away from the river banks on the foot hill zones. All these explored sites are of the open air type and are associated either with a thick deposit of red soil or with granite gnessic outcrops. These sites consists of more than one locality and some times the number of localities goes up to five or seven. The assemblages mainly consisted of both heavy duty tools and microliths of same nature as found earlier in the area in district Phulbani. Ota concludes by saying that "this findings confirm that the Mesolithic sites found so far (in 3 years) in both the districts, belong to one and the same cultural complex fixed on the basis of typological similarities in respect of the nature of sites and stone tool assemblages." (I.A. 1983-84. A Review. pp. 60-61)

KEONJHAR DISTRICT

Explorations in Ghasipur and Harichandanapur taluks of this district by P. Mohanty (I.A. 1983-84 – A Review) resulted in the discovery of 12 primary Mesolithic sites. The majority of the sites are in association with the granite outcrops and a few are on the foothills close to the tributary rivers. The sites are Karadapal, Tikira, Noapara, Kachiladarah, Karadabani, Sanahudi in Ghasipur Taluk and Palarpur (Rebna), Golibeda, Chilikadach and Bhagamunda in Harichandanapur taluk. Four of these sites are quite large with the artifacts found spread in an area measuring 100m x 100m.

Besides the above sites at a few rock outcrops stray microliths and heavy implements were reported. Although these spots cannot be called as sites but their significance for interpreting the working of the Mesolithic cultural system cannot be ruled out. The microlithic tools consisted of retouched blades, truncated blades, blunted backed blades, truncated blades, points, borers, crescents, traiangles, trapezes, side scrapers, scrapers, hallow scrapers, knives, flake cores, blade cores, worked nodules and chips. Chert was the principal raw material found in most of the sites. Quart, chalcedony and agate were also utilized for making the tools.

At Karadapal, Tikira, Noapara, Kachiladarah, Karadabani, Sonahudi, Palaspal, Galibeda, Chilikadarah and Bhagamunda, heavy-duty implements made of dolerite and quartzite in association with microlithic artifacts have been reported. Their types included uni and bi-facial choppers, points, discoidal cores having steep edges, scrapers, flakes, lunates, knives and celts. The celts lacked finishing at the cutting edge.

Exploration work at Champura, Gasipura, Ghatagaon, Harichandanpur, Palespal and Patna Taluks by P. Mohanty (I.A. 1986-87 – A Review) in this district further brought to light 57 Mesolithic sites. Most of the sites discovered are located in the granitic outcrops, whereas others were found in the foothill regions close to the streams. The area of spread of the sites differ. The site with the widest spread measures 20,000 m^2 where as the smallest ones have an extent of only $100m^2$. At present mostly all of them are located within dense forests and are located on the banks of smaller streams originating from the western hill, all of which join the Baitarani river, that drains the eastern portion of the district. The sites are now under dense forests. Most of the sites were primary sites and were undisturbed and still preserved habitational deposits. At places isolated Mesolithic artifacts in association with rock outcrops was also observed at quite a few plàces, which Mohanty believes to be short duration, single episode spots involving an individual or a small group engaged in food gathering or food-processing activities lasting from a few hours to a few days or might have served as satellites of larger sites.

The lithic industry of Keonjher consists of two distinct components : microlithic and heavy duty tools. Of the 58 sites 14 have only microliths, 5 have only heavy-duty tools and the remaining 39 sites they occur together. There is no stratigraphical evidence to separate the two components or to suggest they were deposited at different times. Thus it is clear that the heavy-duty tools found in this area form an integral part of the Mesolithic culture.

The tools discovered show that the blade technology was well developed. The main tool types reported are backed blades, obliquely truncated blades, retouched blades, burins, knives, triangles, trapeze, crescents, lunates, side scrapers, steep scrapers, thumb-nail scrapers, flake-cores, blade-cores, microblade cores, utilized blades, flakes and chips. The technique used were fluting, soft hammer of bone or wood, punch, or by pressure technique and then various types of retouchings were done on them. Chert was the main raw material used, besides these quartz, chalcedony and doletite were also used.

Along with these tools, heavy duty implements made of dolerite, quartzite and limestone are found. These differ from the microliths both in terms of raw material and their typo-technological features. The heavy duty implements comprise of chopper-chopping tools, horse-hoof scrapers, picks, knive, large scrapers, limaces and flakes. Celts fashioned by means of flaking grinding and polishing is another interesting category of implements. Mohanty on the basis of other parallels believe that core scrapers with edge-angle of 55-60° and above were used as wood-working tools and the edge-angle analysis of core-scrapers from Kenjhor sites shows that most of the core scrapers are having an angle between 55-80° thus confirming the belief. The horse-hoof scrapers is predominant among these heavy duty implements. These tools have steep edges obtained by means of steep flaking. These artifacts are mostly made on thick dolerite slabs and nodules. Most were prepared by minimum flaking along their margins, leaving much cortex intact. In all cores, the flat bottom of the raw material has been retained. Flake scars are generally shallow and do not show any prior preparation of the core. The nature of the flaking suggests the use of a controlled hammer technique, and secondary flaking along the margins is not very common. The raw material used was mainly chert, followed by quartz, sandstone, diorite, granite and geneiss.

As no fossil remains or organic remains were available at the site it is not possible to give absolute dates to the culture but on the basis of the blade technology and edge-ground tools these sites are dated tentatively by Mohanty between 5000 to 2000 B.C. (Mohanty, P. 1989, 1992, 1993)

SUNDERGARH DISTRICT

Upper Mahanadi Valley : In the Upper Mahanadi Valley in this district P.K. Behera (I.A. 1983-84 – A Review) undertook exploration work and brought to light many a pre-historic sites. In these Mesolithic sites were also reported from sites like Misankund on the Koel, Shigudighat near Bisra town and Pitamahal and other sites. Hundreds of microliths were found from the surface, lying on compact reddish brown weathered sandy silt deposits. The tool types collected comprised of blunted backed blades and bladelets, lunates, micro-gravette points, borers, burins, a variety of side and end scrapers and a solitary trapeze. Typical geometric forms are completely absent. The raw material used for manufacturing these tools is mainly metamorphosed shales and milky quartz.

Manikmunda : Here during the course of documentation work of the rock paintings by the Prehistory Branch of Archaeological Survey of India (I.A. 1991-92 – A Review) a large number of microliths were noticed embedded under the collapsed roof debris of the originally extended roof in front of the present rock shelter.

The microlithic assemblage comprised of both modified and simple artifacts. Blades were thin and small in size, some of which show utilization marks. Modified artifacts comprised of very small sized round scrapers, truncated flakes and retouched blade. The noteworthy feature of this assemblage was the occurrences of solitary chisel, grounded and polished at the working end. Artifacts were quite fresh and were made mainly on chert, chalcedony and quartz. Quartzite was rarely used.

Giripur : Near this village, which is located at a distance of 6 km from Heming road Railway station, Pradhan (I.A. 1991-92 – A Review) discovered a closter of rock-shelters locally called as Tango. Here on the back walls of these rock-shelters 250 specimens of paintings were reported. Below on the surface microliths such as blades, crescents points and burins along with a few specimens of hand-made pottery were found.

Sukhamankar : Sukhamankar, which is located in the Chhengaphar reserve forest, Pradhan (I.A. 1993-94 A Review) here, discovered some rock-shelters. Here in and around the rock shelters on the surface microlithic blades of different sizes without any micro-retouching; points, blade-points, crescents lunates, trapezes along with varieties of flakes, chips and cores and cores of chalcedony and quartz were found.

Hemagir – Kanika region : In this region Pradhan (I.A. 1992-93) located 12 rock-shelters. The paintings found here on the walls and the ceilings of the rock-shelters are dated stylistically and composition wise to the Prehistoric and Protohistoric period. Of these paintings Pradhan believes can be dated to the Mesolithic period for large number of microlithic tools were collected from in and around the rockshelters.

BOUDH DISTRICT

Boudh region consists of two geographical regions forming a part of the northern most extremity of the eastern ghats (1) Riverine plain drained by the Mahanadi and it's tributaries and (2) Hilly zones in the frontier of the district, which is inhabited by the tribals. In the exposed sections on the river banks can be seen red soil overlying the primary deposit of the laterite formation. In some parts of the region, particularly in the riverbank areas, can be seen black soil overlapping the alluvium deposit.

Balaram Tripathy (Basa K.K. Ed. 2000) undertook exploration work in this district and identified 14 Mesolithic sites at the following places Khuntiapara, Jogibhugra, Moryakud, Dholpur, Isisnga, Baghiapara, Paljhar, Bankapara, Tharasahi, Krsnamohanpur, Pargalpur and Boudh proper. All these sites are located in the Mahanadi and Salunki valleys, an tributary of river Mahanadi. The Mesolithic sites here occur in 3-context (1) river bank deposit (2) foothill region and (3) raised land/upland deposit, on the banks of the rivers and small nullahs. Few of the sites were manufacturing sites, while the rest were secondary sites. All the sites are open air sites and the Mesolithic sites are found in the alluvial deposit which varies from 1m to 3m, which was determined from different exposed sections.

The artifactual assemblage of Mesolithic in Boudh is of two types, namely, microlithic artifacts and heavy duty tools. The microlithic artifacts consists of both geometric and non-geometric shapes. The main tool type are blades, points, cresent, borer, scrapers, cores, flakes and chips. The occurrence of blades is more in comparison to the other geometric and non-gemetric tools like lunates, trapez, triangles and borers. The percentage of retouched blades are less and mostly comprises of parallel sided blades. The raw material used is siliceous material like chert quartz and chalcedony. The heavy duty tool consists of choppers, chopping tools, knives, large flakes, and cores and the raw material used is dolerite. Ring stone are also reported from Mesolithic sites here. The heavy implements have been convincingly explained as forming an integral part of the Mesolithic cultural stage. The occurrence of heavy duty tools has been explained with the help of local ecological conditions such as high rainfall areas covered with tropical deciduous forests (Paddaya 1994 : 12). Most probably the heavy tools were used for forest cleaning, wood working, house construction and food preparation (Mohanty, P., 1992).

ANGUL AND DHEKANAL DISTRICTS

In these districts Singh (Singh, 2000) carried out research work for a period of 6 years (1980-86). During the course of which he was able to identify sites belonging to different stone age periods, among these 6 belonged to the Mesolithic phase (Sarang, Meramandali, Talcher, Gotamara, Balaramprasad and Kurudale). All these sites are open air sites and the artifacts were collected from the loose rocky surface which rests above the kankrised layers. In all 472 tools of this period were collected. They comprised of 13 fluted cores, 2 fluted flakes, 150 flakes, 97 simple blades, 35 used blades, 62 backed blades, 47 small blades, 44 points, 11 scrapers, 11 lunates. The raw material used is mainly black chert and its different shades i.e. red, green and brown.

All the sites except Gotamara are located close to the Brahmani river and its tributaries Nandira and Lingara. At the site of Gotamara large number of flakes, blades, cores, reject materials and fragments of crude potteries have been recovered in large quantities and spread on a wide area. Where as in other sites the finds are distributed over a small area. Singh believes that the former one was the workshop-cum-habitation site whereas the later sites were used for temporary work. Earlier Mahapatra had reported some microliths from this area.

KORAPUT DISTRICT

Nanda (Nanda, 2000) during his exploration spread over an period of 12 months during 1975 to 80, he discovered 85 Mesolithic sites in the forested areas in the eastern part of the undivided Koraput district along river Indravati and its tributaries. Nanda has grouped the sites as foothill sites, hill slopes site, hill tope sites, plain land sites, elevated waste land sites and cultivated sites. Some of the sites have got disturbed due to cultivation. Majority of the sites occur within 1 to 7 km distance from the rivers. Average distance between the two sites is 2-5 km and most of the sites are in close vicinity of present tribal villages.

In all more than 8709 artifacts were collected from these 85 sites. The main raw material used is yellowish red chert. The other materials used but occasionally are chalcedony, quartzite, jasper and quartz. Typologically Nanda has classified them into two main groups i.e. shaped artifiacts or finished artifacts (844) and simple artifacts or unfinished artifacts (7865). The ratio between the simple artifacts and shaped artifacts is 9:1. The shaped artifacts are distinguished by an intentional retouch and blunting on micro-blades, blades and flakes, etc. they consist of 200 microliths and 624 flake tools. The main tool types of the microliths are retouched blades, truncated blades, blunted back blades, blunted back and truncated blades, points, crescents, triangles and trapeze of these the blunted back blades and crescents predominate. Where as of the flake tool variety, side scrapers, dejected scrapers, denticulates, notches, end scrapers, points, borers, burins, knives, etc. are the types.

The main component of simple artifacts are flake cores, blade cores, microblade cores, flakes, blades, micro-blades, chips, worked nodules and micro-burins. Nanda also made a comparative study between the blades of the Mesolithic culture and the Upper Palaeolithic phase. He found that the blades of Mesolithic phase are shorter and narrower than the Upper Palaeolithic blades but the thickness range of the blades was nearly the same in both the cultures. So he concludes that there has been an gradual reduction in the length and the breadth of the blades from Upper Palaeolithic to Mesolithic culture.

Trial Excavation a Girla : At Girla a large number of Microliths were found on the surface in an area of 42 sqm. This lured Nanda (Nanda . 2000). to undertake a small scale excavation here with the aim to determine the stratigraphic position and to define the nature of the industry. With this purpose a trench of 2×2 m was taken, then it was further divided into 4 squars of 1m each and they were named as A1, A2, B1 and B2. In each, digging was done up to a depth of 75 cm, of these the cultural material was confined up to a depth of 50 cm only. The largest catch of artifacts was recorded from the first 35 cm. The sections on the basis of colour, context and composition was divided into 3 layers :

Layer I – It was 5 cm thick, slightly loose in composition and reddish in color. But it was observed that the color of the soil darkens as one goes down.

Layer II – It is 30 cm thick and its color is reddish but is darker than layer I. According to Nanda this is the main cultural zone. The cultural material does not differ from that of layer I.

Layer III – The deposit in this layer is 40 cm thick and its color is red. The deposit here is more compact than the previous layers and is much humid and contains few angular debris. Of the 40 cm the cultural material is confinded to the upper 15 cm and the remaining part of the debris is sterile.

The finds were collected from 5 cm digs, they were sieved and sorted and documented. Then the find were classified on the basis of morphology, technology, raw material and functional aspect of each artifact.

The Tool Industry : The industry is dominated by mcirobIades and tools made on microblades. In all total of 3350 artifacts were collected from all the four squares, of these 338 were shaped artifacts and 3012 simple artifacts, there ratio being 1:9.

Of 338 shaped tools 279 are microlithis and 59 are flake tools, the main variety of microblades reported are : margin retouched micro-blades, oblique truncated micro-blades, transverse truncated micro-blades, backed micro-blades, margin backed micro-blades with oblique truncation, points, crescents, triangles and trapezes. The flake tools comprised of notched, end scrapers, side scrapers and points on flakes.

The simple artifacts comprised of microblades cores, flake cores, worked nodules, microblades, blades, utilized microblades, and utilized blades, flakes, chips and micro burins. Along with the above tools 3 pieces of hammer stones, one fragment of ring stone, two pieces of rubber stone and twenty-two pieces of rubbed iron oxide were reported. The main raw material used for making the tools are yellowish, reddish and greenish chert, they comprise of about 80% of the tools. Besides this quartz, chalcedony, granite and agate were also used in the same descending order.

Nanda on the basis of his collections, both from the surface and the excavations conclude that "there is no much difference in the proportion of the tools and the use of raw material in the two collections. There is no much discrepancy in the ratio in which the shaped and simple artifacts were reported from both the collection. The occurrence of the flake tools, flake cores and micro blade cores, knife is higher in the surface collection than those found in the excavations. The occurrence of microliths and micro-burins, triangles, trapeze in the excavated collection is much higher than those reported from the surface".

Among the flake tools, side scrapers, predominate the surface collection, while end scraper is the dominant type in excavated collection. Crescents dominate the microliths in the excavated collection, while the backed-blade is the dominate type in the surface collection. Thus from the above discussion it is evident that technologically there is no much variation among the two collection but typologically and morphologically the variation is very distinct.

JAIPUR DISTRICT

Darpankhas : Sahoo (Sahoo, D. 2000) did extensive surface exploration in the area in the year 1987-88. This resulted in the discovery of 6 Mesolithic and Neolithic sites, all of them were open air sites. The area of Darpankhas was divided in two parts i.e. North and South. The sites that fell in these zones were, Darpankhas, Sunamukhi Janghar and Ranibandhi in the norther; Dhanmandal, Kahanikia Tangar and Mahagiri Tangar in the southern zone respectively.

Research was carried out in a areas of 18 sq. km. approximately. The area included the hill ranges of the Barunavant, locally called the Baruna pahar or the Mahavinayak pahar and its surroundings erosional, undulated rocky foothills and lateritic plains. The Barunavant hill range is oriented east to west and is 6 km. long and 2 km. wide thus dividing the area into two.

The tools were collected applying random sampling technique as well as grid layout, at places where archaeological remains were suspected, few sections were studied to understand the stratigraphy and cultural chronology of the area. Further the artifacts collected during the surface exploration were analyzed and classified from typo-technological point of view.

The tools were collected from the surface as well as insitu. Altogether 1760 tools were collected of these only 1001 were complete tools. These included 974 microlothic and 27 Neolithic artifacts. The Mesolithic tool industry here comprised of cores (simple cores, polyhedral core); flakes (simple flake, utilized flakes and fluted flake); blades (simple blades, single sided blades, parallel blades, pen knife blade, backed blade, micro blade); scrapers (side scrapers, end scrapers, round scrapers, thumb scrapers and notched scraper); lunate, points, awl and borers. Besides this chips, spalls, nodules of different cryptocrystalline and crystalline rocks are also considerably found in the area. The raw material used for making the tools are mostly opaque to translucent rocks, ranging from medium to fine grained silicone rock types i.e. different shades of cherts, quartz, milky quartz, crystal quartz, cherty quartzite and jasper. The technique adopted for making the tools are impulsive pressure or punch and by wood. On many of the artifacts uni-facial and bifacial re-touchings are also observed.

From the above it is clear that the artifacts of Darpankhas are of the non-geometric type dominated by the core and blade industry. Here the tools show a gradual development from application of simple techniques to complex typologies. The tools are comparable with those, reported from Udayagiri hill in Jajpur (Mitra 1959) district, Bhubaneswar, Khurda district (Tripathy 1970) and Tangi (Tripathy and Kar 1993, and other parts of the state. The blades, cores and core scrapers especially resemble those reported from North Orissa and its neighbouring states.

On the basis of relative dating technique, it is believed that the Mesolithic culture of this area can be pushed back to the Holocene period and before the advent of Neolithic.

Stratigraphy : To reconstruct the Chrono-cultural sequence of the area, 3 sections were taken. The first one was at the site of Ranibandhi and the other two were from Dhanmandal. At all the three places similar type of stratigraphic deposition was observed from bottom the top with little metric and structural variations. In two sites out of the 3, bed rock in the form of laterite was not encountered i.e. one at Ranibandhi and another at Dhanmandal. On the other hand a section at Dhanmandal has the same stratigraphical sequence but has the laterite bed rock below the lower loose laterite. Thus the composit stratigraphy of the area reconstructed on the basis of the finds in the three areas is :

Silt (Recent humus);
Redsilt;
Lower loose gravelly silt;
Lower loose laterite;
Laterite (Bed rock)

Here from the red silt, from the depth of 28 cm ground and polished implements have been reported. Where as the microliths have been collected from the laterite rock surface. Thus establishing stratigraphically, that the Mesolithic people roamed this area and made tools prior to the emergence of Neolithic.

NEOLITHIC CULTURE

Neolithic is the youngest period of stone age history of man. In this period he becomes sedentary, which was due to change in his economy. He took up agriculture, which made him land tied. Sedentism gave rise to two distinct attributes. They are : firstly for agriculture large areas had to be cleared and then the land to be cultivated. For this new tools were produced adopting new techniques. The tools produced was axe or adze for cleaning the forests. For preparing it, first a hard and compact rock is selected and flaked, then the unwanted protrusions on the flake are removed by pecking and then finally the tool is rubbed on a hard rock surface with water and sand, resulting in metal-like smooth and sharp axes. The last stage being referred to as "grinding and polishing".

Secondly, agriculture is linked with surplus and even uncertainty. This gave rise to the need of storing for regularity and security of supply. This gave rise to pottery making, initially un-backed and later burnt. Thus management of land and also its produce became the main features of this period. It is therefore seen that, archaeologically when ever, either in exploration or excavation, ground celts, potsherds or permanent dwelling structures either individually or together are found are taken indicate a Neolithic culture. In Indian context till 1950's only the Neolithic finds were collected and reported but it was only in 1959 that V.D. Krishnaswamy for the first time gave them a regional treatment. His division was purely on the basis of techno-morphological characters of the celts, microliths or ceramics. He identified 4 zones, which were :

(1) The northern zone, covering the Kashmir valley and this was characterized by pit dwellings and painted butt-celts.

(2) The eastern zone, comprising of Bihar, Orissa, West Bengal and Assam. The artifacts reported was mainly from the surface and was characterized by varieties of shoulder celts.

(3) Central and western zone, this included some of the excavated and explored sites of Malwa region and Northern Maharastra. Neolithic here was characterized by microliths and potsherds and the occurrence of celts was less.

(4) Southern zone, this included the sites in south India and it was characterized by broad butt ended celts.

In 1962 Sankalia, who was working in the last two zones on the basis of his findings for the majority of sites which do not fit in within either a pure Neolithic or a pure calcolithic picture and hence these could be identified as Neo-Chalcolithic (Bhatacharya, 1996, pp. 135). According to him Indian Neolithic is of two types :

(1) True Neolithic : It could be said the sites(1) in Bihar, Bengal and Assam, which were characterized by ground axes with shoulders and very little pottery. (2) the Kashmir sites that are characterized by ground axes, bonetools, pottery and pitdwellings.

(2) Neo-Chalcolithic : The sites in South India in the states of Andhra Pradesh, Karnataka and Tamil Nadu. This phase was characterized by ground stone tools, microlithic blades, and handmade pottery and round huts, on hill terraces. From a few sites here even metal is reported.

Then he counts the sites at Baghor in Bhilwara as forming a separate Neo-Cahalcolithic group. Microliths, copper arrowheads, pottery and huts with wooden posts characterize this phase.

He even included the early Baluchi cultures in this category. The sites here show much developed habitational structures and ceramics, often wheel made. The cultural material reported consists of ring-stones, saddle-querns and celts.

Another noteworthy thing that daunts Indian Neolithic is that almost all the Neolithic sites in India can be dated at the most up to 2500 B.C. At around the same time the Harappan culture is also datable which is not only Chalcolithic but also associated with well developed literature, urban metropolis. Where as in the western and eastern neighbouring countries it can be dated to the 8000 to 6000 B.C.

What ever the case at present the Neolithic cultures in India have been divided into the following six geographical regions.

(1) The Northern Region, covering the Kashmir valley.
(2) The Vindhyan region, covering the Belan Valley and the Vindhyan plateau in district Allahabad, Mirzapur, Reva and Sidhi.
(3) Mid-eastern region, covering the northern Bihar district of Saran.
(4) North-eastern region (Assam complex) covering Assam and adjacent sub-Himalayana regions.
(5) Central eastern region (Bengal, Bihar and Orissa complex), covering the Chota Nagpur Plateau with its peneplains to West Bengal and Orissa.
(6) Southern region, covering peninsular India.

Besides these there is possibility of another Neolithic region, that of Gujarat and Rajasthan. The above divisions are done following broad physiographic sub-divisions displaying an apparent diversity in their ecological setting and cultural equipment. But at the same time it must be admitted that except for the Belan Valley, no where else in the other five regions have any one tried to figure out the details of the transition from the stage of food gathering to that of food producing and primary and settled village farming been worked out. Thus, Thapar is very apt when he remarks "our understanding of the origins and early spread of farming is therefore still very fragmentary." (Thapar 1985, pp. 25)

Orissa has a rich repository of the Neolithic stone tools. Different types of Neolithic implements have been found from various parts of the state. The find spots include former districts of Mayurbhanj, Sambalpur, Keonjhar, Sundergarh, Koraput, Puri, Ganjam, Dhenkanal, Phulbani and Bolangir. The first Neolithic implement was reported from Baidapur near Baripada in 1923-24 by P. Acharya . After this Neoliths have been reported from a number of places like Kiching, Rairangpur, Kuchai in the Mayurbhanj; Sarsara of Sambalpur; Sisupalgarh near Bhubaneshwar in Khurda District, Jaugada of Ganjam; Sankerjan and near by areas of

Angul; Taming in Koraput; Naira of Rayagada; Manmunda of Phulbani; Jangra of Sundergarh; and Udaypur, Ramala and Dengaposi in Keonjhar.

The earliest excavation was undertaken in the 20's by R. D. Banerjee and found Neoliths in association with pottery. The pottery are hand made, are thick and coarse and look like fragments of bricks. Some sherds have black slip at the base. But nothing was written about the tool type or the stratigraphy.

The excavation at Kuchai made by B.K. Thaper in 1961-62 has substantiated the fact that Neolithic culture has followed the Mesolithic cultures of Orissa. At Kuchai, Neolithic tools are found to be lying over a non-geometric microlithic culture. Stratigraphically the Neolithic implements occur in the late dry period of the Holocene period. These are generally found in the seasonal floods, silt and gravel of the river basins.

The Neolithic cultures of Orissa is distinguished by ground and polished tools along with celts fashioned by means of flaking and pecking, indicating the stage before they were grounded or polished. The raw materials used for manufacturing the Neolithic tools in Orissa are dolerite, basalt, genesis, sehist, epidiorite and diorite stone. These are usually hard and fine grained stones, exhibit a decent look when ground or polished and make the tools effective for agricultural pursuits. The associated finds with Neolithic tools in Orissa are pottery. Evidence of cultivation of rice and cereals are found from the excavation at Baidipur. The Neolothic tool types of Orissa includes axes, adges, fabricators, puch, stone hammer, wedge grinder, shouldered celts, bar-chisels, chisels and ring stones. The associated pottery of this period was mainly hand-made and grey-red in colour. Neolithic pottery have been found only in sites from Mayurbhanj District, Sarsara in Sambalpur and Taming in Koraput District. R. N. Das (Dash : 1987-88, 1990-93) has done extensive work on Neolithic cultures in Orissa.

The technological development of Neolithic tools indicate four stages in their preparation. Such as flaking, chipping, grinding and polishing. These also reveal grinding, alternate pecking and facet orienting. The shouldered celts are possibly developed at the later phase of Neolithic period. Postulating metal association. The shapes include triangles, rectangular and square along with few irregular ones. The butts indicate pointed, rectangular, square and round forms. Where as the working edge reveals convex, straight and oblique outlines. The ring stone are prepared by perforation from both the sides. The tools may be grouped under two categories. Category I has Indian types, while Category II shows a mixture of foreign types, well known as S.E.Asian Neolithic. In recent years Neolithic implements along with bone implements, harpoons and worked bones have been discovered from surface as well as excavation at Golabai in Khurda District (by Rath and A. Nath 1986, 90 and B.K. Sinha 1991-93). The excavations have revealed the association of pottery, circular house plans and secondary burials in association with copper. The evidence of animal life is provided by the discovery of antler and bones of (probably) bovine species and also the harpoon discovered in excavation at Golabai. P.K. Roy found similar evidences of Neolithic implements with burials and copper along with stone beads at Sankerjang in 1971. Absolute dating of Golabai and Sankerjang along with their cultural horizon are awaited. Scholars tend to call this cultures variously as Neolithic-Chalcolithic phase and some others think these have Neolithic and Chalcolithic phases separately.

Mahapatra (Mahapatra, 1962) on the basis of comparative study of the polished stone celt and shouldered celts with south-east Asian types, suggests Ist millinium B.C. as the date for the Orissa Neolithic culture.

Sarkar has dated the Nagarjunakonda Neolithic between 2500 to 1500 B.C. and since the pottery found there are similar to those found at Baidipur. He believes the date may be applicable for Orissan Neolithic also. According to Thaper (Thaper, 1985), this culture flourished in the last quarters of the 3rd millennium B.C. as the date on the basis of available evidences.

The Neolitic cultures of Orissa, particularly those sites, yielding pottery, have been compared with similar culture of Daojaliharding and Pandurajadhibi in Assam and West Bengal respectively. The Neolithic culture in Orissa seems to have started with the domestication of wild plants and animals, settled life in habitations along with the development of a ceramic industry and burial practices.

Neolithic Research in Orissa

Orissa is included in the East Indian Neolithic zone. So the high land as well as alluvial plains of Orissa forms a part of Thapar's Central Eastern

Region as far as Neolithic culture is concerned. In 1923-24 evidences of Neolithic was first reported by Padmashree Paramananda Acharya is his native village Baidipur area in the Mayurbhanj district (Acharya 1923-24). After him, Banerjee (1930), E.C. Worman Jr. (1949), Mitra, Ghosh and Chakrabarty (1958-59). Thapar (1976) have reported some more evidences from the same area. Discoveries of artifacts of this phase have been made fro Babaikala, Jadiapali, Dukura, Basipitha, Panchpir, Baripada, Khanua and Deodhipa in the district of Mayurbhanj. In the subsequent years scholars have reported large number of Neolithic sites from different parts of the state i.e. (I.A., 1958-59- A Review) Singh (1985 and 1988-89), Angul (Basa et al 2000; Mishra 1996-97), Keonjhar (Mitra and Ghosh 1958-59), Sundargarh (Datta-Majumdar, 1955; Mahapatra 1963; Tripathy 1982-83; Behera 1989, 1992 a, 1992b), Sambalpur (Mishra 1982-83), Bolangir (Tripathy 1972), Phulbani (Ota 1986), Boudh (Tripathy 2000), Koraput (Tripathy 1967; Prusty 1972), Kalahandi (Dash 1994; Singh Deo 2000), Ganjam (Mitra 1956-57), Puri (I.A., 1984-85 A Review), Khurda (Prusty 1996), Nayagarh (Kar and Basa 1998), Cuttack (Lal 1953; Dash 1987; Sahoo 1987-88 and Basa 1997).

P.K. Ray of the Archaeology Department, Govt. of Orissa, undertook an excavation at Neolithic-Chalcolithic burial site at Sankerjang in the district of Dhenkanal, presently in the distrct of Angul (Senapati and Tripathy, 1972). Similarly excavations at Golabai in the district of Khurda by B.K. Sinha of A.S.I., here period I revealed the prevalence of Neolithic. (Sinha 1993).

H.C. Chakladar (Chakladar, 1952) states that the Neolithic in Orissa is represented by ground tools, pottery and cultivation of cereals. Most of the tools collected are surface finds and they have been described by several people. But no one has ever tried to shed some light on the pottery discovered in association with them. He further states "potsherds indicating pottery of two distinct types, one pretty thick and the other comparatively thin, have been discovered with the Neolithic implements at Baidipur in Mayurbhanj, and at other stations also. Potsherds collected with the tools in the valley of the Sanjai, show on examination that in the preparation of the paste for manufacturing pots, husks of grains (Paddy) have been used with the clay for giving it greater binding strength".

In Orissa fourteen Neolithic tool types have been reported as per the availability. These are axes, adze, chisel, shouldered tool, ring stone, muller, corn-crusher or freak, flakes, indeterminate tool portions and rejects. The last three do not make proper tools but by products or un-ascertainable discards parts of tools. (Das 2000, pp. 201-221).

Das has done a detailed study of the tool types, for example only in the study of the cross section he has given so many types i.e.biconvex, Plano convex, rectangular, square, lenticular, oval, concave convex, parallelogramatic, circular, trapezoidal, elliptical and triangular types. In case of the blade edge of the axes, they are convex, straight oblique and indeterminate. (Das 2000, pp. 201-221).

The technology of making the axes in particular and other tools of these period is generally a contribution of different methods. According to Dash the proforma of combinations are in a permutation basis, such as, flaked and less ground, flaked and pecked; flaked and chipped and less ground; flaked, chipped and pecked; flaked and ground; flaked, pecked and less ground; chipped; chipped and flaked; chipped and less ground; chipped and ground; chipped, pecked and less ground; chipped, pecked and edge-ground; chipped, pecked and ground; chipped, pecked, ground and polished; pecked and ground; pecked, ground and polished; fully ground; ground and polished. (Das 2000, pp. 201-221) techno-typological analysis of the celts from various parts of Orissa has been carried out by a few scholars (Tripathy 1966-72, Behera 1989, Dash 1990-93).

The axes from the dominant type in the Orissan Neolithic, followed by chisels, chisels are of two varieties, namely chisels and elongated or bar chisels. They have been categorized so on the basis of their length i.e. 130 mm or less are termed 'chisel' and 140 mm or more are bar chisels. One of the distinctive feature of the Orissan Neolithic is the finding of shouldered tools. For these tools are typical to Northeast India and the southeast Asia, which also speaks about the probable trade or cultural links during that remote period, which share these cultural relics. Shouldered tools were generally used for agriculture in the form of hoes. But from the Orissan types their use as wood working tool, especially as adzes, and for various other purposes are indicated.

Distribution : River Mahanadi divides Orissa into two distinct Neolithic areas. The Northeastern part of Orissa is rich in bigger and flatter axes, and chisels of both smaller and bar types, whereas the southern part of the Mahanadi yielded more of smaller tools and the ring stones varieties, indicating two separate cultural units. But at micro level the distribution pattern shows further variation. Mayurbhanj region is dominated by the heavier-axes with broad cutting edges, though smaller chisels are also found. In Keonjher and Dhenkanal districts, bar-chisels along with smaller chisels form the main tool type. But to the south of river Mahanadi the tools are mostly small and lighter having affinities with the Chinese, Assamese and Kashmir Neoliths. In the districts of Koraput and Ganjam along with smaller tools, cylindrical heavy axes are reported, which is believed to be south Indian influence or intrusion. Even ring-stones are found in large number from the areas south of Mahanadi.

The eolithic culture in Orissa can be soundly placed in between the Mesolithic and the Chalcolithic cultural phases. Which has been tentatively dated to 3500-500 B.C. This is done on the basis of the excavations at Kuchai, Golabai and Sankaerjung. The date of Orissa is further strengthened on the basis of the C14 dates available for the sites in the neighboring states like Bihar, Andhra, Assam and West Bengal.

Scholars believe that the Neolithic of Orissa did not originate, all at once. It has undergone at least 5 stages in course of its development till it was replaced by the early metal culture. According to Dash (2000) these five stages are:

1. The oblong axes resemble the Palaeolithic types with arched butt and broad cutting edge appeared first.
2. This was followed by oval forms towards the last phase of the oblong type.
3. In this stage the tools were of triangular types with rounded corners and cylindrical types.
4. Quadrangular forms without the cornered edges belonged to this stage.
5. In the last stage were found purely quadrangular and facetted forms and at its fag end shouldered tools and bar-chisels appeared. The metal culture is initially represented by copper-chisel, awl, needle and

bangles, which probably appeared with the bar chisels and shouldered types to overthrow ultimately the Neolithic culture.

Pottery : Potteries have been reported from this phase in explorations and regular excavations. They have been found in association with the Neolithic tools and they even show primitive features. They have been reported by Acharya (1930), Banerjee (1930), Lal (1950), Ghosh and Thapar (1961), Prusty (1972), Dash (1978), Mishra et al (1982-83), Nath and Rath (1985-86), Singh (1988-89) and Dash, Tripathy and Prusty (1991). The potteries are of varied nature, their section varies from being as thick as brick to thinner types. scholars have identified 4 stages in its development. In the first stage thick to medium varieties of pottery are found i.e. brick sized from Baidipur and red gritty Micacious ware of coarse variety from Kuchai. The second type is a cord marked tapering body with painted base, high necked, grey and brown pottery. The 3rd type is black ware which have their types available outside India i.e. Thailand. The last type is a bigger round vessel with small round face and dull brown colour. Later these pottery types were replaced by a Chalcolithic pottery type as have been reported from Golabai and Gopalpur.

Rock Paintings

From Orissa rock paintings belonging to this phase have been reported from a large numbers of sites in Kalahandi, Sundargarh and Keonjhar districts. The paintings can be chronologically dated on the basis of their depictions i.e. the paintings at Manikmunda is believed to be the earliest. They depict the trapping of bull probably for domestication, which is a characteristic of the Neolithic period. Then from Yogimath we get a pastoral scene, which shows success in domestication of plants, which is also another development of the Neolithic period. From here only, depictions of ringstone, an artifact of the Neolithic period proves its Neolithic affliation. At Vikramkhol we have engravings depicting social and pastoral scenes having affinity with Mesolithic and Chalcolithic phases.

BARIPADA DISTRICT

Kuchai : It is about 8 Km to the north of Baripada along the national highway to Keonjhar. Here excavations were undertaken by B.K.Thapar in 1974 (Thapar 1985). The excavation revealed a 40-45 cm thick occupational deposit, yielding Neolithic artifacts together with a coarse grit tempered red ware. Which were sometimes slipped and had incised and finger-tip decoration, and an orange brown ware. Although a shouldered celt had earlier been collected from the area, no such tool was recovered from the excavation. The stone artifacts unearthed here comprised of rounded butt end axes, faceted hoes, chisels, maceheads, pounders and grinding stones. From the deposit below it that was composed of gravel mixed with grayish earth and loose laterite, microliths of essentially non-geometric industry were obtained. No pottery were found with these tools.

SUNDERGARH DISTRICT

Upper Brahmani Valley : Here in the upper Brahmani valley and its tributaries P.K.Behera (I.A.1983-84. A Review) undertook did exploration work. This resulted in discovery of a few Neolithic sites at Riu, Misankund, Jakeikela, Garjan and Brahmanimara near Jangla. From these sites ground stone axes, chisels and ring stones were reported. At Gajaran and Jakeikela a black burnished pottery was also encountered.

Deoposh : Excavations were carried out at Deoposh by Behera and Adhikari (I.A-A.R, 1984-85, pp-60-61) with the objective to ascertain the stratigraphy and potentialities of Upper Palaeolithic and Neolithic cultures in the region.

The site is situated on the northern extreme of a hill locally known as Burhapahar, on the left bank of the Brahmani, about 1 Km south of Bonaigarh township. Two small trenches measuring 1.5 × 1.5 m and 2 × 2 m were taken up at 2 different localities. One of the trenches yielded numerous potsherds of grey and coarse-gritty red ware and from the other was found' countless waste flakes and a few Neolithic celts.

The first trench yielded a total deposit of 50 cm , which was divided into 3 layers, resting directly on the reddish deposit of stone fragments washed down from the hill. The upper layer is formed by a light reddish brown silty gravelly sand, about 10-12 cm in thickness, which did not yield any cultural material. The second layer was composed of light colored gravelly sand, measuring 10-15 cm, which was found to be the cultural horizon of the site. The lower most layer comprised of lateritic gravelly sand and was sterile. The cultural materials retrieved from this trench, included sherds of grey and coarse gritty red ware, mostly wheel-turned and ill fired, reed impressed burnt clay and two dolerite chips, which Behra believes were taken-off during the process of manufacturing Neolithic celts.

The excavation in the second trench yielded only dolerite waste flakes and a solitary unfinished bar chisel at a depth of about 10 cm. However no potsherds were encountered here.

Bonaigarh : Bonaigarh sub-division is on the south east of the Sundargarh dist. The region comes under the northeastern hill regions of Orissa highland. Geographically, the area is an isolated hilly tract, surrounded by rugged forest clad hill, intersected by a few narrow valleys, which are the only outlet to the neighboring regions. Most of the area is about 200m MSL. The area is drained by the river Brahmani and its several tributaries. The area has a "Tropical Deciduous forest" type of vegetation. Behera (Behera P.K,2000) undertook extensive survey in the area in the years 1985-88 which resulted in the discovery of a large number of celt manufacturing localities as well as a few sites associated with celts and ceramics.

Most of the sites here are open air sites. The open air sites here have been found in two different geographical contexts viz. sites on the alluvial surface of the river banks and those in the foot hill or piedmont area. Except a few sites most of them are located on the banks of river Brahmani. The workshops that are on the foothills were also hear the riverbanks. This type of selection must have been due to ready availability of food, drink and raw material for making the tools. Behera has identified two types of sites i.e. workshop sites and habitational sites with celts and ceramic. He has further divided the workshop sites into two on the basis of the finds from the 18 sites explored by him i.e. Minor workshop sites and Major workshop sites.

Minor Workshop-Sites

These sites are mostly confined to the southern part and are generally found on the cliff surface of the rivers and foothills as well as piedmont areas, usually not very far from the river Brahmani. These sites are believed to be used for a short duration for the stone implements and debris found from these places are very substantial. From these sites mainly finished and semifinished celts of different types along with pebble tools, axes, adze, chopper-chopping, bored-stones, spearhead, grain pounders, elongated knife on pebble etc and debris were found of these axes of various types and chisels formed the main tool types in these workshops. The raw material used mainly was dolerite, particularly for fabricating celts. But at the same time it was observed that selection of specific raw-material for specific tool-types was also prevalent, as is seen in the core of bored pebbles, worked split pebbles and the waisted flat pebble. All the tools made of dolerite have patination of various degrees from reddish brown to yellowish color.

Major Workshop Sites : Of the 18 sites in Bonaigarh only one has yielded evidence for mass production of semifinished celts. The site is in the form of four massive debry mounds, located near village Sulabhdihi. The mound measures (1) 3 m high and having a diameter of 160 m. (2) 1 m high and 90 m in diameter, (3) 2.5 m high and 140 m in diameter and (4) having a height of 3 m and a diameter of 95 m. On the basis of the dimention of the mound and its context it is presumed that this site must have served as a very large Neolithic celt manufacturing center in this part of 'Central Eastern Neolithic zone' for a long period of time.

All over the mound can be found large dolerite boulder cores, numerous partially or fully flaked large celts in various stages of manufacturing process, besides tons of thick broad flakes and blades, waste chips and broken implements and hammers. So far, only at Shevray hill ranges in Tamilnadu such evidence of existence of extensive manufacturing of celts have been reported. (Narasimhai 1980)

No excavation was taken up here, but through mound I a pathway had been cut. The section exposed has a height of 2 m and rests over a natural layer composed of yellowish- brown compact silty clay soil mixed with weathered dolerite cobbles. The deposit consisted of artifact debris consisting of numerous rectangular shaped dolerite boulders with marks of core preparation on their surfaces, numerous specially struck flakes and blades, innumerable waste chips, which constitute 80% of the total debris deposit, consisting of primary, secondary and tertiary flakes of various length width and thickness, large number of prepared as well as unprepared dolerite pebbles and cobbles of different dimentions and lastely hundreds of broken as well as complete specimens of unfinished and semi-finished celts. Besides this one semi-finished axe and 4 semi-finished adzes were found. The surface preparation marks shows that two types of flakes technique was adopted by the workmen here i.e. quadrilateral and trilateral technique, of these the quadrilateral technique was more prolifically used.

Thus, it is seen from the above description that the artifacts reported from Mound I shows that this centre was more a manufacturing site for large scale production of semifinished chisels having chipped surfaces but were not micro-chipped and ground of the surfaces and hence were, semi-finished. In this context Behera states "every site need not be necessarily a place where implements were manufactured and also used. In the present case it appears that only semifinished as well as unfinished chisels were produced at Sulabhdihi, leaving final stage, like micro-chipping and grinding of the implements to the people who used them in their habitations and areas of activity."

It is presumed that the large-scale production of semi-finished chisels with medial rectangular cross-section was meant for local consumption, whereas the bar-chisels with triangular cross-section were manufactured by the knappers of Sulabhdihi with an intention for trade.

Sites with Celt and Ceramic : A throughout exploration of the area, it was revealed that the Neolithic people of Bonaigarh region preferred the alluvial plains, located on the river banks for habitation. To confirm this a trial excavation was taken up. The site chosed was located to the west of the Bargaon village at a distance of 1 km and the village is located on the left bank of the river Brahmani. The mound measured 40 × 25 m and had a height of about 3 m. on the surface itself potsherds belonging to different ceramic traditions were found scattered. Towards the southern side of the mound a small trench measuring 1.5 × 1.5 m was laid. The excavation revealed a total habitational deposit of about 140 cm, which had three distinct layers, which was done on the basis of the cultural contents in them. The soil composition, as such, in all the 3 layers is similar. The soil is composed of reddish brown sandy-silt.

The first layer had a deposit of 30 cm and yielded wheel made pottery and some iron objects and some iron objects, which include one broken part of a bowl, one nail and a double ended point. Most of the potsherds are of the red ware variety and has section of medium thickness. In some instances the potsherds are treated with red wash, and one example has a red slip. The shapes are vases being the most common followed by bowls, basins and occasionally carinated handis. The surface treatment included besides wash and slip, decorations with concentric grooves, notches and applique pattern.

The second layer measured 75 cm in thickness. It yielded wheel made potteries of red ware, grey ware and few suspected sherds of black and red ware. The potsherds are thick and wheel made with evidence of the use of quartz powder as tempering materials.

The third layer Measured 10 cm from this layer few shopeless, caorse and gritty red ware sherds, several celt, dressed flakes and a broken Semi-finished chisel were reported. The potsherds are thick wheel made with evidence of the use fo quartz powder as tempering materials.

The excavations suggest that the Neolithic culture complex of the Bonaigarh sub-division belonged to pre-iron phase and was associated with a coarse gritty-tempered red ware, a feature also noticed at Kuchai in the Mayurbhanj district of Orissa (Thapar 1985:45). The thermoluminencence dating of the Neolithic complex of Kuchai dates it to latter half of the 2nd millennium B.C. Thus, as Kuchai shares some characteristics with the Bonaigarh Neolithic culture, it could also be dated roughly to that period i.e. second half of the 2nd millennium B.C.

Dadhari : During exploration at a site called Dadhari located at a distance of 8 km north of Birsa township, yielded a few Neolithic celts and ring stones (Behera, 2000).

ANGUL AND DHENKANAL DISTRICTS

Singh (Singh.P.K. 2000) during the course of his survey carried out between 1990-85 in the districts of Angul and Dhenkanal covering a total area of 10,826 Sq Km. During this period besides discovering Lower Palaeolithic and Mesolithic sites, he even identified 19 Neolithic sites. Before Singh's research there was no evidence of Neolithic cultural remains from Dhenkanal except for the stray collections made by Mohapatra (1962). The sites are mostly found along river Brahmani and its tributaries like Nandira, Dingara, Kishinda, Matalia and Takua. The Neolithic sites reported are Nimidha, Sarang, Gotamara, Balaramprasad, Joragadia, Kurudole, Panchamahala, Turang, Ranigada, Sakosingha, Phulapada, Talmul, Jamunali, Parang, Kuia, Sankarjang, Ghantapada, Balhar and Dera.

The Neolithic people of this place generally preferred the locally available rocks like quartz and sandstone and it is in these source areas of raw material that implements are reported in large number. Tools made on dolerites and basalts were also reported. As these rocks are not locally available it is presumed that they might have been quarried from the adjoining localities, the exploitation of elongated quartzite river pebbles has been an interesting feature observed, especially at Kuia.

In all 211 tools were collected from these sites. The tool types are axes, adzes, chisels, bar celts, scrapers, ring stones, shoulder celts, chopper. The other associated materials that were found were crude and backed handmade pottery with grain impressions, pottery, earthern bead and stone beads. Singh further states that the recovery of crude and backed handmade pottery with grain impressions, massive and elongated bar celt, complete pottery containing ring stone, round and circular mud pellets, beads etc speaks about some of the traits of incipient agricultural and social life of the early man in this region.

Pallahara : It is a small town and is the sub-divisional headquarters of Pallahara sub-division of the Angul District. It is on the bank of Mankara river a tributary of river Brahmani, explorations were carried out in the Mankara river valley. (Basa.K.K.et al, 2000). The survey resulted in the discovery of prehistoric sites yielding artifacts belonging to the Palaeolithic, Mesolithic and Neolithic cultures. Of these the Neolithic were found at Somiapalli, Subranapalli, Pond site, between Subarnapalli and Somiapalli, opposite socio-economic development programme office, Pallahara college area, Bajpur, Muktapur, Illisuan and Udaupur. From amongst these sites a trial excavation was undertaken at Bajpur within a grid measuring 10×10 in an area of 1 × 1 m.

In all 205 Neolithic artifacts were recovered from the surface exploration and the excavation. The main tool types of the Neolithic here are axe, chisel, and dimple-scarred rubber, flakes and chips. The axes were usually made with rectangular butt, but a few are also found with irregular butt. Their working edge are beveled and made sharp ended. Chisels both finished and unfinished along with blank of quadrilateral shape are found. The dimple scarred rubber stone, are usually found on flat stones with depression dimple like shallow marks on one side and also on both the sides. The raw material used for making the tools here is predominantly dolerite, which are abundantly available locally.

Sankarjang

The site was visited by members from the Excavation Branch IV, Bhubaneswar and state Archeology. Here they found a few Neolithic tools which comprised of rigstones and small celts. Later Anthropology Department of Utkal univeristy also took up excavation work here.

Bajpur : The site is located on the left side of the National highway 6 towards keonjhar and 1 km away from Pallahara college. Here from the surface finished and unfinished axe, chisel, flakes, chips and potsherds were found. Here except an area of 200 sq m. all the rest are ploughed. On this site two trial trenches of 1 × 1m were laid. The lst trench 'T1' was from a square of a grid 10 × 10 m. From this trench no cultural material was retrieved except charcoal. In all a dig of 20 cm was taken in it.

'T2' was taken outside the grid area to its northwest on a relatively flat surface. In all the habitation deposit in this trench was 85 cm. The deposit is divided into 3 distinct layers. The Ist layer is 13 cm thick and is yellow reddish in colour. Layer 2 is 30 cm^2 thick Layer 3 is 42 cm thick and is reddish in color. In all 53 lithic artifacts belonging to the Mesolithic and Neolithic was recovered. Neolithic artifacts were recovered from the first two layers and microliths from the last layer. The Neolithic artifacts consisted of flakes, chips and no finished tools, all made on dolerite. Where as the Mesolithic tools comprised of bladelets, blade and crescents made on chert. Three body sherds of the coarse red ware were unearthed from this trench.

Pottery : Potsherds were recovered from the surface and excavation at Bajpur. Most of the pottery was, made on slow-wheel but few show coil method being also used. (coil method of preparation is inferred by existence of few ridges and grooves in the outer surface and inner surface of the potsherds). The potters have mixed fine sand with clay as tempering material. Two main types of pottery are identified i.e. coarse red ware and black and red ware.

The black and red wares are doubtful potteries for diagnostic or large fragments were reported nothing can be said about the shapes they formed. But the outer surface looks red and the inner is blackish so it is taken to be black and red ware. Whatever the case the black and red ware are in section where as the red ware are medium in section and is of coarse variety.

The potteries found here can be compared with those found at Kuchai. There are at least 3 similarities identified i.e. (a) coarse red ware (b) of bowls and tools (c) the use of red slip, between the Neolithic pottery at Kuchai and Bajpur. Further the sequence obtained at Trench 2 at Bajpur also broadly corresponds to that obtained at Kuchai by B.K. Thapar (Thapar, 1985). Scholars have tentatively tried to date them on the basis of chronology of the Early Metal Age sites in the same region to around 2nd millennium B.C.

BOUDH DISTRICT

Boudh : Tripathy (Tripathy 2000) undertook intensive exploration for 3 years (1993-96) in Boudh Dist of Orissa. The Exploration resulted in discovery of 6 Mesolithic, 1 Neolithic and 2 Early Historical sites. Boudh region consists of two geographical units forming a part of the northern most extremity of the eastern ghats (1) riverine plain drained by river Mahanadi and its tributaries and (2) hill zones in the frontier of the district which is inhabited by the tribal populations.

Here in some areas, a few celts of dolerite have been reported. At Manamunda also in the excavations a few implements belonging to the Neolithic culture were reported, but the main problem lies in the fact that without a clear cut cultural phase one cannot ascertain a particular nomenclature to a cultural phase. In the Boudh region the Neolithic celts are refered to as 'Charak Pathar' and are kept by the people in their houses to ward of lightening or thunder. Here till now also one site called Salalkata has yielded some polished stone implements and a variety of crude red ware. The site is 30 km south of Boudh town proper. But the site is badly disturbed due to agricultural activities. So till further research is carried out in the area nothing can be said about the Neolithic phase here, firmly.

PHULBANI DISTRICT

Members from the Excavation Branch IV, Bhubaneswar and State Archaeology undertook exploration in the estuary of the Tel and on the right bank of the Mahanadi, discovered a Neolithic celt made on chert from a mound locally known as Manmunda Asurgarh. A similar celt was picked up earlier at Malapadaghat near.the village shrimal (I.A-A.R. 1981-82, p-54)

JAJPUR DISTRICT

Sahoo (Sahoo D. 2000) did extensive surface exploration in the area in the year 1987-88. This resulted in the discovery of 6 Mesolithic and Neolithic sites, all of them were open air sites. The area of Darpankhas was divided in two parts i.e. North and South. The sites that fell in these zones were, Darpankhas, Sunamukbi janghar and Rani bandhi in the northern Dhanmandal, Kahanikia Tangar and Mahigiri Tangar in the southern zone respectively.

The area of research was 18 sq km approximately. The area included the hill ranges of the Barunavant, locally called the Baruna pahar or the, Mahavinayak Pahar and its srrounding erosional, undulated rocky foothills and lateritic plains. The Barunavant hill range is oriented east to west and is 6 km long and 2 km wide thus dividing the area into two.

The tools were collected applying random sampling technique as well as grid layout, at places where archaeological remains were suspected, few sections were studied to understand the stratigraphy and cultural chronology of the area. Further the artifacts collected during the surface exploration were analyzed and classified from typo-technological point of view.

The tools were collected from the surface as well as insitu. Altogether 1760 tools were collected of these only 1001 were complete tools. Out of the 6 sites explored at only one site Mahagiri Tangar did not yield any Neolithic relics. From the other 5 sites a total of 27 Neolithic tools of various types have been reported and the rest 974 were Microlithic tools. Of the 27 Neolithic tools two are rare types of implements an adze and an arrow head, which were recovered from a rain gully section at Dhanmandal near Konark Jute Limited. All the artifacts are generally found in the red silt deposit.

The Neolithic implements found here include ground axes chipped axes, adzes, chisels, shoulder axes, arrow head and broken ring stones. Of these some are unidentifiable but were collected and included for they possessed chipping and grinding marks. Some flakes made of dolerite and diorite are seen in the north western hills in the nearby areas of Darpankhas with granite outcrops and dykes.

The axes reported from here are of various types, they are pointed to rectangular butted, straight to round working edged and unibevelled to beveled longitudinal section. Except one chipped axe all others found were fully ground and polished in nature. Some of them even have chipping marks on them. The tools even have a developed shoulder. Those type of tools are reported from other parts of the state also. Its presence in Orissa implies that there was probable links with north eastern India.

The adzes found in the area is a proto type of modern Iron adze of a carpenter, showing unibevilled longitudinal section and rectangular cross-section with straight and highly utilized lateral working edge without an intact hafting end. Sahoo typo technologically sees a lot of akin ness of the adzes of this region and those collected from Sankarjung in Angul dist of central Orissa.

The ring stones are made of khandolite. They are not always circular but semicircular also with original cortex on it. They were bored from both side with a central perforation measuring about 1.5 cm to 3.5 cm in diameter.

The arrowhead, which has two straight sharp blade edge and a prominent ridge in the middle tapering towards the ends. It is devoid of its tip and tang portion. The raw material could not be identified.

Thus it is seen that the occurrence of adzes and polished implements and ringstones implies a gradual development of Neolithic culture from early stage of Neolithic to Late Neolithic period.

KHURDA DISTRICT

Golabai: Excavations were under taken here by the Excavation Branch IV of Archaeological Survey of India under the Directorshi of Dr. B.K. Sinha (Sinha, 2000) in the year 1991-92. Golabai Sasan in Khurda district is located in the laterite zone. It is on the left bank of river Mandakini, which is a tributary of River Daya. Earlier in 1986-87 during exploration here evidence of polished stone tools, bone pieces showing secondary work in association with painted pottery were found here.

The excavations here exposed 8m of habitational deposit giving a cultural sequence consisting of 3 periods:

(1) Period I : Neolithic	Circa 2300-2100 B.C.
(2) Period IIa : Osteo-Chalcolithic	Circa 2100-1100 B.C.
(3) Period IIb : Ferro-Chalcolithic	Circa 1100-900 B.C.

Here we shall only discuss the Ist period and the rest two in the proto historic section.

Only a small area belonging to the Neolithic period was exposed. The total height of this deposit is a little over 1m, consists of five layers. The layers were composed of compact clay of blakish dull red and bluish colors. In this level, traces of post holes and floor levels were noticed. No stone tools were reported but bone tools were found. One piercer made of bone and some bone pieces showing secondary work on them were found along with them a number of pieces of antlers and pieces of semi mineralized bones, which served as raw materials for making tools were found.

The potsherds recovered shows that both hand made as well as wheel made were used. They were generally of dull red and grey variety. Besides this a few sherds with red slip on them, having 7 mm thick section was also met with. The other types of surface treatment observed on some of the pot sherds, are (1) Grey ware, having chocolate slip or wash. (2) Post firing paintings in the form of bands around the neck were noticed with red ochre color. (3) hand made potteries were decorated with chord or reed impressions. The cord or reed impressed pottery is comparable to the Neolithic pottery unearthed at Daojali harding in Assam.

The main shapes, the wares form are shallow bowls and vases in dull red and grey wares. An interesting potsherd found here was a pot/lamp stand. It was both wheel and hand made, is in grey ware and is given a chocolate slip/wash on the exterior.

In this level even some structures were come across. The structures are of stone rubble set in mud. Sinha postulated that this structure possibly served as a boundary of the settlement for it was running north-south and its traces were noticed in the rain gully upto a considerable length.

NAYAGARH DISTRICT

Gopalpur (Jagati) : To the north of the Gopalpur village there is a small mound locally known as Jagati. The mound is north south oriented and it measures 140m x 115m and has a height of 9 m. A small stream, called Khatiari flowing from west to east has cut the mound in north south direction. The section of the mound is visible clearly from the eastern side. The exposed section contains many varieties of artifacts such as celts, potsherds, burnt clays, fragments of rubbing stones and bones. Such materials were collected from the surface and river bed.

The tools found are celts, perforated stones, fragment of rubbing stones, fragment of sharpeners, fragment of grinding stones and the raw material of which they are made are dolerite, basalt, sandstone and quartzite.

Potteries of various types have been collected from Jagati. Most of them have been collected from the surface randomly. They are of various types and in wide range of colors. The main varieties are red ware, red slipped ware, dull red ware, grey ware, cream slipped ware, chocolate ware, black and red ware and burnished black ware. The potteries are handmade, turntable made and wheel made.

The main shapes formed are storage jar, vases, handis, basins, lids, dish on stand, dish, bowls and minature pots, basins, high necked jars. Besides application of slip and wash the other surface treatments were chord marks, vertical parallel chord marks, uneven chord marks, applique designs, horizontal grooves and also finger pinching designs.

During the exploration no metal objects were recovered but according to the villagers they have collected metal implements made of copper, iron and gold from the river bed and surface. From the exploration faunal remains of cattle, buffalo, nilgai, chital, wildpig and rhinoceros have been reported. The faunal remains were analysed by P. Joglekar of Deccan college.

Kar (Kar, 2000) has compared the artifacts of Gopalpur with those found from Golabai, since it is situated just 20 km away from Gopalpur by road. Kar has classified the artifacts from Jagati on the lines of Golabai into IV cultural phases i.e. Phase I-Neolithic, Phase II-Chalcolithic. The other 2 being Historical.

At Golabai from Period I no stone tools were recovered. but some bone tools and wastes and raw materials were reported. The potteries were handmade; wheel made and were also made by slow wheel method. Dull red ware and grey ware have been noticed. The main shape was vases.

Where as from Gopalpur no bone industry is reported. The only criteria on which the finds of Gopalpur can be compared with Golabai period I is some specimens of dull red ware and grey ware. These are also made by hand, wheel and turn table and the main shape reported in these wares is the vase. This phase on the basis of the C14 dates available at Golabai can be dated prior to 2100 B.C. as the C14 dates for period IIa obtained is 2100B.C. to 1100 B.C.

Period II which is Chalcolithic shall be discussed in the next chapter on Proto history.

KALAHANDI AND NAUPADA DISTRICTS

Here in these districts explorations were taken up by Singh Deo. (Singh Deo 2000). In the rock shelters of Gudahandi, Yogimatha and Ghatghumar rock paintings have been reported. Of these the rock paintings at Yogimathdangar have been assigned to the Neolithic period as they show occupation of early men, to have been food producing or in agriculture and domestication of animals.

CHAPTER VI

PROTOHISTORIC CULTURES

According to Dhavalakar (Dhavalakar, 1997), Indian Protohistory is the period between 3000 B.C. to 600 B.C, which covers the Bronze Age, Chalcolithic cultures and part of the Iron Age. The generally accepted view is that Protohistory is the period when the knowledge of writing was there but we are not decifer able to decifer it, as has happened in the case of the Harappan script, or that literary evidence is available but there is no archaeological evidence to corroborated it i.e. the references in the Vedic literature.

(a) CHALOCOLITHIC CULTURE

The culture is so called for the tool assemblage of the people of this phase was Chalcolithic in character, they used copper on a restricted scale for the metal was scarce and a specialized blade-flake industry of siliceous stone like chalcedony and chert. It is presumed that there were all rural cultures, which did not develop into an urban status obviously because of inadequate technology for exploiting the environment. All of them flourished during the 2nd millennium B.C. and most of the settlements were deserted by the end of 2nd millennium B.C.

Our knowledge about the many aspects of the material culture of the Chalcolithic farmers is yet sketchy for the simple reason that most of the data are from explored sites and all the excavations except Golabai have been small exploratory digs. Consequent to this our knowledge about their origin, various stages of development and decline are all in a very incipient stage.

In Orissa, with regards to Protohistory scholars were skeptical about the very existence of this stage. Except Kuchai, which was excavated in 1964 (Thapar, 1975), no other site of this period is excavated. But recently not only has the number of Protohistoric sites been reported fiw of them have also been excavated.

Chalcolithic Research in Orissa

In Orissa it is believed that Protohistory or copper age culture commenced with the introduction of shouldered celts, both of the stone and metal. At the present state of our knowledge it is difficult to say, which one is earlier. Towards the end of polished stone celt culture of the Late Neolithic period, there are evidences that man knew the use of metal (Mahapatra 1962). Similar shouldered celts have been found in the Malaya, Hongkong etc, and they have been assigned to circa 1500 B.C. so it is probable that this culture began here around 1500 B.C.

A typical shouldered celt of Orissa is characterized by a clear cut angle and parallel sides, which is characteristic of metal type. It is also opened that metal tools were used for preparing stone celts. (Mahapatra 1962). It is generally believed that the culture of shouldered celt came from southeast Asia and the Knowledge of metal and its technology came from northwest India. Thus it can be presumed that Orissa was the junction of northeast, north west and southern Protohistoric or later Neolithic culture. The extension of the southern protohistoric culture is attested by the find of pottery of Baidipur type at Nagurjunakonda.

The oldest specimen discovered in Orissa is interistingly a copper plate grant of king Purushotamadeva of the Suryavamsi dynasty (1470 to 1497). It is an old copper shouldered axe. On the basis of its distribution it seems that, this culture has a wide distribution. Some of the excavated and explored sites are discussed below.

KHORDA DISTRICT

Golabai-Sasan : The Excavations were conducted by the Excavation Branch IV of ASI in the year 1991-92. Digging was taken up to a depth of 8m, which gave a cultural sequence consisting of 3 periods :

(1) Period I : Neolithic	Circa 2300-2100 B.C.
(2) Period IIa : Osteo-Chalcolithic	Circa 2100-1100 B.C.
(3) Period IIb : Ferro-Chalcolithic	Circa 1100-900 B.C.

An area of 175 sq. m. was excavated in seven trenches belonging to this phase and the total habitational deposit assignable to this period was 5m, which was divided into 14 layers (I.A. 1991-92 A Review, Dhavalikar 1997).

During period IIa (Period I has been discussed in the previous chapter) a new group of people arrived here but in the present state of our knowledge nothing can be said about the origins of the people who occupied Period IIa. They had a well developed ceramic industry, had knowledge of metallurgy and used bone, stone and copper tools, learnt the art of living a well settled life and took pleasure in making plastic arts. It is believed that the earlier people who occupied the site were assimilated within the new group.

In this phase at the lower level circular huts with post holes and hearts were noticed. In all 13 hurts having different dimension were found. The smallest of these had a diameter of 3.90 m while the largest, encountered, had a diameter of 7.90m. the biggest hut, possibly served as a community hut or could be the hut of the head of the settlement. In most of the cases the floors of the huts were made with rammed red clay and its borders made with yellow clay. The exception being in two cases the boundary of the hut was made of grayish clay, while in one case a clay wall formed the boundary. To support the super structure mostly small postholes were noticed on the periphery as well as on the inner side of the floors. In the bigger huts along with small postholes a few larger size postholes were also reported. The postholes on the periphery were ment for supporting the roof while those on the inner side were intended for internal partitions and the large one for supporting the super structure. From within most of the huts, a hearth in one corner was found and from the floor potsherds and tools were found. In the upper levels, handmade pots, possibly for storage purpose were found placed on these floors.

The tools unearthed from the excavations can be catogarised into 3 wide groups i.e. Lithic, Bone and Metal (copper). The lithic industry can further be divided into 2 groups :

(a) Microliths : Very few specimens of microliths have been reported. They consists of cores, points and parallel sided bladelets. The raw material used for making them are green chert, jasper and quartzite.

(b) Polished Stone Tools : They comprise of celts, adzes, chisels and edge sharpners. Of these adzes outnumbered others, in the number of occurrences. Adzes and celts were found in small as well as big sizes. A edge polisher was found which had a groove on its wider edge in to which edges of all adzes fitted. In addition a beautiful shouldered adge was found embedded in the mud floor of yellowish clay belonging to middle level of this period, speaks of its antiquity, than in the level it was found in. Besides these tools, pestels, grinding stones and grain. Powder of stone were also recovered from this period.

It is the first excavated site in Orissa that has yielded bone tools in large number. The tools have been made on antlers, semi-mineralized bones of humped cattle, sheep, goat and tusk of wild boar of these mostly the semi-mineralized bones have been preferred over the others. Discovery of adzes on semi-mineralized bone is the only one reported so far from Chalcolithic sites in India. In case of other bones, they have been charred in order ot provide compactness and strength. The tools yielded are polished, unpolished, crude and developed types. The excavator of the site has divided the bone tools into 3 categories. (1) Hunting Tools, (2) Domestic tools and (3) Digging tools :

(1) The Hunting tools consisted of points, spears heads, barbed spear heads and long points, (27 cm long) and single-row harpoons.

(2) Needles, engravers, burnishers, adze, blades, scrappers, side scrapers, borers, awl and denticulated blades comprised the domestic tools.
(3) Chisels and long tools with pointed edges were used as digging tools.

The technique used for making the bone tools were the same as used for making the stone tools i.e. percussion, flaking, splitting, cutting, notching, grinding and tempering. Stone adzes were used for flaking, splitting and scrapping.

Very few metal tools were recovered from the excavation, except for a chisel and a fish hook. This shows that the people knew the art of making metal, this is attested to by the find of a furnace from the middle level of period IIa. A large number of crucibles, long, narrow and tubular in shape and having rounded bottoms have been reported.

In this period leaving a few specimens of hand made pottery, all are wheel made. The main wares of this period are (1) Red burnished slip ware (2) Cholcolate burnished slip ware (3) Black slipped or black burnished slip ware (4) Black and red ware (5) Chocolate and red ware (6) Blakish grey or grey ware (7) Buff ware (8) Buffish red ware and (9) dull red ware, in this assemblage, the dull red ware dominates. Surface treatment of various types are observed on the potteries. The potteries have been provided with slip of red, black and chocolate colors, evidence of burnishing is seen and are also decorated with paintings appliqué and incised and painted designs. The incised and appliqué designs consisted of bands or loops of oblique cuts forming a pattern. These are found on the lips, neck and shoulder and sometimes on the inner side of the rim. The paintings are mostly post fired and are executed in red olive color. They are mostly horizontal bands, oblique and vertical lines and hatched triangles. These are also found on the lips, neck and shoulder and sometimes on the inner-side of the rim.

The shapes found are vases, bowls, handis, carinated handis, dishes, narrow beaked vases with lids, jars, basins, troughs, potsherds or lamp stand, dish on stand and Katoras (which is the most distinctive shape of this period). Of these shapes the most common shape is the carinated handi with a splayed out rim and short neck and these are in most of the cases having incised designs at the rim and the neck. Besides these shapes, miniature pots, about 5 cm in height, with featureless rim and curved base, were found from all levels of the period. These miniature pots were found in fairly good number and possibly were used as crucibles for smelting copper.

The people of this period subsisted partly on agriculture, livestock breeding, hunting and fishing. From the excavations rice, mong and kulth grains were found. On analysis they showed they were cultivated. Besides these finds of pestles, grinding stones and grain ponders also indicate that they practiced agriculture.

Bones of humped cattle, sheep, goat and cattle suggests that these animals were bred and domesticated. Hunting of wild animals and birds supplemented their diet, is attested to by finds of hunting tools like points, spearheads, barbed spearhead and long points 27 cm long. Find of bones of wild bore, deer and other members of the antelop family confirms this.

Fishing is attested to by the find of large number of fish bones and fishing tools like fish hook, barbed spear and harpoon. Sinha (Sinha 1996) believes that fishing was not limited to the near by water bodies but up to the Bay of Bengal. It is so believed due to the finds of 2 teeth of Shark from the early and middle levels of this period.

From the upper level of this period an extended burial was found. The burial was found under a floor and was oriented in east-west direction. The skeletal analysis revealed that it belonged to a female having a age below 10 years. Plenty of potsherds and other materials were found in its association. The bones were found in very brittle condition due to which many parts of the bones have been damaged. No skull was found with it even the legs below the knee were missing the first cervical vertebra was smashed and as no teeth are found, it is presumed that the individual was beheaded and the head was not placed in the grave. One such headless skeleton was found in the Chalcolithic levels at Pandu Rajar Dhibi in Bengal, and the absence of the fortion of th elegs below the ankles was a distinguishing feature of the burial luston in the Deccan Chalcolithic Dhavalakar (Dhavalkar 1997) states that the portion beow the ankles of the dead was deliberately chopped aff by the Jorwa people of Maharashtra, Probably with a view to prevent the dead from becoming a ghost. This be believes could have been the belief among the Chalcolithic Population of Orissa also. A copper bangle was found on the right wrist of the skeleton. Though this is the only burial from the period but it speaks a lot about the burial practice of the Chalcolithic people of this period. As the skeleton was not completely exposed its exact length could not be confirmed.

During the course of excavation leaving the above discussed, some other remains of material culture and art were also retrieved i.e. ornmanets, objects of daily use made of bone, copper, terracotta and faience.

Among the copper objects three rings and a bangle were found. Pendants and ear studs made of fish bones, one rectangular pendent of ivory are the items recovered that were made of bone. Terracotta objects comprised of sling balls of different sizes, hopscotch, discs, spindle whorls. Besides these a crude human figurine, handmade, measuring 3×2 cm has also been reported. Slight thinning at the top marks the head of the figurine, whereas blunt and horizontal projections mark the shoulders. Three beads of faience have been reported of these 2 are microbeads and the 3rd one is short and tubular in shape.

Then it is observed that the pottery types reported from Golabai have similarity with those found at Chirand. Even the bone tools have similarity but those found at Chirand are more developed than those found at Golabai. Two things, which are not reported from Chirand, are the Katora (Bowl) and the Harpoon. As the C14 dates found from both the sites gives an early date for Golabai by about 500 years Sinha (Basa 2000) states "Golabai owes nothing to Chirand but on the contrary Chirand shows a development on Golabai IIa".

The sites reported in the Middle Gangatic plains, as far as its material culture is concerned show affinity with Period IIa of Golabai but chronologically like Chirand they are also later than Golabai IIa.

Period II b

This period has been designated by Sinha (Sinha 1996 & Basa 2000) as the Ferro-Chalcolithic phase. The habitational deposit of this period was of over one meter. Excavation for this period was undertaken in only one quadrant. This 1m deposit was divided into 3 layers. As such there is no break between period IIa and Peiod IIb, only that degenration creeps in towards the last stage of IIa and further. All the attributes of period IIa such as stone tools, bone tools continue in this phase also. No house plan were encountered but floor levels with post holes were found. Two things, which separated IIa from IIb, are :

(1) Pottery : Though the burnished varieties of red, black and chocolate ware continue but are in a degenerated form and make their appearance. Then are (a) Tumbler, in black and red ware with internally sharpened rim, flaring sides and with a disc cut or ring base. (b) Convex sided bowls, again of black and red ware with feature less rim and incurved sides.

(2) Iron celt : This is the only and the most important find. It is akin to the other stone celts reported from the site and so is believed to have been copied from them. The celt measures 7.1 cm x 4 cm x 1.5 cm respectively. The technology of making of the tool seems to be very primitive and crude. It shows layers and appears to have been hammered into shape.

The material culture reported from Golabai is very rich and advanced. It is till date the only site of its kind reported from Orissa. The most important aspect from this site is the knowledge of metallurgy of iron. For in pan Indian context the date for iron is around 1000 B.C. but from the evidences from Golabai sasan this date can well be pushed back by at least another two centuries.

ANGUL DISTRICT

Shankerjung : It is located on the northern bank of the dried up stream Pandiani, a tributary of Brahmani. The site is in the form of cluster of mounds and the main group of the mound lies roughly 300m southeast of the peak of the Jaminia hill. The site is situated on the eastern fringe of the Athmallik hills and on a lateritic shelf at an altitude of some 200m above the sea level. The site was excavated by the State Archaeology Department, Orissa.

The mounds are spread over an area of 500 x 500 m and is cut across by a cart track that also crosses the Padiani. Three mounds were taken up for excavation. In all three layers were identified on top of the natural soil in all the mounds. The upper two layers were culturally sterile i.e. layer (1) and (2). The upper most was composed of a detrital deflated gravel, followed by a layer consisting of a packing of small quartzite chips and clay. Layer (3) was composed of reddish clay soil and yielded napped and ground Neolithic stone axes, adzes, chisels, shouldered celts, ring stones, copper bangles, chisels, celts and awls. The other objects found were large quantity of human bones and beads of shell and steatite, but no pottery was reported nor other cultural traits of Chalcolithic culture were found.

Due to presence of human skeletal remains in the pits in layer (3) the site may be considered as a burial site of a late Neolithic and Early Chalcolithic period. According to Yule and Rath the burials consisted of simple pits due to which lithic tools were found irregularly scattered along with the bangles and skeletal fragments. The teeth recovered from the 3 mounds gave evidence for at least 5 children and 4 adults and their diet is believed to have consisted of food rich in soft carbohydrates, perhaps rice, grain or peas. Stone and metallic grave goods were also derived from the same stratigraphic/chronological units.

The site is not important, for the cultural material recovered, but for giving the first radio-carbon date for Orissan Archaeological sites. The radiocarbon date available from the site is 2596+60BP, which comes to calibrated 795 B.C.

There is controversy about the probable use of the bar celts reported from the site. Yule (Yule et al, 1987) argues that the bar celts from Shankarjang were the earliest musical instruments in India and that they were similar to those reported from Vietnam. Whereas Dash (Dash 1986) believes that these tools bears thrashing marks of grain and hence, might have been used in pounding or corn-crunching or as mallets or even as nut crackers.

SUVARNAPUR DISTRICT

Khambesvaripalli : It is in Survarnapur district. The site of Khambesvaripalli is located at a distance of 4km from the Tahsil headquarters of Biramaharajpur. It is oriented SE-NE along the left bank of the river Mahanadi, the mound is partly eroded by the river and partly occupied by the present Khambesvaripalli village. It is approximately 130 m in length and 50m in width and has a height of 7m above the present bed of the Mahanadi. Trial vertical excavations were undertaken here in order to ascertain the cultural sequence of the site, by the Post-graduate Deptt. of History, Sambalpur. Trenches were laid at three places over the mound, covering a total area of 23 sq. m. The excavations revealed a habitational deposit of 2.20 m and it was divided into 3 periods i.e.e Period-I, Period-II and Period-III, of these Period I was further divided into Period IA and IB.

Period IA & B : These periods represented the Chalcolithic phase. The main pottery types reported were fine and lustrious specimens of plain as well as white painted black and red wares, plain as well as white painted red-slipped wares, plain red wares and cord impressed red wares. Most of the pottery were made on slow-wheel and were burnished; a few sherds of hand-made pottery were also reported. The shapes included bowls, bowls with perforations at the bottom, basins, convex-sided bowls with or without incipient lug handles, handis with splayed out rims, vases with ring bases, shallow bowl-on-stand, miniature handis with four legs and lids with hand made handles at the center. The surface treatment besides burnishing and wash/slip included painting of black and red ware of fine to medium fabric with cremish white color in the inner side. The painted designs included dots, rows of wavy and straight lines, zig-zag lines and 'w' patterns. Even red ochre pigments were observed used on the rim edges of some black and red wares.

The antiquities reported from this phase were stone celts, T.C. discs with or without perforation at the center, stone discs, bone points, T.C. spindle whorl and a few stone beads. But no metal was reported which Pradhan (Pradhan 1999) does not rule out at the site but believes it could be due to limited area of excavation. The first settlers lived in wattle and daub houses as was evident from burnt clay lumps with reed impressions.

Period II : The deposit in this phase is very different and is composed of black cotton soil. In this phase copper fragments have been found along with a few bone points and carnelian beads. Though the cultural material is the same in this phase also but degenration is seen, especially in case of the pottery and the occurrence of white painted black and red ware decreases in this period.

Period III : The deposit of this period was brownish to grayish colored sandy soil. This layer is disturbed for it yielded pottery types of the earlier phase and along with them was also found iron objects, glass bangles and cowri shells.

Though the excavations can not be said to be very fruitful due to the limited nature of the excavation, but it is important for it is the first reported Chalcolithic site from the Upper Mahanadi valley. The site can be compared with those of Aahar in Rajasthan with regards to the discovery of white painted black and red ware; with Chirand in Bihar, Pandu-Rajar-Dhibi and Mahisdal in W. Bengal with regards to the finding of bone tools and implements, which is an important trait of the Chalcolithic cultures of Eastern India.

NAYAGARH DISTRICT

Jagati Near Gopalpur : Here to the north of the Gopalpur village is a small mound locally known as Jagati. The mound is north south oriented and measures 140 m by 15 m and has a height of 9 m. A small stream called Khatiari flowing from west to east has cut the mound in north-south direction. From the eastern side the section of the mound is clearly visible. From the exposed section various types of artifacts were obtained such as celts, potsherds, burnt clay, fragments of rubbing stones and bones. Such materials were collected from the surface and riverbed.

The tools found are celts, perforated stones, fragments of rubbing stones, fragments of sharpeners and fragment of grinding stones. The raw materials used are, dolerite, basalt, sandstone and quartzite.

Potteries of various types have been collected from Jagati. Most of them have been collected from the surface randomly. They are of various types and are found in various shades of colors. The main varieties are red ware, red slipped ware, chocolate ware, black and red ware and burnished black ware. The potteries are made by hand, turntable and on wheel. The main shapes found are storage jar, vases, handis, basins, lids, dish on stand, dish, bowls and miniature pots, basins and high necked jars. The different types of surface treatment found are chord marks, appliqué designs, horizontal grooves and also finger pinching designs.

No metal objects were found but according to the villagers they have collected metal implements made of copper, iron and gold from the riverbed and surface. From exploration in the area faunal remains of cattle, buffalo, chital, nilgai, wild pig and rhinoceros have been reported. The faunal remains were analyzed by P.Joglekar of Deccan College.

Kar (Kar 2000) has compared the material remains from Gopalpur with those found from Golabai, since it is situated, just 20 km away from Gopalpur by road. He has classified the artifacts from Jagati on the lines of Golabai in to II cultural Phases i.e. Phase I Neolithic and Phase II Chalcolithic.

Here shall be discussed Phae II which is Chalcolithic and is comparable to Period IIa of Golabai. In this period potteries like black and red ware, burnished black ware and chocolate ware have been reported from amongst the specimens collected from Gopalpur, which are akin to the same type of potteries reported from Period IIa at Golabai sasan. A fragment of a base of a tumbler and a miniature pot are also having affinity with Period IIa of Golabai. But no bone tools or copper objects have been reported from Jagati so far. But the local people explained that they have collected many metal objects made of copper, iron and gold from the region.

Among the lithic tools reported from here are polished celts, varieties of rubbing stones and saddle querns, which are also a part and parcel of the period IIa at Golabai. But as the finds are not from stratified layers but surface finds, the comparison doesn't sound reasonable and rational.

KEONJHAR DISTRICT

Kanjipani / Kunar : It is a mound located on the right bank of tributary of Baitarani river called Masani mallah. The area is thickly forested. The mound has a flat top and has a height of 6.2 m from the bed of the Masani nallah. Masani and Ghumura nallaha surround the mound on three sides. It is accessible from the west. The site is oblong in shape, measuring about 196.15 m in length, running east to west. It is more or less kidney shaped; the narrowest part is about 9.3 m wide. The northern side is badly damaged for a number of tunnels cut through it. From these tunnels a large number of tools and potsherds were found. The souther slope though less disturbed, also yielded large number of tools on top also tools were found not in so profound number. Here both exploration and excavation were carried out for systematic collection of data. (Ray 1993). The artifacts collected from the site consists of large quantity of stone tools, potsherds, terracotta pieces, burnt clay pellets, charcoal and metal ornaments.

Stratigraphy for the site was reconstructed on the basis of the trial digging and observations made along the cliff section of the streams surrounding the mound. The top soil which is thin and rich in humus, is brown in color. Below it is a thick deposit of reddish brown silt, below this is a bed of coarse sandy layer mixed with grit. Below this is again a layer of reddish brown soil. The reddish brown soil lies on a thin bed of ghuting, which is made up of tubular lime concretions. Blow the ghuting is a silt bed. The silt bed lies over a bed of gravels lying loose in coarse, sandy matrix.

The tools are found over the bed of coarse and sandy layer mixed with grit and where ever the top 3 layers are eroded, the tools are found lying on the surface of the reddish brown soil.

The tool assembly from here consisted of axes, adzes, saddle queens, ring stone, hammer stone, various types of scrapers, blades, points, awls, burin, borers, knives as well as large quantity of flakes or chips. Tools were also made on flakes and most of the flake tools were scrapers with serrated and denticulated edges. Prepared core technique was also adopted for making awls. All the celts were made by chipping, pecking and grinding technique. Besides these saddle querns with ground and pitted surfaces were also reported.

The raw material used for making them was mainly basalt. Fluted cores on chert and quartz are reported but no tools were found. On the basis of the total assemblage from the site it is infered that the site was a workshop for tools both finished, unfinished and large quantity of waste flakes and cores are found all over the site.

The potsherds reported are mostly fragmentary so are undigonstic. But what could be known from them is, that the potsherds are red and buff in color. Due to use of tempering materials like sand, grit, husk and straw, they are coarse and in the cross-section of every sherd porosity can be seen. The rims show a tendency of thickness with slight rounded edges where as the necks are slender. The bases of the pots were mainly flat this is discerned from that is found. A very thick sherd with slugs embedded on it is believed to be part of a crucible. The analysis of which revealed that the metal is a very old type of brass, alloy of copper, zinc and tin. This makes one to believe that perhaps smelting was also carried out at the site.

From the site a few nonescript pieces of burnt earth, were reported which are small in size and ovaloid in shape and are burnt. They have protrusions present at one of the ends. These are believed to be used as pellets for slings.

The metal objects collected from the site are all ornaments comprising of nine bangles and two rings. They are made of bronze and its laboratory tests give the following composition for it. Copper-54%, Tin-8.5%, Zinc-33%, Lead 1.0%, Iron 2.5%. On the nine bangles two types of engraved designs are observed. Ist type has a number of protrusions intervened by parallel lines and the 2nd is designed with parallel lines engraved at equal intervals along the width of the bangle. The two rings are also having different decorations, one has parallel lines engraved at equal intervals along the width of the ring and the other has pyramid like protrusion made in a sequential order along the periphery of the ring. But both have a internal diameter of 60 mm.

The celts reported from here are chipped and ground from Barudih and Dueri these are cruder than those found by Sen and Chaturvedi (1958) at Chakradharpur. The findings from Kanjipani may broadly be placed after Neolithic and before the Iron Age (Ghosh et al 1984). As no full scale excavation was takenup it is necessary to have further exploration and excavations to get a fuller picture of the cultural pattern in the area.

DHENKANAL DISTRICT

Dunria : It is in Dhenkanal district in central Orissa. The site has yielded copper celts, its cutting edge is not sharp and it is shouldered type.

MAYURBHANJ DISTRICT

Baghada : Hoards of ten copper implements have been discovered from the bank of river Gilpha near Bahagada at a depth of one feet. Some of them are double-edge battle-axe type.

The other sites from where metal implements have been reported are Kiching, Panhapida, Khetra, Panchipir, Bamanghati, Kshetra in Mayaurbhanj District. Ladarpada in Keonjhar district.

At present nothing more could be said about this culture as we only get a faint out line of it from the discovery and distribution of the implements. Further work especially through excavations will help throw more light in future on the chronological phase in Orissa and throw more light on the pottery types, burial practices, diet and other aspects of this period.

(b) MEGALITHIC CULTURE

Megaliths are a variety of sepulcheral and commemorative monuments, which are either built of large stones, rude or chiseled or else associated with a some what homogenous group of the black and red ware and an equally homogenous group of iron tools and weapons. Generally they are group burials in which post exposure bones of more than one person are buried. Megalithic burials are generally found located in waste lands often over looking a tank or a river valley and cultivated fields. In many a instances they do not have most of the features of the Megalithic burials but even when one or the other diagonastic trait is present, if not then they can not be categorized as Megaliths. The Megaliths of North India compared to that of peninsular India are very different both in structural details and associated cultural complex. They are even believed to be of a little later date than the peninsular Megaliths. Here the Megaliths are not associated with homogenous group of pottery nor metallic objects or the mode of disposal of the dead and sepulchral monuments. The types of Megaliths that are reported from here are Cairn burials, chist burials, menhirs, pits curved in the rocks, simple slabbed cists, a cairn burial within a circle of stones etc.

Megaliths as such are found all over India but they have a very high concentration and are of various types in peninsular India, in the states of Tamilnadu, kerala, Karnataka and Andhra Pradesh. The concentration of Megalithic sites in other states are Maharashtra followed by Madhya Pradesh, Uttar Pradesh, Northeast Rajathan, Kashmir valley and Ladakh. The areas where they are not found are plains of Punjab, the Indo-ganga divide, the Ganga basin, the desert of Rajasthan and in parts of North Gujarat. (Ghosh, A., 1989).

The main types that are available are menhirs, dolmenoid cist, topical, kundan-kudai or hood stone, cairn-circle, multiple hood stone, alignment (series of menhirs, urn burials, rock-cut cave, porthole cist, trancepted cist, sarcophagus within a dolmenoid cist.

The Megaliths on the basis of themselves only have often been dated netween 1000 B.C. to A.D. 100 time bracket. But this is just an assumption for no C14 dates are available from any of the Megalithic graves. The second problem that plagues its dating is that, a number of tribal people in Northeast, East and South India still raise Megaliths as commemorative monuments. Then a few C14 dates that are available gives a very wide disparity i.e. date from Hallur is 1000 B.C. where as that from Pykara is 1000 A.D. Thus considering all the above facts, keeping in mind the concentration of C14 dates and the relative chronology on the basis of Archaeological data retrieved it is believed that the most affluent period of the Megalithic was between 600 BC and 100 A.D. for a period of 700 years (Ghosh, A., 1989, pp. 111)

A long lingering problem in the field of Orissan archaeology is to establish the Megalithic culture as a distinctive cultural phenomenon. Most of the works carried out are mostly based on ethnographic observations. In Orissa, erecting Megalithis is prevalent among the tribes inhabitating the hilly regions of Koraput and Phulbani. (Haimendorf, F.C. Von., 1943). But as yet not a single Megalithic burial site is excavated in the whole of Orissa, and therefore except the casual observation made on the Megalithic practices among the tribes of Orissa, no scientific research has yet been carried out to ascertain the actual nature of these burials. But the problem of its date and value as an integral part of iron age culture is not yet done, though a large number of sites have been reported. R.N. Das reported of dolmenoid chist near Rajbhawan in Bhubaneswar and dolemens were reported near Sisupalgarh in 1948 by A.S.I. Das also reported about stone circles near Gangadhar minor irrigation project, and reported iron implements from Gudaveda and Kharligarh in Mayurbhanj district. It has been seen that most of the sites of the stone circle variety are found in western and central Orissa but not a single site has been reported from coastal Orissa. So far not a single Megalithic burial site has been excavated in the whole of Orissa. Thus we are not sure whether they carry any sort of skeletal remain or any material culture associated with it, so as to have a clear picture of the burial practices, the extension of this culture and to see if any similarity existed with the South Indian Megalithic culture.

It has been suggested by some scholars that some of the black and red ware shapes found from the excavations at Sisipalgarh in 1948 and collected from the surface at Manamuada in Baudh district and Nehana near Khariar can very well be compared with similar shapes found from Megalithic burial sites of south India. The black and red ware found in western and central Orissa occurred in the lower strata and they are generally dated between 900 to 400 B.C. This ware has graffiti marks, which are not floral or faunal motives but carry some ritualistic symbols, as have been found in the Megalithic burials of south India. (Wheeler 1948,).

BOUDH DISTRICT

In the Boudh region both Menhirs and Stone circles are found in large numbers but nothing can be said about its contains unless and until systematic excavations are taken up at any of these sites. In this area the stone circles are called 'Punja Pathar' meaning a heap of stones and are found in places like Mohuli, Maryakud, Nanden, Birgarh, etc. whereas Menhirs are noticed in places like Tileswar, Jamtangi and Boudh proper. One of the menhirs has been taken from its original location, is locally worshipped as a village deity and is placed on the outskirts of the village.

KALAHANDI AND NAUPADA DISTRICTS

Megaliths are still raised in these areas. (Singh, Deo, 2000). Survey conducted by Singh Deo revealed Megalithic remains on top of the Rishipititi hill near Tukla Village and at Chandel dangar, the heighest peak of Kudal reserved forest, situated to the south west of Khariar at these sites, the stone boulders are noticed in a wall like heap with ritual spot at the centre.

At Sandohel, which is on the left bank of the river Sundar, a Megalithic twin urn burial is reported. Besides that in the village itself a circle or cairns, measuring 9m in diameter exists. A trial excavation was taken in its centre. The excavations yielded one twin burial associated with thick black and red ware, red ware, iron objects and one huge iron spear, measuring one and a half meter. Few fragments of human bones were also recovered from within the twin-urn. Along with them few sherds of black ware was also found. Singh Deo, on the basis of the Megalithic chronology of Vidharba and south India postulates a tentative date for the Megaliths here to the middle of 1st millennium B.C.

At another site called Nehena which is located close to sandohel and is on the bank of the same river sundar has revealed some remains of Megalithic culture along with a few ringstones and lithic celts. Black and red ware with white painting at the outer black suface has been refuted besides this a funnel shaped potsherd has also been reported which has resemblance to those found from Brahmagiri in Karnataka.

SUNDARGARH DISTRICT

Jangla : Here at Jangla evidences of some Megalithic monuments have been reported but no details have been given.

Thus the need of the hour is systematic exploration, excavation and proper documentation of the sites to solve the problem existing in the context of Megalithic culture in Orissa in particular and this will also fill in the gap between the Megalithic cultures of the Vidharba region and south India, in general.

CHAPTER VII

ROCK ART OF ORISSA

All types of artistic expressions noticed on the rock surfaces of caves, rock shelters and boulders is termed as rock art. The earliest artistic expressions of the prehistoric men are found executed on bare rock faces in the naturally formed caves and on rock surface using paints and bruishing. Rock art is found all over the world and it dates back to as early as 30,000 B.P. and is reported from more than 150 countries and regions across the world, if put together, would number over a million. Art is the genuine reflection of human mind, inner thoughts and beliefs and are of great help to us in determining the contemporary environment, means of subsistence and the mode of man-nature relationship of primitive people. Further we don't get any authentic records other than the artifacts, so these rock art comes handy and provides us clues about their society, customs religion, rituals, implements, technology, contemporary flora, fauna, dress etc.

Rock art is divided into two categories viz. Pictographs and petroglyphs (Pradhan, 2001). Pictographs are done with pigments on rock surface, the pigments are made out of minerals of different hues like ochre, white etc. Pictographs are otherwise also called as rock paintings. Petroglyphs are made by engraving, scooping on the rock surface. As the pre-historic man was primarily a hunter, his paintings depict the scenes of hunting. Scholars have different views over the probable purpose and function of these art. Some believe that the function was magical, it was the fear of the animal, religious, for some it was purely aesthetic and for personal delight i.e. "art for arts sake", where others attribute to the early paintings some mystic, religious beliefs, because of the representation of certain animals and the absence of human figures in them.

The discovery and study of Rock Art is a global phenomena since they are reported from all over the world barring a few countries in Europe, having a wide distribution and lasting for a longe period. In the history of men, ranging from the pre-historic to the historic period.

The discovery of magnificent painted Bison in the caverns of Altamira, on the North coast of Spain has ushered a new era in the Stone Age painting studies and researches. Every continent claimed to have vestiges of pre-historic paintings in global context except Antarctica. The devotion and talents of scholars have brought to light stone age engraving, carving, modelling and painting from Europe, Northern and Eastern Asia, North, Central and South America, East, South and Savana Africa and Australia.

India ranks 3rd in the world, next only to Australia and South Africa as far as rock art is concerned. India played the role of pioneer as far as rock art research is concerned, as the first rock bruising work (Petroglyphs) of pre-historic man was reported by Henwood from Almora in India in 1856 (Henwood, 1856). Rock painting by Carlleyle in 1868 (prior to the discovery of Altamira in Spain) at Sohagighat in Mirzapur District of U.P (Pradhan 2001). John Cockburn was the first British scholar to publish for the first time a scientific article on painted Rock Art of Kaimur Rangs in 1883 (Cockburn, 1883). Thereafter many scholars took interest and the report of exploration and research started coming from different parts of our sub-continent viz. Kozhikode (Kerala) in 1901, Ladakh region in 1902, Rock art of Distt. Banda in 1907, Rock art of Raigarh in Chattisgarh in 1918, M. Ghosh studied Rock Art of Mirzapur, Adamgarah and Raigarh in 1932, Vikramkhol by Prof. K.P. Jayaswal in 1933.

Mention may be made of the contributions of D.N. Gordan (1958) F.R. Alchin, R.K. Verma, J. Gupta, V.S. Wakankar, S.K. Pandey, A. Sundara, Y Mathapal, Giri Raj Kumar, Sonawane, K.K. Chakravorty, G. Mahapatra and S. Pradhan in bringing to light their painstaking discoveries of Rock Art Shelters and sites in different part of the country (India).

It is seen that now after a period of 150 years since the discovery of Ist rock-art site, today we have rock art reported from throughout the length and breadth of the country. According to an rough estimate in India we have more than 500 rock art sites, consisting of several rock art shelters in each site.

In the north, rock art is reported from altitudes as high as 4000 m. in Kargil and Leh, Ladhak region (Neumayer, 1983, 1993). From this area mostly petroglyphs have been reported. In the Himalayan region both pictographs and petroglyphs are reported from the stratified belts of sandstone, limestone, shale, granite and schist.

About 66% of the rock art of India are reported from central India, in the quartzite and sandstone beds of the Vindhyas. Here in a area spread over 40,000 sq. miles are found 457 painted rock shelters in the Betwa source region, spread over a chain of 31 hills; 400 rock shelters with paintings within a cluster of 542 rock shelters at Bhimbetka (Mathpal 1984); 250 painted rock shelters in Mirzapur (Tiwari, 1990) and 650 painted rock shelters in 63 complexes in the chambal valley (Kumar, et.al, 1992). This central Indian zone has reported more of rock painting and negligible number of petroglyphs.

Peninsular India is too rich in rock art, which are found on the granite hillocks. They are found and are well distributed in all the 4 south Indian states i.e. Karnataka, Tamil Nadu, Andhra Pradesh and Kerala. South Indian rock art is mainly known for its petroglyphs, though paintings are also found but in insignificant numbers (Pradhan, 2001).

Besides this rock art is found fairly distributed in the states of Gujarat and Maharashtra in the West Bengal, Bihar and Orissa in the east and also from the Northeast in the states of Assam and Manipur. (Indian Archaeology Review, 1982-83 : 104, 1983-84 : 59-60).

The study of rock art in orissa started as early as the early 30's of the 20th C. It was Dr. K.P. Jayaswal who in 1933 discovered one of the earliest rock engraving site in India at Vikramkhol in Jharsuguda District (erstwhile Sambalpur district (Jayswal, 1935). But after this there was a lull in Rock art research for about two decades. Then S.N. Rajguru (1950) and J.P. Singh Deo (197) reported about discovery of two important rock art sites namely Gudahandi and Jogimath in the erstwhile districts of Kalahandi and Naupara respectively. Ulap in Jharsuguda district,

Ushakuthi and Manikmoda in Sundargarh district were reported in the District Gazetters of 1971 and 1975 respectively. (Senapati, N. (ed.) 1971, 1975). Rock Art at Pathanpathar near Jamda in Mayurbhanj distrit was reported in 1975 in the Indian Archaeology A. Review 1975-76, p. 37. Behera and Neymayer (1992 and 1993) reports about the discovery of 5 painted rock-shelters in Chhiengapahad in Sundergarh district. (Behera, P.K., 1992).

Then the most detailed survey and documentation work was carrid out by S. Pradhan, who identified 40 new rock art sites and re-documented the earlier 15 sites thus giving a new dimension to the rock-art research in Orissa. According to Pradhan (Pradhan, 2001) there are 2241 specimens of paintings and 3534 speciments of engraving reported from 55 rock shelters. Of these 31 rock shelters have only engravings, 9 have engravings and paintings and 15 have only paintings. It is surprising to note that all the rock art sites in Orissa are reported from the western part of the state comprising of the ditricts of Jharsuguda, Kalahandi, Mayurbhanj, Sambalpur, Sundergarh and Suvrarnapur. Out of these the largest concentration of sites is seen in the districts of Sambalpur and Sundergarh. This is due to the favourable gemorphological situation, for being part of the Vindhyan sandstone formations and being extension of chotanagpur plateau and the Chhattisgarh basin. Here the rock system is represented by the sedimentories of fossiliferous purple, ferruginous sandstone, siltstone, shales and grits. In the fringes and cliffs of these rock formations that nature has created caves and rockshelters hidden under thick foliage, giving a strategic location for keeping an watch on the movement of wild animals and games. So were chosen by the prehistoric hunter-gathers as places to reside and for ages they were in use by different hunting-gathering groups. In course of these stays, the people have left behind their imprints in the form of artifacts and other refuges lying embedded on the floors of the shelters and paintings and engravings on the walls and roofs of the rock shelters. Though a large number of rock shelters exist in the geological formations but rock art is found in only a few of them.

An interesting aspect of the rock art sites is that, they are locally known either as 'Lekhamoda' meaning rock shelter with writing (Lekha-writing, Moda-shelter), or 'Ushakuthi' meaning worship hall (Usha-

worship, Kuthi-hall), or 'Ushakupa' meaning ritual cavity. (Usha-ritual, Kupa-cavity) or 'Lekhapathar meaning stone with writing (lekha-writing, pathar-stone). Many of these are even associated with characters in the epics i.e. Rama, Sita and Bhima. So they are known as Sitakund, Bhimamandoli etc. (Pradhan, 1999). Lekhamoda and Ushakuthi are the two most frequently used terms for shelters irrespective of their locations and subject matter of depiction. So to identify one Ushakuthi or Lekhamoda from the other, the hills in which they are located is identified and named accordingly, i.e. Deulluga Ushakuthi or Ulapgarh Ushakuthi. Even some of the reserve forests are named after the rock shelter located in them, like the reserve forest cf Vikramkhole in Jharsugada, reserve forest of Ushakothi near Rajbahal in Sundergarh etc. scholars for convenience of documentation and for its easy identification and to avoid confusion to identify one rock shelter from the other located on the same hill. The sites are given short forms i.e. for Ushakuthi UKT, Lekhamoda LMD etc. and numbered in roman like UKT-I, II, III; LMD-I, II, III. Then the numbering is done on the basis of priority of their discovery and documentation.

The following are the main characteristics features of the rock art of Orissa :

1. The rock shelters are situated deep in side the forests, several kilometers away from the present day habitation. The paintings and engravings are executed in the fringes and cliffs of the sandstone hills and are at approachable heights.
2. The color pigments used in the paintings are minerals dark red, purple, white, yellow, blue and black, blue and in combination with red and white in the polychrome paintings of decorative patterns and symbols. The paintings are done directly on the back walls and marginal roof of the rock shelters.
3. The paintings in Orissa on the whole appears as jumble of indefinite geometric and non-geometric pattern and forms with a host of wavy, zig-zag, criss-cross and parallel lines randomly executed all over the surface of the wall. Only a few motifes are similar to the central Indian wavy and rhombic designs, these paintings are all independent patterns unlike the central Indian

style of filling the geometric body of the animal and human figures.

4. The unique feature of the Orissa rock art is the complete absence of hunting and chasing scenes, restricted depiction of human and animal forms, and the popular depiction of human and animal forms, and the popular depiction of certain patterns like the harpoon and broom, which is not found any where else in India.
5. In the rock art of Orissa engravings constitutes a special feature along with the paintings, both being complementary to each other, which is rarely found else where in India. The engravings are linear, boldly incised deep into the soft sandstone faces measuring 20mm x 10mm (width and depth) and they were filled with paste of deep red ocher. Nothing can be said about the chronological attributes of these engravings for they lack evidence of superimpositions, stylistic differentiation and narrative pictoral depiction so commonly found in the rock paintings of central India. The engravings have been executed with much care and precision but they are abstract in their conception, which is believed to have some kind of mystic or ritualistic significance or both. The engravings mostly constitute of geometric patterns like zig-zag lines, triangles, circles, grid of vertical and horizontal lines, squares and spirals. But the anthropomorphic forms are absent, other popular motives found are female genitals, rhombic patterns, palm, foot, brackets and cobra hood marks with dots, some of the motives have faint resemblance with the central Indian paintings of the Mesolithic period. The carving of the female genitals of various shapes and sizes with natural or carved out holes and slits predominate the carvings in these rock shelters. What do they mean? Do they have any thing to do with the fertility rites? Do they depict the primordial mother, the source of creation of all beings? All these questions baffle all interpretation.

Some of the important rock shelter sites have been described below are as follows :

KALAHANDI DISTRICT

Gudahandi : It is situated at a distance of 20 km. from Kaksara in Kalahandi district. It is located on the left bank of a nallah. The site was first reported by S.N. Rajguru in 1950. The site in all preserved 24 specimens of paintings which are badly eroded. The paintings are executed in red, blue and yellow colors. Th rock shelter at Gudahandi is oriented east west and is facing north. The motifs include a human figure in red and variety of geometric patterns of single or double squares, rectangles, either empty or filledin with straight or diagonal lines with or without dots on the borders, circles, wheels, apsidal patterns, oval shapes with dots executed either in mono chrome or in poly chrome of red, blue and black. The notable scenes are genital pattern cobrahood, a large canine animal, wheels with spokes etc.

NAUAPARA DISTRICT

Jogimath : It is in Naupara district. It is located on top of a granite hillock near the village Risigaon at a distance of about 10 km. from Khariar. J.P. Singh Deo reported it in 1976. Here the paintings are found at two rock shelters. The rock shelter is made of boulders and in all 27 paintings have been reported, they are painted in dark red, purple red and bi-chrome of red and white. The paintings include a variety of astronomical and geometric forms like circles one upon the other, circles within circles, simple squares, bow like shapes one upon the other, dambaru like shapes, stick like human figures, bull with or without humps and many other shapes. The treatment is linear. The early paintings suffer due to large-scale disfigurement by human vandalism and superimposition of ritualistic symbols, like tridents, swastika and other auspicious symbols drawn upon with paste of vermillion and ghee. The early paintings are also of two periods. They are identified on the basis of the color used i.e. in the earlier phase paintings were mono chrome in red color, where as in the later phase they are in bichrome of red and white and are believed to belong to later historical period, as is evident from the exaggerated circles with their radiating lines and other astronomical symbols.

JHARSUGUDA DISTRICT

Vikramkhol : Situated at a distance of 8 Km. from Belpahar within Reserve forest named after the rockshelter. The theme here consists of engraving and paintings. The rock shelter here is facing northeast and the engravings are spread over an area of 11m x 2.10 m. K.P. Jayaswal discovered it in 1933. He opened that the engravings are pictographic inscription, which is partially incised and partially painted, and they belong to a period between the Harappan script and the Brahmin. Many other scholars also share the same view. He further opined that the writing was from right to left. Here also we get the usual depictions of the triangular pattern resembling the female genitals, footprints, double triangles, cobra hood marks, brackets with dots, geometric and floral patterns. The rainwater streaming on the rock surface has eroded most of the engravings and paintings. The engravings were originally filled with paste of red ochre whose traces are still available in their grooves. Besides the engravings the rock surface was also painted with various motifs a few traces are available here and there. Altogether 68 specimens have been studied at Vikramkhol.

Pradhan (2001 : 29) states that on the basis of his observations of the engravings documented by him from 40 rock shelters, numbering 3534, comes to the conclusion that the engravings at Vikramkhol are definitely not a script for he finds no difference between the engravings at Vikramkhol and other motifs reported from elsewhere in Orissa.

Ulapgarh Ushakuthi : It is in Jaharsugadha district. It is situated at a distance of about 7 km north west of Belpahar town and near the village Ulap. Here both paintings and engravings are found. In all 400 specimens are reported of these 280 are paintings and the rest 120 are engravings. The paintings are done with monochrome of red, bi-chrome of red and white and polychrome of red, white and yellow. The paintings consist of geometric and non-gemoetric designs, wavy and zigzag lines, spirals, series of triangles, honeycomb, broom or beaten brush marks, ladder, wheel with spokes and a host of intricate patterns and designs. Here also over lapping of paintings is seen, the bi-chrome red and white overlap the monochrome red color.

The engravings are painted in red. The engravings are mixed with the paintings. The forms that they make are palm, foot, triangular female genital patterns, zigzag lines, circles, brackets, dots, loops, hoofs, cobra-hood marks and many other, which can not be described or interpreted. They are mostly linear and non-figurative in representation.

SAMBALPUR DISTRICT

In Sambalpur district in 1999 Dec S. Pradhan discovered 25 rock shelters. These are all located in the Rairakhol tehsil in the two hill ranges namely Rail and Landimal and they house 12 and 13 rock shelters respectively. The local people believe that the works of art in these shelters are the handiworks of the gods and goddesses who lived in them. So the hills are highly venerated by them. May be, due to this, the rock shelters are locally called 'Ushakuthi' for easy identification of the sholars they have been numbered serially depending on the priority of their discovery and documentation i.e. UKT-I to UKT-XII at Rail and those at Londimal also as UKT-I to UKT-XI, for the other are located at Bhimamandli. At all the 25 rock shelters only engravings are found and not a singl specimen of painting could be found. The engravings have been filled in with ochre pigments.

The engravings are done in two types. In the first instance, drawing the outlines of the figures and motifs by deep incisions and in the second case by making shallow depression of the specimen, specially of the animal forms by scooping th rock surface after the outline is drawn. The main motives engraved consists of : triangles resembling female genitals, these are most profuse, geometric and non-geometric patterns and motifs with criss-cross, wavy, straight and parallel lines, hoofs, strokes, palms, cupulas, dots and foot. The animal forms represented are deer, antler, boar, samber, birds (peacock, crane) Serpentines, lizards, turtle, fish etc. besides these of special interest are the anthropomorphic form with a large vulva suspending at the bottom of UKT-XII and along with it is depicted a male genital. The other is a long necked animal superimposed by a series of triangles at Rail UKT-X, which could either be a giraffe or an ostrich or nilgai.

Here at all the sites it is seen that the engravings have been superimposed over several a times due to which engravings below them have been distorted. It has been observed that the scooped out patterns are later works for they have been executed over the earlier engravings in the form of line drawings. The subject matter here is also non-thematic (Pradhan, 2001).

SUVARNAPUR DISTRICT

Chandli Ushakuthi : In this district in the reserve forests of Pujadumguri, a rock art site has been reported. The rock shelter is called Chandli Ushakuthi for it is located near the village Chandli. The rock surface has both paintings in ochre and engravings but most of them have been lost due to weathering and erosion. Of what survives the representations are those of deer, boar, foot and cupules.

MAYURBHANJ DITRICT

Pakhanpathar : Rairangpur tehsil of Mayurbhanj district has also yielded Rock art site at Pakhanapathar near village Jamda which are the Eastern most limit of rock art boardering West Bengal. In Pakhana Pathar rock painting are noticed in three shelters. According to Dr. S. Pradhan, the largest of them has a different kind of unusual painting documented for the first time in Orissa. The composition made of series of Roman 'S' like forms, circles, dots, strokes, superimposed one upon the other connected by crescents and semi circles drawn in monochrome of red are beyond any interpretations and probable usages and are drawn at an unusual height of 7.26m.

In other two shelters traces of ochre are quite prominent, a lizard like figure on the rock shelter no. 2 is the only form that could be identified.

SUNDERGARH DISRICT

In Sundergarh district 24 rock art shelters have been identified. They are Baurikupa, Chormoda, Imlimoda-I, Imilimoda-II, Jhinkamoda,

Jodabilmoda, Lekhamoda group consisting of 12 rock shelters, Manikmoda, Tango, Ushakupa and three other under the name Ushakuthi.

Baurikupa

It is located in the reserve forest of Jangir in Himgir tehsil, 2 km further north of Ushakupa. Here both paintings and engravins are reported. These have been made on the back walls of the rock shelters, spread over an area of 14m x 4 m. The representations here are hoist of triangles, rhombic patterns, animal forms, palm and a series of cupules and strokes. The engravings have been filled in with a paste of Ochere.

CHORMODA

It is situated in the Bagh-Chagha-Kendu reserve forest. The site is so called for this used to be a hideout for the thieves on the highway between Raigarh and Sundergarh. All over the shelter walls 826 specimens of couples are referred executed along with only one specimen of engraving. The cupules are of various sizes, with an average of 2.5 cm radious. The largest one is of 6.5 cm and the smallest one is 5mm in radious. Pradhan (Pradhan 2001) on the basis of their distribution has classified them as (a) linear forms of straight and/or parallel lines, (b) somewhat circular, apsidal or triangular forms and (c) the independent marks being isolated from each other without forming any pattern. These constitute the largest number of cupules. In the lenear form the most interesting is 2 parallel lines consisting of 4m on the western wall. In the same wall there are cupules in small alinments of single, double and lines of three, then we have 15 cupules arranged in 5 rows with 3 cupules in each row. In yet another instance there is a vertical alignment of two parallel lines consisting of 20 cupules in each line, above a horizontal alignment made of 11 cupules on the eastern wall. Another interesting formation is that of 17 cupules forming a apsidal/triangular pattern with a big cup-mark at the centre. Pradhan states that "the distribution of the cupules appears to suggest an attempt to represent the enigmatic starry sky with all its stars and planets in constellations and in isolation". On the floor of the rock shelter rested a thick habitational deposit from over which microliths and potsherds were recovered. The cupules were also treated with ochre.

Imlimoda-I

As a tamarind tree overlooks the rock shelter it is so named. It is situated in the Dhanubauns reserve forest on the right bank of Sapnei nalla. In all there are 109 specimens of engravings, of which 89 are only those of female genital patterns. They are of different shapes and sizes i.e. oval, apsidal and triangular and they measure between 0.7 cm x 0.05 cm to 40 cm x 28 cm with an average dimension of 22 x 12 cm (LxB); with or without a central line and a shallow depression at the lower edge or in the center. The other engravings are obliterated rhomboid, palm and cupules. The engravings are treated with ocher color.

Imlimoda - II

It is situated on the right bank of Kerkuti nalla in the reserve forest of Dhonubauns and is so called due to an tamarind tree near it. Here on the rock shelter 24 spcimens have been reported of these 23 are triangles resembling female genitals in different shapes and sizes and the one left is an obliterated rhombic pattern. These are also treated with ochre.

Jhinkmoda

It is located on the right bank of Ranitarha nalla and is about a quarter km from Chormoda rock shelter. The rock surface is badly damaged, of what remains, consists of seven triangles and a few cupules and other eroded specimens beyond recognition. Ochre is used here in the engravings. The site is so called as lots of porcupines are found here.

Jodabilmoda

It is located in the Diagarh reserve forest and is on the left bank of Bhalu-Juria nalla. It is so named as there are two large subterranean pits present in the shelter. The rock shelter has been occupied by hundreds of Mud-dubber nests (a kind of wasp), which has covered much of the paintings and engravings here. Of the area that is unoccupied, traces of paintings and 21 specimens of engravings can be seen. The engravings consists of usual traiangles and they have ochre in their grooves.

Lekhamoda group

In this group are found 12 rock shelters distributed in the reserve forests of Chengapahad and Garjanpahad. This group has the richest repository of rock paintings in Orissa. As Lekhamoda is a generic name so the shelters have been numbered as LMD-I to LMD-XII. Paintings are reported from all the 12 shelters but engravings are found only on two of them. The shelters have in all 502 specimens of paintings and 36 specimens of engravings. The figures given above are of the existing paintings, these must have been many more but they have been washed away, obliterated and disfigured by natural agents like rain, water, micro-biological and exfoliation of rock surface, etc. The paintings include a variety of geometric and non–geometric forms mostly in bi-chrome of purple red and white, which is about two third of the total painted forms. Yellow is occasionally used in mono chrome and in combination with red and white in polychrome. The decorative patterns are the zig-zag, wavy, criss-cross and parallel lines within circular, square, rectangular or oblong shapes and they give the look of carpets, harpoons, blade, saw, net and honeycomb patterns. These are reported from LMD II, LMD IV, LMD V, LMD VIII, LMDX and LMD XI. The other forms found are those of a few human forms in dark red wearing head gear and carrying sticks, the animal figures found are those of deer's, monkeys, humped bull, goat, lizard, snakes, peacocks and crane than these human palm and foot are quite popular and are found at LMD VI, LMD VII, LMDX and LMD XII. Depiction of a hearding scene at LMD X is the only thematic depiction noticed in the assemblage of pictures in this group.

The engravings found in the two rock shelters of LMD III and LMD VI include a variety of geometric shapes, mostly triangular resembling the female genitals, foot and palm etc. The engraving of two animals, of which one is upside down is very interesting at LMD III. The engraving were filled in with paste of red ocher which is now mostly lost.

LMD VI exhibits 61 specimens of engraving of usual triangles, entwined lines, circles, palm and foot. Here also all the engravings have been filled with ochre. The shelters floor has a thick depositional layer above the bedrock, on which a trial excavation was taken up. The excavation unearthed a large number of microliths, faceted hematite nodules and pottery.

Manikmoda

It is located 8 km south of Himigir the tehsil headquarters. The rock surface has a large panel of paintings in monochrome of red, white and yellow colors. The shelter has only one specimen of an engraving, which is an serpentine measuring 2.52 m in length. The artists chose 7 locations on the wall for execution of the paintings, repeaditly superimposing a new composition over the earlier one and thereby completely distorting the underlying the earlier and original paintings. Some of the specimens have been destroyed due to human vandalism. The subject matter of the paintings are varied, they consists of antler, humped cattle, human figures wielding sword, shield, musical instruments both in red and white, geometric and non-geometric intricate patterns in dark red.

Pradhan (Pradhan, 1994) has identified 3 phases after a detailed study of the superimpositions. According to him "in phase I the paintings were drawn in monochrome of dark red concealed under the thin film of white patina being super imposed by the paintings in monochrome of white of phase II. Paintings of phase III are drawn in monochrome of orange red and buff red and are without any layer of patina". In the IIIrd phase the main subject are human figurnes shown wielding soword and shield, musical instruments and have different typed of draperies. The floor is marked with 19 cupmarks and has also yielded large number of microliths.

Tongo

It is located near village Giripur. The rock shelter is east west oriented and is facing south. Of the total 50 m spread of the rock wall only 351 × 2.68 m area at present houses 190 specimens of engravings. The triangles resembling the female genital pattern predominate the engraved forms. The other representations are palm, foot prints, rhomboid, honey comb, serpentine and a host of forms resembling roman characters like X, Y, T and H, which Pradhan believed to be reminiscences of an original elaborate pattern either that of a rhomboid or a honey comb. Ochre has been used in the grooves of the engravings.

Ushakupa

It is located at a distance of 4 km. north of village Girisma Ushakupa in the reserve forest of Jamkani. On the rock shelter backwall over an area of

17m x 3.60m, 200 specimens of paintings have been reported. The paintings have suffered erosion due to the work of natural agents and has suffered disfiguring and super-scribing due to human vandalism. The paintings here were executed in monocrome of red, white and yellow and bichrome ofered and white. Other representations include animal figures like tortoise and fish midst of a variety of geometric and non-geometric patterns and motives like saw, harpoon, heart, honeycomb, broom pattern, palm, etc.

Rajbahal Ushakuthi

This group has 3 rock shelters, they are Risikund, Sitakund and Sargagumpha. They are located in the Ushakuthi reserve forest at a distance of 6 km north of village Rajbahal in Lefripara tehsil. The locals associate these rock shelters with the epic hero Rama, who is believed to have visited these places during the period of their exile. This is the most inaccessible rock shelter site in Orissa. Paintings are reported from all the 3 sites but engravings are reported from only Risikund and Sitakund. At Risikund the engravings have been made on a well prepared rubbed surface of the back wall, which has subsequently been smeared with ochre. The engraved representations include a host of triangles, rhomboid, honey comb and couples. The engravings at Rishikund are spread over a surface of 8.57 m x 0.73 m and the engravings are smeared with red ocher. To the right of these engravings is a space of 1m x 0.60m which has an elaborate panel of intricate polychromatic patterns drawn in red, white and yellow, in midst of a broom pattern in dark red. This broom pattern is found in all the 3 rock shelters, executed randomly all over the wall of the shelter up to a height of 3m. The idea behind such paintings is unimaginable. But according to the local people these broom pattern in red are the menstrual blood of Sita, after whom one of the rock-shelter is named as Sita Kund. At Rishikund, two cup marks on the floor and the collection of microliths from the adjoining slopes amply attest to the archaeological significance of the rock shelter.

Three phases have been assigned to the rock art of Orissa on the basis of the subject matter of the engravings and paintings, color composition, style of execution, superimposition and the state of preservation.

In phase I we get animal and human figures in monochrome of darker shade with a film of white patina. The engravings at Vikramkhol, Ushakoti, Tongo and Lekhamoda belong to this phase for their association with the patinated red pigments noticed in the grooves of all these engravings.

Phase II can be distinguished on the basis of their super imposition over the dark red paintings of phase I. The paintings in this phase are monochrome as well as polychrome paintings of animal forms and decorative patterns and symbols executed in purple red, white and yellow.

In Phase III all the paintings are in monochrome white and orange red depicting bull, deer, and human figures carrying swords, shields, superimposed over the paintings of the earlier two phases, the color is also fresh than that of the earlier two phases.

Thus we see that the rock art of Orissa ranges from prehistoric Mesolithic to the early historic period through the Neolithic-Chalcolithic period. At the present state of our knowledge it is difficult to say weather these line drawings and the symbols are pictograph or just drawings evolved from the imagination of the pre-historic artists. So till further research on scientific lines and detailed study made nothing definite can be said.

Out of the 55 rock shelters, 31 shelters contain engravings, nine engravings and paintings combined. In Orissa petroglyphs are entirely non-thematic. The popular motifs notices are rhomboids, honey combs, palm, foot, serpantine, entwined lines, cupules, dots, brackets, cross hatches etc.

Faunal remains include boar, deer, antler, samber, tortoise, lizards, snake.

What tools were used for preparing these petroglyphs is difficult to say with certainly but some harder rocks with pointed ends must have been used like burin of dolarite, quartz etc.

The rock shelters yielded large number of microliths lying embedded in the floor suggest these shelters were in human occupation. Besides microliths substantial number of potteries have also come to light. According to Dr S Pradhan (Pradhan 2001) who under took trial digging in some of the shelters floor, supports that three occupational level were encountered viz. (1) Blackish loose soil with 30 cm depth with pottery and microliths. Pottery types are redware, red slipped ware and black slipped ware. A few fragment of black and red ware deserve special mention. The potteries are made of well levigated clay, wheel turned, well potted and well backed and can be compared with the chalcolithic and early historic potteries found in the plains.

The microliths found are classified as blades, points, crescents, scrapers, flakes, triangles, trappers, lunate, fluted cores.

Layer (2), deposit of brown granular soil. In this Neolithic celts in association with haematite, three ring stones, one pounder as well as potteries were found.

Layer (3) has a deposit of 20 cm over bed rock and below layer (2). Soil composition is granular dark red soil, Microliths like lunates points were encountered but this layer is devoid of potsherds.

Another significant aspect noticed within rock shelters is the circular holes on the floors of the shelters, possibly used by the premitive people for grinding corns, one painting within the rock shelters at Kahhotia attest to this fact, where in a lady is shown pounding grains in a conical hole with the help of a stick.

Thus rock art of Orissa has a hoary antiquity like that of India. The rock paintings discovered within Orissa survived in different stages of their disappearance and disfiguration, they have at present largely become faded, eroded, obliterated and are at the verge of extinction. The increased flow of tourists and their behaviour towards these paintings are becoming a burning problem and if no protective measures are taken by the Government agencies and the villagers to protect those precious heritage they may get deteriorated faster due to natural cause and partly due to human vanalism.

CHAPTER VIII

CONCLUSION

In the chapters discussed above, we have seen that Orissa, like the other parts of the country has a rich cultural heritage spread over many millenniums, in an unbroken sequences right from the Lower Palaeolithic to the Protohistoric period and which ultimately led to the Historical period in about 800 to 600 B.C.

Then like other parts of India, Orissa during the Pleistocene period also witnessed three wet and three dry phases and it was at the end of the first dry phase and the beginning of the second wet phase that we get the evidence of the earliest activity of man in Orissa. The Early, Middle and Upper Palaeolithic cultures flourished during the first dry, second wet and dry phases. In the third wet phase deposits, we get the Mesolithic cultural remains, and the Neolithic flourished in the last dry phase or in the early Holocene period.

The Stone Age tools like in other parts of the country occur in the successive river gravels. All the Stone Age cultures and the Chalcolithic and Iron age culture sites are widespread in Orissa, but they are mostly concentrated in the west, north and southern parts of Orissa, eastern Orissa shows very scanty distribution of sites (may be due to no proper exploration and neglect on the part of the archaeologists). And it is believed that these cultures show chronological continuity (this can not be said with certainty for not much excavation work has been undertaken). But in Orissa till date no fossils have so far been recorded from the river beds, therefore estimation of their chronological status is done purely on a typo-technological basis.

The Lower Palaeolithic tools as seen are found in the coarse gravel deposits over the bed rock. They also occur loose in the beds of the rivers, on the surface in the forests, slopes of the hills and in the secondary laterite. In Orissa the Lower Palaeolithic is characterized by its tool type 'hand axe – clever and chopper-chopping tool industries' like that found in rest of the country. Stratigraphically the evolution of the tools in this phase cannot be marked as both the crude and the developed tools occur together (Mohapatra: 1962). The tools have been classed in to three stages on the basis of their technique. They range from the crudest to the most developed ones. In stage–I the tools were prepared by block-on-block technique. So, they are crude, asymmetrical, rough with crude working edges and most of them have remains of cortex on them. In stage-II, besides block-on-block technique cylindrical hammer technique was introduced. The flake scars are small, shallow and uniform, which denotes to more control over the flaking technique and the tool size also becomes smaller and handy. Stage-III sees complete mastery over the cylinder hammer technique. The tool types become more varied due to introduction of a variety of miniature tools. Clactonian and Levalloisian techniques of preparing flakes, which was earlier believed by Mohapatra (Mohapatra: 1962) to be absent have been reported from sites in Orissa. Further, it is seen that there is no distinction between the flake and core industry as such.

The raw material used are generally the coarse grained quartzite (of red, pink, white, greenish, brown and blackish shades) and majority of them are on pebbles only. In central Orissa they are found made on sandstone and grit, and encrustation of laterite is seen on the tools. But from no were patination is reported on the tools. The main concentration of the sites is in the districts of Sambalpur, Sundargarh, Bolangir, Mayurbhanj, Keonjhar, Dhenkanal and Koraput. The tools, typologically and technologically correspond with the Abbevillian, early Acheulian industries of Europe and Africa. So, we can rightly call it belonging to the Abbevillo-Acheulian tradition of India.

The Middle Palaeolithic tools, stratigraphically occurs above the Lower Palaeolithic tools yielding layer. It has been seen that due to change in the raw material used, the Middle Palaeoiithic sites are away from the Lower Palaeolithic sites but in Mayurbhanj district the middle Palaeolithic tools are found in association with Lower Palaeolithic or Mesolithic or both. The tools can be said to be belonging to the highly advanced upper Acheulian phase. The technique adopted is basically soft cylinder-hammer technique and the tools were generally made on small flakes but it is seen that the people of this phase had no complete mastery over the technique of retouching. The raw materials used for making the tools are fine grained rocks like-chert, jasper, opal chalcedony and fine grained quartzite. The tool assemblage consisted of scrapers, borers, burin, point, scraper-borer, nodules, cores and blades. No fossils have been reported till date from this phase.

It was only in the early 80's that Upper Palaeolithic was identified in Orissa. The characteristic feature of the tool types of this period are 'Blade and Burin'. Technologically and typologically this culture's industry is divided into two groups i.e. shaped artifacts and simple artifacts. The tool assemblage of the shaped artifacts consisted of knife, scrapers, denticulates, notches, borers, burins, backed blades, micro-crescents and that of the simple artifacts were the by products of shaped tools like cores, flakes, bladelets, chips and worked nodules. The technique adopted for making these tools were-indirect percussion or punch technique, chest-pressure and direct percussion techniques; besides these various types of retouchings were also done. As a whole the industry represents a very crude craftsmanship. The raw material used was mainly chert. Most of the sites reported are explored sites. From the data collected it is evident that the upper Palaeolithic sites are open air sites located on top, slope and foot of hills, on the plains and on waste lands. So, only with more discoveries of sites and their proper identification stratigraphically in the riverine sections or in proper excavations that we will have a better insight into this phase of prehistoric culture in Orissa and its distribution pattern.

The Mesolithic tools appear within the layer of the third wet phase. They are generally found loose on the surface or in the dry beds of the rivers. It has been seen that Mesolithic sites are mostly found at the sites where the Middle Palaeolithic tools have been found and this can be attributed to the similarity in the raw material used. The tool assemblage is mainly of non-geometric type (borers, points, lunates, scrapers, denticulates, knives, blades, burin both of single and backed variety. Fluted and ordinary cores and flakes also occur in sizable number) along with geometric types (triangles and trapezes) and no pottery or evidence of fire has been reported along with the tool assemblage. The non-geometric microliths of Orissa can be compared with Singrali basin (Mirzapur), Giddlur II, Nagurjunakonda and Sanghankallu Phase I (Andhra Pradesh). A typical aspect of the Orissan Mesolithic culture is the association of heavy-duty implements such as horse hoof cores or scrapers, choppers and pointed tools with the microliths. The raw material used for the manufacture of heavy duty tools and microliths are completely different. For making the microliths-chert, quartz, chalcedony, jasper, opal and agate were used whereas for heavy duty tools-dolerite and quartzite were used. The industry as such is crude and in some cases the tools are found rolled and weathered. The microliths of Orissa typologically presents some similarity with the Mesolithic non-geometric microliths of Europe.

The Neolithic tools are found in the last dry phase or the early Holocene period deposits. They have been found from various parts of Orissa. Unlike the Palaeolithic and Mesolithic artifacts, which are primarily found in the hilly terrain of Orissa, the Neolithic artifacts are found both in the plateaus of hilly areas as well as on the plain land of coastal Orissa. Neolithic sites have been reported from the districts of Mayurbhanj, Sambalpur, Keonjhar, Sundergarh, Koraput, Puri, Ganjam, Dhenkanal, Phulbani and Bolangir. The main excavated sites of this period are Kuliana, Kuchai, Baidapur, Golbai and Shankerjang. The Neolithic culture of Orissa is distinguished by ground and polished tools along with celts made by means of flaking, pecking, grinding and then polishing. The tool assemblage consists of axes, adzes, fabricators, punch, stone hammer, wedge grinder, shouldered celt, bar-chisels, chisels and ring stones. The raw materials used are dolerite, basalt, genesis, schist, epidiorite and diorite stones. Pottery has been reported in this period and they are of coarse handmade type. The pottery is similar to those found at Nagarjunakonda, Daojali Harding and Pandurajardhibi in Andhra Pradesh, Assam and West Bengal respectively. The other distinguishing features are the find of evidence of cultivation of cereals from the excavations and evidences of rock art. The material life of this period is better known than that of the other cultures due to large number of excavations and proper research work. On the basis of Behera's (Behera: 1992b) study of Neolithic culture around Bonaigarh, it can be inferred that there was an exchange network not only between the neighbouring places but also among far off places in the Neolithic period. Further it is believed that the population affiliated with the Austro-Asiatic linguistic groups moved from main land Southeast Asia to Orissa via northeast and Chota Nagpur plateau during this period (Basa: 2005: 72). The tools can be placed in to two heads/groups, Group I belonging to the Indian type while Group II show a foreign influence well known in Southeast Asia (The shouldered adze is regarded as the archaeological evidence of this cultural contact between Orissa and mainland south-east Asia).

The study of archaeobotanical remains from Golbai and Gopalpur shed light and are evidence of economy of the sedentary prehistoric settlements of the Orissan lowlands (Coastal plains) the main crop types that have been recovered are rice, a number of pulses and millets. The find of an array of bone and copper hunting tools speaks that small game hunting and fishing besides animal husbandry and cultivation formed an important part of the economy (Harvey et al: 2006 & Kar: 2000). The archaeobotanical remains from the coastal region have certain similarity with those found in the Vindhyas culture sites in the Belan valley, Gujarat and southern Neolithic. Whereas, in the hilly region of the plateaus some evidences of transient sites exists. This is evident from the small-scale excavation and flotation undertaken here, which are not good enough to shed light on early agriculture in this area. These sites are believed to be contemporaneous with the settled farming societies in the lowlands and may represent a subsistence choice of shifting cultivation or more mobile people with seasonal camps. The little amount of organic samples collected from sites like Malakhoja (Angul), Banabasa (Mayurbhanj) and Bajpur (Keonjhar) suggests short-lived nature of the sites (Harvey et al: 2006), which scholars believed could be due to use of these sites for quarrying and making lithic tools, or were used for shifting cultivation, or absence of pottery suggests that the people depended on crops like tubers, which could be readily pit roasted, rather than seed crops.

Hence it is suggested on the basis of the above finds that two different types of settlement types with different subsistence pattern existed in Orissa at the same time i.e. one with settled agricultural life in the coastal plains and the second with a more mobile life incorporating shifting cultivation or seasonal mobility in the highlands. The Orissa Neolithic as a whole is included in the Chottanagpur zone of Bengal, Bihar and Orissa complex of Eastern India. The date tentatively, assigned to this period is between 2500 to 1500 B.C.

In Orissa it is believed that the Chalcolithic cultures emerged in the second millennium BC. It is associated with the introduction of shouldered celts of stone and it is difficult at present to say as to which came first. It has been observed by the end of the late Neolithic period that men knew the art of making metals (Mahapatra: 1964). It is also seen that the shouldered celts found here have Southeast Asian influence over them and it is presumed that the knowledge of metal came from the northwest, and the south Indian influence can be seen in the potteries found. The pottery from Golbai IIa has similiarity with those found at Chirand. Bone tools have been reports only from the excavations at Golbai, which Sinha (1993) believes are not as developed as the ones reported from Chirand. Copper objects in the form of bangles, ring, and fishhooks have been reported but their number is limited. From Golbai in Periof IIb which Sinha (2000) calls the Neo-Chalcolithic; the finding of an iron celt is one of the most important aspect for this pushes back the date of knowledge of metallurgy of iron by at least another two centuries for the date of iron in India is around 1000 B.C. The evidence of settlements is available from the hilly regions of the plateaus and from the coastal plain. From Golbai IIa, from the lower level 13 circular huts with post holes and hearths were reported (Sinha: 2000). In the light of recent researches it can be said that the period witnessed the emergence of chiefdom in Orissa, and is also associated with the expansion of agrarian base, which is evident from the plant remains rice and kulthi from Golabai (Sinha: 2000). The human tooth recovered from Sankerjang show consumption of food rich in carbohydrates, which imply more dependence on agriculture of the Chalcolithic population. The animal remains from Gopalpur (Kar et al: 2000 & Basa: 2005) shed light that animal husbandry must have also been practiced during this period.

This period also saw the emergence of arts and crafts. The find of different kinds of pottery implies the existence of potters. The repertoire of a wide range of bone artifacts from Golbai implied a skilled group of tool makers. The copper artifacts like bangles, ring, fishhook, etc speaks about the existence of a group of copper smiths. Beads recovered imply either of local bead-making tradition or of trade. The existence of copper in Mayurbhanj and Chota Nagpur plateau entail that there must have existed an intricate exchange network between the above areas with the sites in central and coastal Orissa. According to Basa (Basa: 2005) 'all these factors would imply an emerging complexity in the social and political organization of prehistoric Orissa. The chiefdoms might have emerged as a mechanism for effective maintenance and management of such social complexity. This also implies about the ranked nature of Chalcolithic society in Orissa'. At Golbai, out of thirteen circular huts with post-holes and hearths, the biggest hut may be regarded as belonging to the chief, then the association of scarce copper artifacts with the grave goods from Golbai and Sankerjang could be interpreted as belonging to the members of the elite group in the society. The period assigned tentatively to this phase lies between 1600-1400 to 900 B.C.

Though Orissa is endowed with a fairly good distribution of Megalithic burials but at present nothing conclusive can be said, since in many parts of Orissa the present tribals practice these types of burials. So, till systematic excavation is not carried out at few of the probable sites nothing can be said about this culture. It has been observed that Megalith's are mostly concentrated in western and central Orissa (this may be due to preferably good ecological and environmental conditions). The discovery of a rich Megalithic complex by A.K. Sharma of Archaeological Survey of India in Kankarbhat near Raipur district of Chhattisgarh has provided enough evidences of migration of Megalithic stock communities to Orissa through Kalahandi district, as it is bordering Raipur, but still no systematic attempt has been made to trace Megalithic complex in Kalahandi and Koraput districts to enrich our knowledge on the much neglected aspect of Megalithic cultural phase in Orissa. This aspect requires immediate attention and encouragement from Anthropology and Archaeology departments of Universities; Department of Archaeology, Government of

Orissa and the Branches of Archaeological Survey of India, Bhubaneswar (Excavation Br. IV and Bhubaneswar Circle).

Orissa has a rich legacy of rock art. They are mostly found in the rock shelters, which are mostly located in inaccessible hilly and forested areas of western Orissa in the districts of Jharsuguda, Kalahandi, Mayurbhanj, Sambalpur, Sundergarh and Svarnapur. An important feature of Orissan rock art is the engravings found along with paintings, which are engraved on the soft rock surface and have colour paste filled in them. The rock art sites are mostly known as Lekhamoda (Shelter with writing), Ushakuthi (worship Hall), Ushakupa (ritual Cavity), Lekhapathar (stone with Writing) and are also named after the characters in the Epics. In Orissa till date 92 rock art sites have been reported, of these 44 rock shelters have only engravings, 34 have only paintings and 14 have both engravings and paintings. From these 92 rock art sites 3878 specimens of engravings and 2492 specimens of paintings have been reported (Pradhan:2001& Pradhan *et al*: 2006). Habitational deposit with cultural remains has been reported from the floors of some of these rock shelters.

The subject matter of the rock paintings is patterns which are mostly geometric and non-geometric (Including figures of human, animal, birds, reptiles, etc). It is observed that there is almost absence of hunting and chasing scenes but the depiction of harpoons and broom are typical to Orissan rock art. Some of these patterns have similarity with the central Indian paintings. The colours used are mainly organic and mineral. The colours used are dark red, purple, white, yellow, blue and black. The engravings consist of geometric patterns, female genitals, rhombic patterns, palm, foot, brackets and cobra hood marks with dots. Some of the engravings are similar to the motives found in central India belonging to the Mesolithic period. The rock art in Orissa can be put in the time bracket ranging from the Mesolithic to the Early Historical period.

But still study of rock art like other fields of prehistory is in incipient stage. Very little systematic and scientific research work is being carried out. Till date, no absolute date could be assigned to them nor has any attempt been made to correlate the prehistoric cultural materials available, to rebuild the material culture or the cultural phase to which they could have belonged.

As a whole, though a lot of exploration and research work is being carried out now a day and almost every now and then new sites are being reported. But, still the researches are in the early stages of study, what is known is mainly from explorations, that too have been conducted very unevenly and unscientifically, and the results are mostly descriptive of the tool types recovered during the field trips. Besides, the researchers have mostly neglected the study of geological context within which the different tools were produced and have never made any attempt to study and reconstruct the environmental background in which the authors of the tools described by them lived. These studies are very important for we can hardly visualise at present the changing pattern of the geography and geology of this vast land mass when man evolved from Lower Palaeolithic to later periods of tool manufacturing. Bose (Bose: 1941&51) in the past had tried to study the implementiferous beds of the Burhabalanga, but the result is still far from satisfactory. A systematic geo-chronology for this region has still to be established. Dani (Dani: 1960) very aptly remarks long back in the 60's and this still stands true through this statement was made in context of whole of Eastern India, when he states, "In the present state of our knowledge only a general geographical and geological background can be given. On the other hand, the stone tools in this sub-continent have been studied mainly on the basic terminology evolved in European and African contexts. The attempt of H.L. Movius to evolve terms like chopper-chopping tools, scrappers and hand axes for the eastern Asiatic tool types is hardly satisfactory. But as long as a comprehensive independent enquiry into the problem of these stone-industries of this sub-continent, based on the nature of raw-material available is not made, a researcher in a limited field has to make the most of the given opportunities." Due to this, still no proper time brackets have been assigned to the different cultural phases. The earliest excavation in the field of prehistory was carried out in Orissa (Bose and Sen: 1948) and now among the subjects of archaeology, prehistory is the most neglected in Orissa.

Further, it is observed that the theoretical and methodological developments that took place in the western world from the 1960's onwards stressing upon the explanatory aspect of archaeology did not have much impact on researches in Orissa. Nor has the introduction of new techniques and methods in the archaeological sciences like physical-anthropology, archaeozoology, palaeobotany, geoarchaeology, metallurgy, etc., being utilised for creating a data base which could have helped in addressing issues focused by new theoretical developments. Further the transformation i.e. from 'culture history' approach to the 'ecological' approach, has not yet been adopted by most of the researchers; as the research works of the scholars are still fixated with typology, description of tools, antiquities and ceramics; origin and authorship of the Pre and Protohistoric cultures. Despite the many achievements and commendable works of scholars, the picture of the Pre and Protohistoric cultures that has emerged as a result of the last fifty years of work, further needs a lot of problem-oriented planning and systematic investigations with the help of various scientific disciplines available in the field of research for arriving at holistic understanding of the Pre and Protohistoric cultures. For this if the following considerations are taken in to account in future investigations, the picture of pre and protohistory of Orissa could be more informative:

The archaeological research design has to be given priority and the research needs to have specific goals other than describing, comparing the data and dating the archaeological remains. More than the quantity of the data, it is the data collected against the background of specific research which can answer questions related to the adaptive and non-adaptive cultural behaviour patterns.

The focus of research should be shifted from 'site' to region/landscape. The site oriented approach in which one or a few sites are partially excavated and a few sites are discovered through unsystematic survey needs to be replaced by a regional approach by incorporating intensive surface survey techniques and if possible, a long term systematic, horizontal excavation incorporating all the scientific methods available for data retrieval and interpretation. Only an intensive regional survey can throw light on the pattern of distribution of the sites and other archaeological remains such as 'off-sites', 'hunting site' 'seasonal camp' and 'regular settlement' sites on the landscape.

The technical and scientific investigation of the findings such as chemical analysis, X-ray diffraction analysis, micro-morphology of living area, study of phytoliths and DNA analysis of biological remains and isotopic analysis of the human and animal skeletal remains, etc., will provide valuable information to answer some of the queries or in other words the parameters proposed by the proponents of the New Archaeology and post-processual archaeology should be employed, both for collection of data and in its interpretation. These findings will no doubt enhance the level of interpretation in the light of recent advancements made in archaeological theory and methods.

So, the need of the hour is that the archaeologists and research scholars should now stop just looking for new sites and concentrate on establishing the stratigraphcial chronology of the cultures, reconstruct the paleo-environment, ecosystem, the material culture, try to co-relate the cultures of this region with that of the neighbouring and rest of the country and many such associated aspect. To achieve this systematic excavations and explorations will have to be undertaken in different parts of Orissa; regional chronology of the cultures to be found out; care should be taken to see that this is done by expert hands and a proper and comprehensive report on all this is brought out so that we can place the pre and proto-history of Orissa at par with that of other parts of the country.

Appendix-I

List of Pre & Protohistoric Sites

Name of the site	Lat. Long	Drainage	Police-station	Name of the Culture	Reference Published/Unpublished	Remarks
(1)	(2)	(3)	(4)	(5)	(6)	(7)
Dashapalla			Dashapalla, Puri	N	Tripathy, K.C. Mohanty. U.C. Microlithic Industry of Bhubaneshwar	
Ranpur			Ranpur, Puri	N	Prakruty, U.U. Journal (SC) Vol. 7(1) pp. 77-92, 1970)	
Sarankul			Puri	M.N.	Tripathy, K.C. "Palaeo-Anthropological Relics of Bhubaneshwar	
Sisupalgarh			Bhubaneshwar, Puri	N	Indian Science Congress, 1977	
Udaygiri			Bhubaneshwar, Puri	M.N.	Tripathy, K.C. "Meghalithic culture of Orissa" Puratarwa, No. 3 Journal of the Indian Archaeological Society, Varanasi	
Unit IV			Bubaneshwar Municipality, Puri	M		
Vani-vihar	Daya Dry Streams		Bhubaneshwar, Puri	L.P.M.N.	Dash R.N. "Collection of Orissa State Museum Mitra D. "Exploration of Udayagiri Hills "Indian Archaeology "A Review, 1958-59 pp. 38-40	
Dhauli	Daya		Ditto	M	Orissa state Museum, R.N. Das	
Darada			Baliapal, Baleshwar	N	Orissa State Museum, R.N. Das	
Chaudwar			Cuttack	M	Ball, V. "On Ancient kitchen-midden at Chaudwar Near Cuttack. PASB 8761, pp. 120-121	

Name of the site	Lat. Long	Drainage	Police-station	Name of the Culture	Reference Published/Unpublished	Remarks
Mathurapur			Athagarh, Cuttack	N		
Khunta			Jaipur Road, Cuttack	N	Orissa State Museum, Das, R.N.	
Jaugarh		Ushikula	Purushottampur Ganjam	N		
Manamunda	83° 5520° 52'	Tol	Manamunda	L.P.	Tripathy K.C., "Lithic Industries in India. A study of South Western Orissa" Delhi-35.	
Bard	Mahanadi		Phulbani	L.P.M.N.		
Kalma	Vamsadhara		Gunupur Koraput	M.P.M.	Tripathy, K.C. "South Orissa Prehistory" The First Record of Stone Tools	
Chalkamba		Sanaval	Gunupur Koraput	Fossil Animal Bone	Sian Perspective, Vol. XV, 1973 Hawaji, pp. 47-59.	
Gunupur		Sanaval	Gunpur	N	Tripathy, .C. "Report on Exploration of Pre-historic Site along the Vansadhara Koraput, Orissa, "Prakruti, U.U.J. (Sc.), Vol. 41, 1967, pp. 55-60)	
Taming			Narayanpatna, Koraput	N	Prusty, R.P. A note on cells from Koraputunpublished Orissa State Museum.	
Bhalitundi		Brahmani	Talcher, Dhenkanal	L.P.	Mohapatra, G.C. "The Stone Age Cultures of Orissa" Poona, 1962, pp. 37-50	
Bhimakanda		Brahmani	Talcher, Dhenkanal	L.P.		
Chakrasil		Brahmani	Talcher, Dhenkanal	L.P.		
Dhenkanal			Dhenkanal	L.P.	Mohapatra G.C. Exploration in the	

Name of the site	Lat. Long	Drainage	Police-station	Name of the Culture	Reference Published/Unpublished	Remarks
					District of Dhenkanal	
Dunria			Dhenkanal	L.P.	Sundergarh, Mayurbhanj Indian Archaeology – A review, 1957-58, p.41	
Durgapur	85° 12'E 20° 52'N		Talcher, Dhenkanal	Cooper Colt		
Gotamara	85° 12'E 20° 52'N		Talcher, Dhenkanal	L.P.		
Harichandanpur		Brahmani	Harichandanpur Dhenkanal	L.P.N.	Mitra D. B. Ghosh, S. "Exploration in the District of Dhenkanal", Indian Archaeology – A Review, 1958-59, p.36	
Hindol Road		Brahmani	Hindol, Dhenkanal			
Jatla	85° 16'E 20° 56'N		Talcher, Dhankanal	L.P.	Dash, R.N. Palaeoliths from Dhenkanal A Brief Study Orissa Historical Research Journal, Vol. XVI, No. 1 to XXII, No. 1, 1957, pp. 51-56.	
Kaliakata		Brahmani	Anugul Dhankanal			
Kankell		Brahmani	Talcher			
Khargaprasad		Brahmani	Talcher/Anugul, Dhenkanal	L.P.M.P.N.	Tripathy, P. "Geo Morphology and Lithic Industries of anarpal, Dhenkanal"	
Kutel		Brahmani	Talcher/Anugul, Dhenkanal	L.P.	Unpublished Dissertation Department of Anthropology U.U.	

Name of the site	Lat. Long	Drainage	Police-station	Name of the Culture	Reference Published/Unpublished	Remarks
					1978	
Meramanda II			Angul, Dhenkanal	L.P.	Government of Orissa, Dsitrict Dhanakanal, 1972	
Muchurigarla	..	..	..	L.P.		
Pala Lahara	..	Mankarnullah in Brahmani	Pala Lahara, Dhenkanal	L.P.		
Parang	..	..	Anugul, Dhenkanal	L.P.		
Pandarbharania	85° 16'E 20° 53'N	Brahmani	Talcher, Dhenkanal	M		
Sana Kerjaag	..	..	Angul, Dhenkanal	L.P.M.N.		Excavated Site
Sardapur	..	..	..	N		
Talcher	..	Brahmani	Talcher, Dhenkanal	L.P.		
Talcher`	85° 14'E 20° 58'N	Brahmani	Talcher, Dhenkanal	L.P.		
Tikaraparha	..	Mahanadi	Angul, Dhenkanal	L.P.		
Anugul	..	..	Anugul	L.P.		
Samal	..	Brahmani	Anugul, Dhenkanal	L.P.		
Kantha	..	..	Talcher, Dhenkanal	N		
Dongar hill	85° 37'E 21°	Jira	Baragarh, Sambalpur	M.P.M.	Ball, V. 'On Stone Implements found in the Tributary State of Orissa' Asiatic Society of Bengal,	

Name of the site	Lat. Long	Drainage	Police-station	Name of the Culture	Reference Published/Unpublished	Remarks
	17'N				1876, pp. 122-123	
Dauli	83° 4'E 22° 22'N	Ang	Paikmal, Sambalpur	M.N.	..	
Girigobardhan	83° 34'E 21° 18'N	Jira	Baragarh, Sambalpur	M	Mohapatra, G.C., 'Lithic ndustries in India. A study of South Western Orissa" Leeladevi Publication, Delhi-35.	
Lasa	..	..	Kuchinda, Sambalpur	N	..	
Rugnie.1	83° 38'E 21° 19'N	Jira	Baragarh, Sambalpur	M	Tripathy, K.C., "Sarsarc, A Microlithic site in Western Orissa" 58th Indian Science Congress. 1971	
Rugnia.II	83° 39'E 21° 19'N	Jira	ditto	M	..	
Sarsara I	83° 36'E 21° 18'N	Jira	ditto	M	..	
Sarsara II	83° 36'E 21° 18'N	Jira	ditto	M	Mishra, S.K., "Surface Survey of Jogra Valley" Unpublished Dissertation, Department of Anthropology, U.U. 1976.	
Ratanpur	..	Lb	Sundargarh	M		
Sundargarh	..	Lb	Sundargarh	M.N.R.S.		
Satkuta	..	Luijhor/Brahmani	Benel, Sundargarh	L.P.		
Tamalghat	..	Bramani	Rourkela,	M.P.		

Name of the site	Lat. Long	Drainage	Police-station	Name • of the Culture	Reference Published/Unpublished	Remarks
			Sundargarh			
Tangaiyadi	..	Lb	Sundargarh	M.P.M.		
Ampali	83° 26'E 20° 26'N	Lant	Saintala Balangir	M.P.M.		
Bairakhama	83° 44'E 20° 47'N	Suktel	Balangir	M	Tripathy, K.C. "Lithic Industries in India. A study of South-Western Orissa, Leeladevi Publications, Delhi-35.	
Banaras	83° 23'E 20° 27'N	Lant	Saintala, Balangir	M		
Banapada	83° 25'E 20° 27'N	Do	Do	M		
Bhanpada	..	Raul	Balangir	M.P.	"South Orissa Prehistory : The first record of Stone Age Tools" Asian perspective Vol. XV, 1973, pp. 47-59, Hawaii, U.S.A.	
Baorikhama	83° 31'E 20° 29'N	Do	Balangir	M.P.M.		
Deuli	83° 24'E 20° 29'N	Do.	Balangir	M.P.M.		
Dhangarh	83°	Do.	Sonapur Balangir	M		

Name of the site	Lat. Long	Drainage	Police-station	Name of the Culture	Reference Published/Unpublished	Remarks
	31'E 20° 28'N					
Ghatkaintera	83° 42'E 20° 46'N	Suktel	Balangir	M.N.	Ditto	"Typo-Tecnology of Mayurbhanj Neolithis, Orissa" Prakruti, U.U. Journal (SC) No. 4, 1967, No. 4, 1967 p.p. 61-70
Haladipali	83° 54'E 29° 55'N	Tel	Sonapur, Balangir	L.P.M.P.		
Khalipat	83° 31'E 20° 51'N	Kusumijhor	Luisinga, Balangir	M		
Khalarkolan	..	Raul	Bhauanpada, Balangir	M.P.		
Khariligarh	..	..		N		
Lachut	80° 26'E 20° 26'N	Lant	Saintala, Balangir	M.P.		
Madhabhati		Raul	Balangir	M.P.		

Name of the site	Lat. Long	Drainage	Police-station	Name of the Culture	Reference Published/Unpublished	Remarks
Ratakhandi		Raul	Balangir	M.P.		
Ramanda	83° 24'E 20° 27'N	Lant		M		
Sandisara		Raul	Balangir	M.P.		
Saragada		Singoda	Balangir	M.P.M.		
Sarekela	83° 42'E 20° 31'N	Niburti	Luisinga, Balangir	M		
Silatapara		Lant	Saintala, Balangir	M		
Tetilipara		Lant	Saintala, Balangir	M.P.		
Thakapali	83° 27'E 20° 31'N	Niburti	Luisinga, Balangir	M		
Vagan	83° 20'E 20° 31'N	Singoda	Balangir	M.P.		
Amata	83° 17'E 20° 18'N		Dito	M.P.M.	Tripathy, K. C., "Lithic Industries in India" : A Study of South-Western Orissa, Leeladevi Publicatino, Delhi-35	
Bilat	83° 21'E 20° 4'E	Sandul (Utai)	Kalahandi	M.P.M.		
Chilpa	82° 46'E	Tel	Dharamgarh, Kalahandi	M.P.		

Name of the site	Lat. Long	Drainage	Police-station	Name of the Culture	Reference Published/Unpublished	Remarks
	19° 37'N					
Chilgan	82° 50'E 19° 46'N		Dharamgarh, Kalahandi	M.P.M.		
Jamtora	83° 20'E 20° 19'E	Tel	Kalahandi	M.P.M.		
Luthurbandh	83° 13'E 20° 14'E		Kalahandi	M.P.		
Panagan	82° 49'E 19° 45'E		Dharamgarh, Kalahandi	M		
Champua		Baitarani	Champua, Kendujhar	L.P.M.P.	Mohapatra, G.C., "The stone age cultures of Orissa" Poona, 1962 pp.48-49	
Dangaposl		Baitarani	Kendujhar	M.N.R.A.		
Jagannathpur		Baitarani	Kendujhar	L.P.M.P		
Patna		Baitarani	Kendujhar	M.P.M.	Mohapatra. G.C., "Exploration in the district of Keonjhar and Maayurbhanj", Indian Archaeology, A Review 1958-59 p.36	
Ramala		Baitarani	Kendujhar	L.P.M.P.		
Thakurani		Baitarani	Kendujhar	N		
Udayapur		Baitarani	Kendujhar	N		

Name of the site	Lat. Long	Drainage	Police-station	Name of the Culture	Reference Published/Unpublished	Remarks
Ambadalisasan		Burhabalanga	Sadar, Mayurbhanj	N	Mohapatra, G.C. "he stone age cultures of Orissa" Poona 1962, pp.37-50	
Amsikida		Do	Sadar Subdivision, Mayurbhanj	L.M.P.M.	Sen, D.Ray, G.S. and Beteille A.M., A new Paleolithic site in Mayurbhanj Man in India Vol. 36, No. 4. 234-46. 1956.	
Badada		Kanu/Nadajora	Rajrangpur, Mayurbhanj			
Bahalda		Kharkal/nesa Bahal	Bahalda, Mayurchanj	M.P.		
Baidipur	86° 41' 54'E 21° 46'22'' N	Banra	Banpada Mayurbhanj	N	Tripathy, K. C. "Typo Technology of Mayurbhanj neoliths, Orissa" Prakruti, Utkal University Journal (SC) Vol – V. 1967	
Bangiriposi			Bangiriposi, Mayurbhanj	L.P.N.R.A.		
Banspal		Sone	Udala, Mayurbhanj	L.P.	Bose, N.K. Sen., D. "Excavation in Mayurbhanj" Calcutta University Press, 1948	
Badsul		Khairbhandan			Chanda, R.P., "Mayurbhanj Paleolithic". Annual Report of Archaeological Survey of India, 1923-24. pp. 100-101	
Barajpur		Burhabalango				
Baramanda		Kharkai			Mohapatra, G.C., Exploratio in the Burhabalanga District of Keonjhar and Mayurbhanj" Indian Archaeology. A Review, 1958-59. p.36.	

Name of the site	Lat. Long	Drainage	Police-station	Name of the Culture	Reference Published/Unpublished	Remarks
Baripada		Burhabalanga	Baripada, Mayurbhanj	L.P.M.P.		
Basipitha		Burhabalanga	Udala, Mayurbhanj	N	Mohapatra, G.C. "Exploration in the District of Keohjar and Mayurbhanj" Indian Archaeology. A Review, 1958-59, p. 36.	
Bijatala		Bankba	Bisai, Mayurbhanj	L.P.M.P.		
Bisai		Panposh	Bisai, Mayurbhanj	L.P.M.P.M.		
Bhussuni		Burhabalanga		L.P.	Mohapatra, G.C., "Exploration in the District of Dhenkanal, Sundargarh, Mayurbhanj" Indian Archaeology. A Review, 1957-58, p.41	
Bonaikela		Kharkai	Badampaharh Bangiriposi Mayurbhanj	M.P.M.N.		
Brahmangan	86° 35' 48"E 22° 2'50"N		Kuliana, Mayurbhanj	L.P.		
Budamara				L.P.	Mitra, D. Chakraborty, D.K., "Exploration in District Mayurbhanj" Indian Archaeology, A Review, 1958-59, p. 58	
Chitrada				N		
Dandbosh	86° 8' E 22° 17' N		Rairangpur, Mayurbhanj	M	Brown, C.J.. "Catalogue of Prehistoric Antiquities in Indian Museum at Calcutta." Simla, 1917.	
Dahikuthisasan Domuhani		Burhabalanga	Mayurbhanj	N L.P.		

Name of the site	Lat. Long	Drainage	Police-station	Name of the Culture	Reference Published/Unpublished	Remarks
Dublabeda	86° 10'E 22° 15'N		Rairangpur,	L.P.M.	Acharya, P. "Annual Report of Archaeological Survey of India, 1923-24, pp.100-10	
Dukura Gadha		Kharkal	Rairangpur, Mayurbhanj	N. M.	Mohapatra, S.c., "Geo-Morphology and Lithic Cultural Sequences of Rairangpur" Unpublished Dissertation, Department of Anthropology, U.U. 1979.	
Gambharia	86° 9'E 22° 20'N	Gadia	Bahalda. Mayurbhanj	L.P.M.		
Gangraj		Chipat	Baripada, Mayurbhanj	L.P.		
Ghantasila		Gangahar Burhabalanga	Mayurbhanj	L.P.	Mishra, Bijoya Laxmi, "Surface Exploration and Lithic Cultural Sequence around Baripada" unpublished Dissertatino, Department of Anthropology, U.U. 1980	
Indupur			Mayurbhanj	N		
Jadipal			Mayurbhanj	N		
Jagudia		Burhabalanga	Baripada, Mayurbhanj	L.P.		
Jaipur			Maurbhanj	N	Pradhan, Anaga Manjari, "Lithic Survey of Rairangpur and Baahalda Area." Unpublished dissertation, Department of Anthropology, U.U. 1981.	
Jiani		Godabhanga	Baripada,	L.P.		

Name of the site	Lat. Long	Drainage	Police-station	Name of the Culture	Reference Published/Unpublished	Remarks
			Mayurbhanj			
Jirda		Sone	Udala, Mayurbhanj	L.P.		
Kamarpal		Burhabalanga	Mayurbhanj	L.P.		
Kamta		Burhabalanga	Mayurbhanj	L.P.N.	Bose, N.K., Son., D., Roy, G.S. "Climatic Change during Stone Age in India. Geographical Review of India, Vol.XIII. No. 11951, p. 18.	
Kundulia		Kunduliakhai	Bisai, Mayurbhanj	M.P.		
Kantaban	86° 10'E 22° 15''N		Rairangpur, Mayurbhanj	M	Sen, D., Typology of Paleoliths in Mayurbhanj, Indian Science Congres, 1942.	
Kaptipada			Kapitipada, Mayurbhanj	N		
Kendudiha	86° 39'E 22° 5'19" N	Burhabalanga	Mayurbhanj	L.P.		
Kalabadria	86°38'7"E 22° 5''20"N	Burhabalanga	Mayurbhanj	L.P.		
Khiching	86° 50'E 21° 55''N	Khairbhandan	Mayurbhanj	N.M.A.		
Kuilisuta	86° 40'E 22° 4'40''N	Burhabalanga	Kuliana, Mayurbhanj	L.P.		
Kuchai			Mayurbhanj	L.P.N.		
Kucheibudi		Kharkal	Rairangpur,	M.P.M.N.		

Name of the site	Lat. Long	Drainage	Police-station	Name of the Culture	Reference Published/Unpublished	Remarks
			Mayurbhanj	(R.S.)		
Kuliana	86° 39'E 22° 41''N	Burhabalanga	Kuliana Mayurbhanj	L.P.		
Kurkutia			Mayurbhanj	N		
Mahulia		Burhabalanga	Baripada, Mayurbhanj	L.P.		
Madhuban		Kharkal	Rairangpur Mayurbhanj	M		
Madhupur			Mayurbhanj	M.N.		
Mahuldiha	86° 10'E 22° 16''N	Kharkai	Rairangpur Mayurbhanj	M		
Alicha		Burhabalanga	Mayurbhanj	L.P.		
Manda			Mayurbhanj	M.N.		
Muruda			Mayurbhanj	M.N.		
Mendhakhal		Sone	Udala, Mayurbhanj	L.P.		
Mondbani		Sone		..		
Murgaghutu	16° 10'E 22° 19'N		Mayurbhanj			
Naraharipur				M.P.		
Naujora		Naujora	Mayurbhanj	L.P.		
Nuaberia	86° 40' 28''E 22°	Naujora Burhabalanga	Baripada, Mayurbhanj	L.P.		

Name of the site	Lat. Long	Drainage	Police-station	Name of the Culture	Reference Published/Unpublished	Remarks
	3'35''N					
Pariako		Burhabalanga		N.P.		
Patinja		Burhabalanga		N.		
Patua		.	Kaptipada, Mayurbhanj	L.P.N.		
Pratappur	86° 38' 22''E 22° 4'34''N	Burhabalanga	Mayurbhanj	M.P.		
Panposh				L.P.M.P. M.N. (R.S.)		
Rairangpur		Kharkal	Rairangpur, Mayurbhanj	L.P.M.P. M.N. (R.S.)		
Ranikudar		Kharkal	Rairangpur, Mayurbhanj	M.P.M.		
Radhiabindha				M.N.		
Sandim	86° 38' 22''E 22° 5'26''N	Bhurhabalanga		L.P.		
Sansimda	86° 8' E 22° 18'N	Gadia	Bahalda. Mayurbhanj	M		
Shyamsundarpar		Kharkal	Rairangpur, Mayurbhanj	L.P.M.P. M.N.M.A. (R.S.)		
Silipunji			Mayurbhanj	N		
Sirsa		Subarnakha		L.P.		
Sudiamba				M		

Name of the site	Lat. Long	Drainage	Police-station	Name of the Culture	Reference Published/Unpublished	Remarks
Tentala	86° 7' E 22° 20'N	Kharkal	Bahalda, Mayurbhanj	N		
Uruchandbali				M		

Appendix – II

LIST OF ROCK ART SITES IN ORISSA AND THEIR DISTRICT WISE DISTRIBUTION

District	*Number*
Jharsuguda	2
Kalahandi	1
Mayurbhanj	5
Nuapara	1
Sambalpur	35
Sundargarh	34
Suvarnapur	3
Bargarh	4
Cuttack	1
Keonjhar	6
Total	**92**

Rock shelters, their distribution and subject matter:

Sl. No.	*Name of Rock Art Sites*	*District*	*Subject Matter*
1	Vikramkhol	Jharsuguda	Geometric Pattern, Triangles, Brackets, Honey comb, Dots Palm, Foot and Cupules
2	Ulap	- do -	Triangles, brackets, Honey, comb, wheel, Broom pattern Rhombic, intricate patterns serpentine, Zigzag, Animal, Palm, foot cupules etc.

Sl. No.	*Name of Rock Art Sites*	*District*	*Subject Matter*
3	Gudahandi	Kalahandi	Geometric motifs, Deer, Human figure
4	Pakhana Pathar	Mayurbhanj	Intricate forms, circles, lizard.
5	Pakhana Pathar - II	-do-	Lizard(1), Intricate pattern, Obliterated
6	Pakhana Pathar - III	-do-	Manipulable
7	Pakhana Pathar – IV	-do-	Concentric circles, Manipulable
8	Pakhana Pathar - V	-do-	Foot print, Curvilinear, Concentric circles, Intricate pattern, Pairs of horizontal strokes, Series of dots.
9	Jogimath	Nuapara	Geometric forms, humped cattle, Human figures.
10	Rail Ushakothi-I	Sambalpur	Intricate patterns, Triangles, Deer's, Lizards, Serpentine cupules.
11	UKT-II	- do -	Triangles, Serpentine, Deer, Bird, Cupules.
12	UKT-III	- do -	Zigzag, Triangles, Deer, Cupules
13	Vushakothi-IV	- do -	Triangles, Cupules, Deer etc.
14	UKT-V	- do -	Triangles & Cupules
15	UKT-VI	- do -	Triangles, Cupules, Miscellaneous
16	UKT-VII	- do -	Triangles, Fish, Deer, Cupules etc.
17	UKT-VIII	- do -	Geometric Patterns Triangles, Deer, Cupules
18	UKTIX	- do -	Geometric Pattern, Triangle, Harpoons, Deer, Boars, Cupules etc.
19	UKT-X	- do -	Triangles, Geometric patterns, Harpoons, Cupules, Deer, oar, Giraffe, Nilgai, Palm foot etc.
20	UKT-XI	- do -	Birds, Deer, Triangles, Cupules
21	UKT-XII	- do -	Geometric patterns, Triangles, Honey comb, entwined line Criss-cross, deer, Antler, turtle, serpentine Lizards, Venus, Phallus

Sl. No.	*Name of Rock Art Sites*	*District*	*Subject Matter*
22	Laudimal UKT-I	- do -	Triangles, birds, Lizards, Deer's, Antlers, Sambar, Fish Honeycomb, Serpentine, entwined lines, Zigzag, Criss-cross lines, Cupules.
23	UKT-II	Sambalpur	Bird (enigmatic), Deer, footprint, lizard, Cupules and entwined lines, triangles.
24	UKT-III	- do -	Triangles, Cupules
25	Ushakoti-IV	- do -	Circles with criss-cross lines X', Triangles, Circles, Cupules
26	Ushakoti-V	- do -	Deer, Antler, Peacock, Hare, Turtle, Fish, Palm, Foot, Honey comb, Rhomboids, Cupules, Triangles etc.
27	UKT-VI	- do -	Triangle, Honey comb, criss-cross, Cupules, Serpentine, Deer, Elephant, Bear, Porcupine
28	UKT-VII	- do -	Triangles, Cupules
29	UKT-VIII	- do -	Triangles, Cupules, Palm, Deer
30	UKT-IX	- do -	Tree-like forms, Triangles
31	UKT-X	- do -	Deer, Antler, Palm, Foot Harpoon, Cupules, Honey comb, Rhomboid, Triangles
32	UKT-XI	- do -	Triangles, Deer, Cupules
33	Landimal UKT-XVIII	-do-	Vulvas, Deer, Miscellaneous, Obliterated.
34	UKTXIX	-do-	Vulvas, Triangles
35	UKTXX	-do-	Vulvas, Deer, Cupules, Obliterated
36	UKTXXI	-do-	Deer, Diamond Chain, Vulvas Palm, Harpoon, Rectilinear
37	Gothamundia	-do-	Pigmented engravings (Deer?)
38	Ambakhol Gumpha	-do-	Vulvas
39	Chhatagarh	-do-	Triangles, Obliterated.
40	Kundapitha Gumpha-I	-do-	Deer, Tortoise, Vulvas, Serpentine, Obliterated, Phytomorphos, Rectilinear.

Sl. No.	*Name of Rock Art Sites*	*District*	*Subject Matter*
41	Kundapitha Gumpha-II	-do-	Deer, Peacock, Geometric patterns
42	Kundapitha Gumpha-III	-do-	Deer, Geometric pattern
43	Bhimamandali UKT-I	- do -	Triangles, Criss-cross, Honey comb, Cupules, Rhomboids, Foot.
44	Bhimamandali UKT-II	Sambalpur	Ladder, Human face, Honey comb, Rhomboid, Triangle, Palm print, Cupules, Deer etc.
45	Rajbahal	Sundargarh	Geometric pattern, Broom pattern, Cupules, Honey comb, Triangles, Diamonds
46	Rajbahal UKT-II	- do -	Rhombic pattern, Broom pattern, Cupules, Triangles
47	Rajbahal UKT-III	- do -	Triangles, Broom pattern and Cupules
48	Rajbahal UKT-IV	-do-	Triangles, Foot print
49	Rajbahal UKT-V	-do-	Triangles, Foot print, Cupules Serpentine, I-shaped
50	Ushakupa	- do -	Geometric forms, Triangles, Palm, Foot, Fish, Turtle, Honey comb, Broom pattern and Heart pattern.
51	Baurikupa	- do -	Rhombi pattern, Cupules, Palm, Triangles
52	Chormoda	- do -	Cupules
53	Jhinka moda	- do -	Triangles & Cupules
54	Jadabilmoda	- do -	Triangles & Cupules
55	Imlimoda-I	- do -	Triangles & Cupules
56	Imlimoda-II	- do -	Cupules, Triangles and Rhombic pattern
57	Tongo	- do -	Palm, Foot prints, Honey comb pattern, Cupules, Rhombic, Serpentine, Triangles
58	Manik Moda	Sundargarh	Triangle, Human figure, Serpentine, Plant, Deer, Humped Cattle.
59	Lekha Moda-I	- do -	Deer, Lizard, Frog, Palm print.

Sl. No.	*Name of Rock Art Sites*	*District*	*Subject Matter*
60	Lekha Moda-II	- do -	Deer, Lizard, Frog, Tortoise, Triangles, Harpoon, Rhombic, Broom and Intricate, Geometric patterns.
61	LMD-III	- do -	Triangles, Deer, Cupules and Miscellaneous
62	LMD-IV	- do -	Triangle, Honey-comb, Broom patterns, Harpoon, Palm; Foot, Deer, Antler, Bird, Frog, Lizard, Tortoise, Cupules
63	LMD-V	- do -	Heart pattern, Deer, Antler
64	Lekha muda-VI`	- do -	Triangle, Cupules, Foot, Palm, Human figure, Welded with Sword, Shield, Musical instruments
65	LMD-VII	- do -	Triangles & Palm print
66	LMD-VIII	- do -	Triangle, Humped cattle, Human figures
67	LMD-IX	- do -	Floral Motif, Triangles, Palm
68	LMD-X	- do -	Triangles, Serpentine, Rhombic pattern, Palm, Footprints, herding scene, Rhino, Deer, Humped cattle, Bird, Lizard, Snake, Fog, Turtle
69	LMD-XI	- do -	Geometric motifs, Triangles, broom pattern, Antler, Frog, Palm.
70	LMD-XII	- do -	Deer Frog, Tortoise, Human-figures, Honey collection scene.
71	Petenmoda	-do-	Vulvas, Deer, Reptile, Geometric pattern
72	Dholmoda	-do-	Lizard, Geometric pattern, Cupules
73	Chirenmoda-I	-do-	Deer
74	Chirenmoda-II	-do-	Obliterated forms
75	Rajamachan	-do-	Triangle
76	Gastimoda-I	-do-	Tortoise, Butterfly, Sun motif , Vulvas , Cupules, Geometric pattern

Sl. No.	Name of Rock Art Sites	District	Subject Matter
77	Gastimoda-II	-do-	Peacock Deer, Unidentified
78	Bhalupani	-do-	Human forms, Deer, Vulva, Foot print, Frog.
79	Chandili UKT	Suvarnapur	Deer, Boar, Foot, Cupules, Geometric motifs.
80	Chandili UKT-II	-do-	Human forms, Serpentine Rectilinear pattern
81	Chandili UKT-III	-do-	Quadruped (Jackal)
82	Debrigarh UKT-I	Bargarh	Human forms, Animals, Rectilinear, Concentric circles, Obliterated
83	Debrigarh UKT-II	-do-	Palm Motif, Serpentine, Obliterated
84	Debrigarh UKT-III	-do-	Lizard, Frogs, Animals, Triangle, Ovals, Rectilinear , Intricate pattern, Wavy line, Lunate shaped motif, Obliterated
85	Debrigarh UKT-IV	-do-	Shield Motif, Triangle
86	Adhai Akshyara	Cuttack	Bird, Human form, Boat, Brahmi alphabetic forms, Fish
87	Santamundia	Keonjhar	Human forms , Animal(tiger?) , Obliterated
88	Sitaghara	-do-	Human forms, animal form, Geometric motifs, Obliterated
89	Bhalughara	-do-	Diamond pattern , Linear form , Obliterated
90	Jarasandha Huli-I	-do-	Manipulable
91	Jarasandha Huli-II	-do-	Palm, Diamond pattern, Obliterated pattern
92	Gupta Ganga	-do-	Triangle, Serpentine, obliterated.

According to Pradhan (Pradhan: 2001: 17-25 and Pradhan, *et al*: 2006: 236-240) there are 2,492 paintings and 3,878 engravings recorded from the above Rock Art sites in Orissa.

Appendix – III

An Out Line ot General Prehistory

By Prof. D K Bhattacharya

Men are messy beings. Nearly 3 million years ago our ancestors began littering the African landscape with stone tools and gnawed bones. From the first tools to today's indestructible glass bottles is the archaeological record. The retrieval material needs to be classified into types and styles on the basis of objective and descriptive attribute clusters. Finally, when these objects are arranged in chronological order, many significant informations regarding culture change and evolution start becoming apparent. To use a modern cultural example we can have pots, pans, ladles and the like which can be broadly grouped into a cluster of cooking objectives. Likewise reading and writing objects, sleeping objects, transport objects, etc. can all be formed to reflect upon the relative specialization and pre-occupation of certain functions in the society. In prehistory, unfortunately, no functional clusters are possible because of obvious lack of any functional indication in the objects themselves. As such, clusters of structural forms are made and through these, attempts are made to reconstruct cultures which have produced these objects. The stone tools which were fashioned by man constitute the main bulk of culture recovered from as early as 2 million years till about 5,500 years ago. This does not mean that man did not fashion tools from wood or bones as well. Apparently the organic medium on which man may have possibly made tools did not stand the test of time. From around 30,000 years onwards, bones are recovered along with the stones but any possible attempts on this material made by man earlier to this date have been destroyed for ever. The usual tool types and the cultural stages defined on them are as follows :

	DURATION	BROAD TOOL CATEGORIES	TOOL TYPES	CULTURAL DIVISIONS
PALAEOLITHIC	10,000 B.C.	Blade tools and Bone Tools	Backed blade knives, Burins End Scrapers	Upper Palaeolithic
	35,000 B.C. (100-80,000 B.C.)	Flake Tools	Awls Poins Side scrapers	Middle Palaeolithic
		Pebble tools	Cleaver Handaxe Chopping tool Chopper	Lower Palaeolithic

2.8 million years ago

Likewise, Mesolithic (10,000 – 6,000 B.C.) is defined on the basis of several tool types made on tiny blades often referred to as microliths. These are 3-5 cm. Long, 1 to 1.5 cm. broad and 0.5 – 0.2 cm. Thick blades which are skillfully backed and mounted on adequate handles to form composite tools. During Neolithic (6000 B.C. – 4000 B.C.) big axes appear with surfaces perfectly smoothened by laborious rubbing on stones. Thus, we see that various cultural stages are discernible on the basis of type identification along. It is not very surprising, therefore, that stone age typology forms a fundamental aspect of research for archaeologists of this period.

Dating the finds forms one of the major problems of prehistorians. Blissfully this problem is also shared by geologists and other natural sciences. Hence a working archaeologist does not have to get much involved in these age estimation processes and their techniques. An archaeologist has to be mainly concerned with stratigraphy and erecting a kind of local chronology on the basis of the depositional process. That is, if the stratigraphy is on an old lake bed (generally referred to as luccustrine deposit) the lowest layer is the oldest and the subsequent layers are successively younger. If it is a river deposit (generally referred to as alluvial or fluvial deposit) in which there are evidences of terraces found on the banks then the uppermost terrace deposit is taken as the oldest and the subsequent terraces (as one approaches to the present flow of the river) as younger; the youngest layer being along the present level of the river. If such local chronologies can have marker fossils of animals or geological indications of climates under which various strata were laid one can easily construct a climatic succession table for a larger area. All these methods of ageing are generally grouped under Relative methods of dating. Since 1950 when the Nobel prize for physics was given to Libby for his work on Carbon-14 and its rate of disintegration, a large number of natural sciences have come out with methods of dating in terms of years. These are grouped under Absolute methods of dating. Without going into these methods and their intricacies we may just look at the calender constructed by these techniques. The time period spreading from nearly 3 million years till about 10,000 B.C. is called Pleistocene. Geological evidences suggest that there were at least 4 great glaciations that occurred during this period. The glacial periods covered large parts of Europe and America upto almost 40° to 35 ^{o} latitude. Areas lying between 20 ^{o} above equator to 20 ^{o} below the equator during the same period experienced a very wet stage causing flood in rivers. Evidence of glaciations from the Northern latitudes and high rainfall (pluviations) from the Southern latitudes are known extensively. The entire period of Pleistocene marks the evolution of both the biological aspects of man and also his culture. Culture from this whole period is called Palaeolithic culture. Evidences from Africa and many new evidences from Europe show that till about the IInd glaciation man did not make any other culture except some very simple pebble tools which can be identified as choppers and the like. It is only about 300,000 to 400,000 years ago that the handaxes and cleavers evolve and show a great degree of slow refinement of technique through a long period of time. The handaxe and the cleaver occur with such a perfect internal homogeneity all over Europe, Africa and Asia that they have often been grouped into a single culture called the Acheulian. Needless to say that we do have evidences of the Acheulians living at the same time with the non-Acheulian chopper types, occurring in neighbouring regions. This left no doubt to the fact that culture in such early part of human history as well shows ramification in preference of adaptation. If our earlier agreement of biocultural evolution can be recalled at this juncture one can argue that such a bifurcation could have led to the formation of two different species of humankind. In all probability it did, but when ever two groups of humankind met they either bred or bled. There is no doubt that both breeding and bleeding had occurred but the Acheulians did reign over a larger period for a longer time than the poorly equipped chopper/chopping groups could do. We shall briefly consider these cultural stages in the following sections.

It will be amply clear that the above cultural interpretations can be possible in prehistory only through the two basic methodologies of Typology and Chronology. Here we do not propose to go into the details of these methodologies but instead survey the results emerging from their careful use.

II. PALAEOLITHIC CULTURE

By definition, the cultural debries recovered from the entire period of Pleistocene (approx 3 million years – 10000 B.C.) is termed as Palaeolithic culture. During the first two-third of this period the climate of various continents in our planet was more or less similar to the present day climate. Man was still in the process of evolution and was more or less of the status of *Australopithecus africanus.* A semi-erect ape like creature who was totally terrestrial and was most probably a scavenging animal. There are some indications that he might have shaped very rudimentary tools on pebbles or broken bones. (hence the name *Osteodontokaratic* culture). The eastern coast of Africa extending from Ethiopia to South Africa seems to be their main area of occupation. Just over two million years ago *Homo habilis* evolves and shortly afterwards a more advanced form called *Homo erectus* comes to the scene. These human types were much better equipped to interact and hence adapt to ground living. Fire was also tamed by them at a later date. This early stage of human culture is termed the *Lower Palaeolithic Culture.* Gathering around fire for equal radiational benefits might have been usually practiced, and this might have also helped in consolidating the social bonds in these early human bands. In Europe this culture is well established by the time of the IInd glaciation while in India it may have entered not before the II interglacial. Africa, however, remains their main homeland where it appears at least 40,000 years earlier than in Europe. Chronologically Lower Palaeolithic starts around 800,000 years ago and continues till 400,000 to 100,000 years. It shows two distinct forms evolving almost side by side in the entire Euro-Asia. In Africa, however, such contemporaneity of the two forms is not discernable. Man did have the ability of creating artificial structures, *albeit* temporary in nature, when a situation demanded but otherwise they lived in the open and hunted animals and collected vegetable produce from the forest.

Europe

The earliest culture in Europe is known from Clacton-on-sea in England and Terra Amata in the French Riviera. Both these sites indicate fairly large human activity dating from the second glacial period. Various types of pebbles were skillfully broken to obtain a broad sharp edge. These are recognized as chopper or chopping tool depending on the manner of their preparation. Large flakes were detached to be used without any further dressing. A single evidence of a wooden spear has also been found along with this material from England. A foot impression in once soft sand at Terra Amata is also another exciting evidence known from this culture. This cultural type has now come to be known as the *Clactonian* culture. By the time the second interglacial sets in, a kind of regional specialization becomes strongly suggestive. Areas spread over England to almost the river Rhine in Central Europe shows a progressive development of heavy core tools with pointed working end and working done on both the upper and under surfaces (biface) of the specimens. These are called handaxes. This cultural type is named *Acheulian* on the basis of the site where this type was first recorded in France (St. Acheul). The Clactonians are earlier in their time of emergence but they continue to survive even when Acheulians have evolved in Western Europe. Mostly they seem to concentrate in Central Europe in addition to a peripheral existence in England as well. Once the handaxes evolve they show a remarkable degree of technological development through time. From 400,000 to almost upto 100,000 years Acheulians flourish in Europe. The non-handaxe makers in Central Europe also show continued survival of chopper-chopping and large flake tools without much change. Nearly around 200,000 years from today, the Acheulians demonstrate a technological revolution by taking to antler as hammer to break their stones, and also devising a planned preparation of previously shaped flake. The former reduced the chance of wastage and breakage of stones in the process of dressing caused by stone hammers and the shattering effect of it. The result was the evolving of very fine medium sized smoothly worked handaxes (often referred to as Upper Acheulian in type). The latter type was a way that the dressed surface forms the upper part of the flake. Since the flake is first conceived and planned and then detached, it is called *prepared core technique,* or *Levalloise technique* after the site (in France) where it was first recorded.

The absence or any possibility to date the Palaeolithic succession originally described in the formative stage lead almost all text books of archaeology to put the event of arrival of man in Europe at least 1 million years later than Africa. Recently, however, some new sites have been discovered and dated which will seem to narrow this enormous gap considerably. This will also require to push the earliest date of human culture in Africa to almost 2.5 million years from 1.8 million years as Issac had earlier commented. Some of the few reliable dates are :

SOLEIHAC in France................900,000 to 970,000

ISERNIA in Italy ....736,000 ± 40,000

CHIILAC in France....................1.9 million years

The northern boundary of human occupation in Europe appears to coincide roughly with the southern limit of last glaciation. That is, about 54° N in Wales, Germany and just south of latitude 51 ° N in Czechoslovakia. This pattern is evidently demonstrative of destructions and re-working of sediments by the repeated advances of Scandinavian ice sheet.

It is generally believed that the intense seasonal variation in the temperate Europe caused short growing season of the vegetable resources and this might have been a strong reason of hominid expansion being more concentrated in the area below 50 ° N latitude. This might also explain why man arrived so late in Europe from his African home land.

E. Africa

The development of lower Palaeolithic in East Africa is most remarkably demonstrative. Here at Olduvai George almost a vertical evolution of early Chopper-Chopping culture developing into Acheulian (Olduvai Levels III & IV) and Kenya Fauresmith (Late Acheulian of Europe with levalloise flakes) is witnessed. But the entire succession shows the evolution occurring much earlier than what has just been observed in Europe. It is in the early Acheulian period of both India and Africa that a variety of handaxe with broad cutting edge evolves. These are called Cleavers. Cleavers are not very common types European Acheulian. Many of these handaxes and cleavers show a special technique of thinning by removing a large flake from one of the surfaces subsequent to finishing the type. This technique is termed the *Victoria West* technique.

India

Lower Palaeolithic in India is known from almost all over the vast country. A vertical evolution of the culture in the manner of Europe and Africa, however, is still not demonstrable. Sohan in the Potwar plateau of North West India shows a Chopper-Chopping dominated development occurring around the II interglacial and continuing till the end of the III glacial. Apparently a developed Acheulian type entered the region around this time. Thus Acheulian forms co-exist with the Soanian in India record two main boulder or gravel deposits belonging to the Pleistocene period.

The cultural materials are all mixed and distributed between these two levels. Thus, the Palaeolithic period is given a two fold nomenclature. Early Stone Age refers to the cultural material occurring in the oldest gravel and corresponds to the Lower Palaeolithic period to the rest of the world. Middle Stone Age refers to the cultural material occurring in the second or last gravel and corresponds to a mixture of Middle and Upper Palaeolithic of the rest of the world. In the last three decades there have been some new evidences coming about a third Pleistocene gravel yielding only Upper Palaeolithic cultural material. The Belan valley in the Pratapgarh district of U.P. near Allahabad, in this regard affords the best stratigraphic succession of the three Palaeolithic stages.

The Early Stone Age tools reported from Kuliana and Kamarpara in Orissa by Sen and Bose and the numerous sites along Burhabalang, Brahmani and Mahanadi valleys reported by Mohapatra have shown a mixed tool assemblage. Clactonian flakes, chopper-chopping tools along with large crude handaxes as well as small symmetrical upper Acheulian handaxes and cleavers have been found to occur within a single stratum. Several of the flakes within the assemblage are distinctly levalloisean. The pattern observed in other sites in the peninsular region by and large continues to be identical. Early Stone Age in Andhra is known from Giddalur and Nagarjunakonda. In Kortalayar valley (Tamil Nadu) a large industry was described from Attirampakkam and Vadamaduri. In Mysore the Malaprabha and Ghataprabha basins yield numerous sites. Kibbanhali from north Mysore yields almost identical Lower Palaeoliths. Nevasa in Maharashtra, Narmada basin in Madhya Pradesh, Luni in Rajasthan and Rohri in Gujarat have all yielded numerous Lower Palaeolithic sites. All these areas show fairly high degree of cleavers made on Clactonian flakes besides showing a marked influence of African Victoria West technique in the handaxes.

Sites with living floors like those of Europe and Africa are rare in India. Recently Bhimbhetka and Adamgarh caves of Madhya Pradesh, and Hunsgi in Karnataka have yielded some additional information regarding the Lower Palaeolithic culture of India. It seems almost certain that handaxe/cleaver (Acheulian) and Clactonian flake/Pebble chopper (Sohanian) were not integral part of each other as the depositional river sites would seem to indicate. Bhimbhetka, for instance, has yielded not a single chopper or chopping tool within its otherwise highly evolved Acheulian complex.

India is a vast country with extreme variations of climate and this has caused variation in animals and vegetations in its different regions. It would, therefore, be natural to expect a fairly high degree of regional variation. The nature of occurrence of our data being completely different such variations, if any, are not so far decipherable. In general the Lower Palaeolithic in India affords a much closer similarity to the same of Africa than Europe.

Middle Palaeolithic

Middle Palaeolithic follows Lower Palaeolithic without any typological break all over the Old World. The earliest date of this culture is dated around 100,000 B.C. and it continues till around 36,000 B.C. The stage of human evolution during the culture is generally attributed to the Neanderthals. These were relatively heterogenous people who spread far and wide over the entire Euro-Afro-Asia. There is no doubt to the fact that they were very accomplished hunters and in course of time adapted to small ecozones with overspecialization. It is likely that survivors of earlier human types also mixed with them in some zones. Yet, whatever be the reasons, this overspecialized group did not survive and the true human race evolved from the earlier stocks. Neanderthals not only loved living in caves but they were sufficiently evolved to have sentiments about their dead. At Shanidar in Iraq a Neanderthal burial yielded evidences of flowers having been offered to the deceased. In many Alpine sites, cave bear bones seem to have been specially arranged for some kind of a religious cult. There are also some evidences of bloody infights between their regional groups. Fire was already tamed by the Homo erectus. Neanderthals made the maximum use of it penetrating into the temperate region right within the glacial region.

Europe

Western Europe, which showed a specialized Acheulian development accompanied by levalloise flakes smoothly enters into a Middle

Palaeolithic variety which is quite famous as Mousterian tradition. The name is borrowed from the site name where this tradition was first identified. It is important to understand that neither Mousterian is a homogenous tradition in Western Europe nor is this known from other parts of Europe. Mousterian is identified as having four distinct varieties right within France. One of this variety, called the Quina tradition, does not even show the famous levalloise flakes which had since long been accepted as characteristic Middle Palaeolithic trait. Another variety called MTA (*Mousterian de Tradition Acheulien*) contains several diminutive handaxes with numerous side scrapers and points made on levalloise flakes. Central Europe, which yielded nearly no handaxes during Lower Palaeolithic, start showing handaxes along with numerous side scrapers during the Middle Palaeolithic stage. Significantly levalloise flakes are not at all preferred in this region. Instead a new refined type makes its appearance. This is an extremely thin bifacially flaked leaf like point which appears in the south German regions and then spread to Hungary and Rumania during the subsequent cultural stage. In small pockets of Yougoslavia and Hungary the Middle Palaeolithic is characterized by tiny side scrapers and points prepared on pebble flakes. East Europe and Ukraini, on the other hand, show a parallel French type Mousterian development.It becomes immediately apparent that Middle Palaeolithic in Europe does not represent a simple or similar tradition. Either there were different kinds of populations already showing the formation of distinct adaptation strategies and hence distinct social formations, or Middle Palaeolithic represents the workmanship of Homo neanderthalesis (in France) and archaic sapiens and east European Neanderthals (in Ukrania and white Russia). Skeletal evidences seem to indicate that there indeed was more than one type of human (kind in biological sense) living in Europe during this period.

East Africa

The third pluviation marks the disappearance of handaxes and cleavers from East Africa. A distinct regionalization sets in at this juncture. In Kenya occurs a clear Mousteroid development with levalloise technique. This is identified as *Proto-Stillbay* and *Kenya Stillbay.* In Uganda, on the other hand, handaxes continue to occur with levalloie flakes worked into side scrapers, points and knives. This tradition is identified as *Sangoan.* Very soon a microlithisation sets in both Kenya and Uganda. These micro-blades along with broad blade tools constitute the Upper Palaeolithic of this region.

India

Middle Palaeolithic or Middle Stone Age of India as a separate culture tradition was not identified till as late as 1960. Although a flake culture as a possible stage in Indian Palaeolithic succession was implicit in Cammaide and Burkitts' reporting of Andhra material in early thirties of this century. It was only in 1956 that Sankhalia demonstrated the stratigraphic context of this flake culture. Since then we have now almost the entire India surveyed and a fairly good understanding of this period.

Middle Palaeolithic forms the second and the last demonstrable cultural phase of Pleistocene. The only carbon-14 date available for this period (from Dattawadi in Pune) shows it to be rather young in age. That is, unlike Mousterian in France which occurs around 90,000 years ago, the Indian Middle Stone Age gives a date of merely 36,000 years. Most authorities believe that either the date is not reliable or the layer which is dated is a later episode and it has incorporated earlier and older Middle Palaeolithic material. An important characteristic of this age is the total change of raw material. Almost all over India the Middle Palaeolithic tools are made of such glossy rocks as jasper, flint, obsidian or chalcedony. Since our sites are mostly depositional and not original living floors, this change of raw material even if it is gradual in reality appears to be sudden in nature. At Bhimbhetka, one of the few sites with primary living floor from India there is a distinct development of an Acheulian which is typically Middle Palaeolithic in its flake element. There is no such cent percent change of raw material observed here. This Acheulian is like *Fauresmith* in East Africa which precedes *proto-stillbay.*

As far as typo-technological character of this age is concerned no remarkable change seems to occur from the preceding culture. While flakes are produced by levalloie technique in some areas, in other areas this technique seems to be totally absent. The most predominant type is a large variety of side scrapers, borers and points in this order. In many of these side scrapers a projected point at one of the corners of the flake seem to have been specially formed. This type is referred to as scraper-cum-borer. At some places such Lower Palaeolithic types as handaxes, choppers and discoids have also been found, even though now they have been produced in the changed raw material.

The important stratified sites of this age come from Maharashtra, i.e. from Godavari valley and its tributaries. Nevasa, Bel Pandhari, Surgaon, Kalegaon and Nandur Madhmeshwar may be mentioned as few of the many famous type-sites from this area. Numerous Middle Palaeolithic sites from the Malaprabha and Ghataprabha basin of northern Karnataka also show the same cultural features. Orissa and Andhra show almost a total disregard for levalloise technique. Here the tools continue, in many cases, to be prepared on Lower Palaeolithic raw material (i.e. Quartzite) and show no appreciable change in size. Handaxes and cleavers are also common in Middle Palaeolithic of this area. Tamilnadu, Madhya Pradesh, Rajasthan and Gujrat are abundant in Maharastra-Karnataka variety of Middle Palaeolithic. Recently several typical Middle Palaeolithic sites have also been brought to light from Bankura and Purulia districts of West Bengal. Mrs. Allchin has added another series of finds from the Rajasthan desert extendingin W. Pakistan.

Middle Palaeolithic in India, therefore, can no longer be considered as an isolated phenomenon as Subbarao thought in the Sixties. It is a well developed cultural stage of Indian Palaeolithic period. Regarding its origin earlier authors were all inclined to subscribe to an exogenous theory linking it with the Sanghao finds of Pakistan or the Tahsik-Tash of Central Asia. With the phenomenal increase in the number of these finds it would appear that there is little doubt about its being developed indigenously in at least the peninsular India. Contact with West Asia for such areas as Punjab, Gujrat or even Rajasthan may be considered as a possibility until more areas of this culture are unearthed.

Upper Palaeolithic

It is a cultural phase which starts around 36,000 B.C. all over the old world and ends around 9,000 B.C. That is, it has a duration of barely

27,000 years which is less than 3 per cent of the duration of Lower Palaeolithic phase and 6 per cent of the duration of Middle Palaeolithic phase. Yet in this small duration archaeologists have identified numerous traditions developing and spreading all over. Upper Palaeolithic is authored by fully evolved human race viz., *Homo sapiens.* It is almost certain that the previous evolutionary stages like the variety of the Neanderthals were totally wiped out by this full grown human group. The scientific attention paid to the otherwise incredible cultural belief of the Nepalese and Tibetan of the existence of an abominable snowman called "Yeti, is primarily based on the suspicion of a possible run away Neanderthal group surviving in isolation. Apparently such a possibility is difficult to entertain as Neanderthals were culturally much more advanced. The early *Homo sapiens* were called Cro Magnon man after the name of the site (in France) where it was first recorded. Both culturally as also biologically these early human groups slowly differentiated to form different human races with their distinct culture. The idea of race is based mainly on perishable features such as skin colour, hair form, face and its relation to the orientation of nose and eyes. In skeletal material most of these morphological features are not demonstrable and hence many authorities do not accept these evidences as conclusive of racial differentiation. It is likely that a large headed generalized type was the emergent man which due to migration and subsequent adaptation within different climates developed specialized Negroid, Caucasoid and Mongoloid features. The occurrence of stone using tribals with typical Australoid features in Japan (Ainu), Phillipines (Aeta) and Ceylon (Vedda) could be taken as an example of Mongoloid differentiation being caused by long spcialization of a different group somewhere in the North-Eastern Asiatic region. We are still quite a distance away from conclusively demonstrating how this racial differentiation took place in the past.

The biggest achievement of these early men were in terms of intensifying only selected aspects of the econiche they adapted themselves to intensification of exploitation in contradistinction to extensification requires progressive technological evolution. Areas where such rapid technological growth is evidenced, therefore, can be taken to be more in equilibrium with the environment at a generalized level of economy. It is important to emphasize that the social structure and the network of relationship that maintains solidarity of generalized economic pursuits become more important. In Europe, while France demonstrates a development similar to the former (Intensification), Central Europe and Balkans maintain a situation similar to the latter type (Extensification). The major development of this period besides the demise of Neanderthals and the appearance of anatomically modern man can be summarized as follows :

(i) The expansion of humans into most of the world's inhabited areas, including the New World and Australia.
(ii) The relatively sudden and widespread appearance of figurines and other artifacts art and rituals.
(iii) The appearance of a wide range of bone tools including eye needles, fishing tools and harpoons.
(iv) There was a decided step towards organizing human groups in closely tied kinship organisation (only indirectly indicative).

Europe

In France there is increased ramification of various traditions in this period. Mousterian is followed by *Perigordian* tradition rather poor in art and bone objects. Perigordians used to blunt a sharp border of the large blades they became expert in removing. Almost parallel to the *Perigordian* developed the *Aurignacians* who never learnt to blunt their blades. Aurignacians retouched their blades instead and made many bone tools of which a variety of lance heads on ivory are quite famous. The Perigordians and Aurignacians are suddently replaced by the Soultreans who prepared fine paper thin leaf points with pressure flaking. These leaf points are so finely prepared that in European prehistory they have come to be nick named as *Laurel leaf* and *Willow leaf.* Solutreans leave the scene as suddenly as they arrived after a brief stay of 2000 years. The *Magdalenians* finally take over the entire Western Europe. These Magdalenians showed a decided tilt in preferring bone tools to those on stones. Further, art executed both on their tools as also on cave walls and ceiling reach its culmination during this period. Most of the Upper Palaeolithic cave art is restricted in the Franco-Cantabrian region (South France & North Spain). These, as a rule, do not depict many human forms.

Mostly animals, that too, horse, bison and reindeer are preponderantly executed.Many of these show animals which are wounded and this has been interpreted as being indicative of the practise of sympathetic magic by the people. There are also some evidences of initiation rituals having been performed in these caves. The caves of Lascaux and Font-e-gaum in France and Altamira in Spain have been studied by many experts and all agree to their function being mainly esoteric in nature. There are numerous specimens of pierced batons found in this culture. Many authorities believe that these could be the roads used by band chiefs as sceptors of authority. On this assumption these are named as *Baton de-commandment.* Towards 10,000 B.C. the climate in Europe starts undergoing a drastic change. Large animals were either dying out or migrating to the polar region. Man had to shift his interest to smaller animals. This required a change in his tool kit and thus evolved the Azilian tradition with its microliths. There is a distinct indication in this period of giving up mass as a clumsy aspect rather than being useful. These tiny tools were used in combination and hafted on organic handles to form light and efficient tools. This emphasis towards lightness can be taken to indicate the evolution of bow and arrow. Indeed many Azilian cave painting show the use of bows and arrow.

East Africa

The Proto-Stillbay of the last pluvial in Africa smoothly gives rise to the Capsian in Kenya and Sangoan in Uganda. These traditions show a strong emphasis or blade tools. End scrapers and blunted back knives of various kinds are found in plenty. Bone tools or art executed on them are not so pronounced as in Upper Palaeolithic Europe. Further, Microliths start occurring in abundance in all throughout the Upper Palaeolithic in East Africa. Ostrict egg shells or poorly fired pottery are also known from some of the younger levels. A true more clearly discernible form the Lower Nile region in the north than in Kenya and Uganda. Capsian industries form the former area shows the Soultrean type leaf points from a much earlier date than in France.

India

Upper Palaeolithic in India still remains to be undoubtably confirmed on stratigraphic ground. Large blades and various Upper Palaeolithic types made on them had been found from as early as 1932 when Cammiade and Burkitt described their culture scheme for Indian Palaeoliths. The Series III of these authors include the Upper Palaeolithic types only, but in the absence of a proper stratigraphical context for these types they had either been described within Middle Stone Age or pushed into Late Stone Age. Since then large number of in-situ finds of Upper Palaeolithic blades have been reported from Rajasthan, Andhra and South East U.P. At Bhimbethka a distinct Upper Palaeolithic layer overlies a flake dominated Acheulean industry. In Andhra in a cave site called Muchchatta Chintamanu Gavi a cultural layer containing more than 90 per cent bone tools was reported recently. These bone tools are, however, not so well finished as the ivory or antler tools of temperate Europe.

Almost all archaeologist today agree about the existence of an Upper Palaeolithic cultural stage in India. It is only a matter of time before all these finds would be chronologically established within Pleistocene. Till then we agree that blades, burins or even simple bone tools formed the main cultural character of the people who took over from the Middle Palaeolithic people. A slow evolution from the preceding culture seems to be more than apparent in almost all the places of its find. Like Africa we can surmise that a specialized bone working and art did not develop in regions which were more forested and were along the sub-tropical belt. It is a matter of great regret that till today we do not have no adequate fossil finds from India to attest the authorship of any of our Palaeolithic stages. Furthermore, social formations or archaeological indications thereof are too rudimentary to forma meaningful interpretation.

In the sequel we need to recount the basic social features of men for this 3 million years of his past cultural history. Archaeologists can not dig out a social system nor can they expose the belief structure of the tool makers. Ethnography of stone tool using communities from contemporary world can throw some strong possibilities. Societies have been classified into Bands, Tribes, Chiefdoms and States in an evolutionary order. The band organization which happens to be the simplest must have been the main type of orgaization of man during the entire Palaeolithic period. In this type of organization there are minor differences among members in the community in terms of prestige. No one has any greater claims to material resources than anyone else. In most of these societies older males who are good providers gain the most respect, but they have no political power. Territoriality, ceremonialism and descent reckoning are usually very weakly developed. Division of labour is along basic age and sex lines and the economic structure is simple. Exchange of gift acts as alliance mechanism but mainly on reciprocity basis. The granting of sexual access to wives or similar procedure (e.g., exchange girls for mating) may be one of the frequently used allied mechanism. One of the most impressive things about bands is their stability and long term success. For a million years this was the only form of cultural organization.

In the succeeding period Mesolithic people underwent many significant changes in their adaptation strategies but the band organization did not change significantly till the onset of full-fledged agriculture.

To conclude, it will not be out of place to point out that economic progress and hence cultural progress has always been linked with surplus economy. This has led to a stereotype of the 'hunting-gathering' cultures being considered as almost prehuman in condition. And the image of a nomadic hunter, his life filled with insecurity and disorder is a deep seated one. Lack of material possessions is visualized as reflecting a chronic poverty. His society has been considered as most barbaric. Anthropologists have now been able to systematically uproot these views. Studies in Kalahari desert Bushmen have shown that only fifteen hours hunting and gathering produces enough food to sustain a small band for a full week. Studies among the Australian aborginies likewise shows that although a complete stone using hunter-gatherer in economy these people had a very complex social and kinship structure.

Some philosophical writings in human history have equated the invention of agriculture with true "Fall of Man" in order to emphasize the positive aspects of the hunting and gathering culture. The most successful adaptation which for two million years or more had ensured a relatively secure and equitable existence for man.

III. PALAEOLITHIC ART

The earliest empirical evidence of art in mankind is recorded from as early as the late Lower Palaeolithic (200,000 years ago) in the form of some engraved series of lines on a mammoth rib. The full flowering of this skill, however, occurs only during the Uppér Palaeolithic period (36,000 years ago). Incidentally, this coincides also with the time of emergence of biologically modern man. This break is best recorded in the numerous rock shelters and caves of France and Spain. Countries previously neglected as "back water" of civilization have for long been not properly explored by experts. In the recent years similar cave paintings have been found from a cave called *Apollo-II* near Orange river in South Africa, from *Naih cave* in Borneo and also from *Bhimbhetka* from India. Although all these are not of comparable dates, their existence all throughout the Old World is enough evidence of the fact that the creative urge was common to all mankind. Further, this seem to have always been more keen on re-creating the animal world around man rather than his own self. The various female figurines nick-named "Venus" are one of the very few exceptions of this rule.

Art executed on movable objects, also referred to as Home art includes these female figures, ivory arm bands and lockets with engraved designs, hair pins, pierced shell and animal teeth necklaces, and a variety of sculptured animal shapes. The cave art or the art executed on cave walls are never so specific. Besides, large panels of multicoloured animals, these show several representation of palm prints. Many of these prints show amputation of fingers. There are many lined figures, usually referred to as *tectiforms,* which could be the representation of valva, or trap or even huts.

Most of these art executions represent large herbivorous animals. More often than not these are super imposed and are drawn in complete disregard of the earlier work. In some cases the superimposed figure use convenient parts of the earlier drawing or painting to complete the new one. Another important characteristic of these works of art is that the orientation of the object depicted is not considered. That is, a horse drawn standing on a horizontal plane has a bovid superimposed with its legs vertically opposite those of the horse. The scales of representations are also completely arbitrary and do not conform to the real sizes of the animals. For example, a small rhinoceros may be superimposed on a huge horse. Another feature of Palaeolithic and is that these are usually found deep inside the cave where it is impossible to reach without crawling through steep ascending or descending crevices.

Palaeolithic art gives the earliest indication of the mind of Prehistoric man. Circumstantial evidences or arrangement of debries have a thrown indications about the Prehistoric society but his mind, by far remained unknown to the analyst. His agonies or for that matter his sources of ecstacies will never be known to us. His art is the sole window we have to his mind, and hence is its significance.

An interpretation of these art works have not been very easy without any clue of the part human behaviour or psychology play. With an increase of ethnographic studies, archaeologists rushed to conclude that the life of Prehistoric people could be comparable to the primitives of today surviving at the lowest level of economy. This eventually led to the drawing of ethnographic parallel in non-economic spheres of life as well. Some authorities, had therefore, concluded that man painted because he had basic needs and also anxieties to meet. That is, when a hunting ritual was done on an engraved animal figure in the cave it helped the artist to capture it in actual hunting. Similarly, the initiation rites of youths in the presence of these hunting scenes by way of some kind of hunting practice gave an assurance to their manhood and to their need of being able to hunt successfully in future. Sympathetic magic or totemistic theories are some of the other explanations given as causative forces of primitive art.

After one surveys all these analyses of art, one finds that contrary to what we expected nothing substantial can really be revealed about prehistoric life ways from their art. All one can say is that man was capable of cumulative symbolic recording of objects, events of phenomena. His mental preoccupation involved hunting animals; fertility in man or may be in the entire biological world; and also identify some animals symbolically as belonging to his ancestry or having special boon granting relationship with him. Initiation cannot be directly demonstrated but preoccupation with life after death is strongly indicative.

The symbolic world reconstructable for early man does not show any remarkable difference from the same in man in preindustrial world. Many authorities, therefore, claim that a proper social structure defined with kinship relations may have already evolved during this period, i.e. at least 4000 years before agriculture started. We may not go that far in the absence of a demonstrative evidence of structured social group. Instead, we may suggest that those socio, psychological ingredients which form a proper peasant after agriculture was adopted did not evolve merely with the adaptation of productive economy but was ingrained in humanity much earlier – may be even as early as the closing of Palaeolithic period (8000 B.C.).

Mesolithic Culture

With the change of climate in our planet after Pleistocene ended (10,000 years ago), many plants and animals went extinct. The ecology changed drastically and man had no alternative but to readjust within the changed environment. Since the subsistence base during the Palaeolithic was always very broad it did not require altogether a new adjustment. For instance, we have evidence of fish and turtles having been occasionally used during Palaeolithic period. In Mesolithic period riverine and maritime food resources are intensified. The tool kit, naturally reflects these changes easily. Racial diversification which may have started around 20,000 years earlier than the onset of Mesolithic culture tends to cause more stable adaptive equation of the various groups with their given ecology. This led to a limit in the migratory range of the various groups. Archaeologically, art and cults act as a very good indicator of the ideological sphere of early man. Upper Palaeolithic remains are, therefore, quite explicit in their generalized meaning. With the onset of Mesolithic these explicit experessions of mind become quite few and far between. The elimination of these tangible remains from our early ancestors' mind is a loss to archaeology. We have enough anthropological studies to indicate that this strongly suggests man's entry into the complicated symbolic world. Man adds the current of implicit meaning to his activities and functioning network with the society. Consequently to say that Mesolithic period shows a regression in art is saying half the truth. Cause of art has merely found alternate channels of expression, which did not leave any tangible remains.

Europe

Mesolithic period is more strongly discernable in areas where during Palaeolithic time the climate was similar to subarctic regions. In Europe, therefore, one can easily identify the new traditions designated as *Sauveterranean, Austrian, Maglamosean, Kitchen Midden, Campignian, Ertboel, Lyngby* and many others. These are all predominantly microlithic cultures where such tiny blade tool types as lunates, trapezes, points and triangles are prepared to be hafted in series on wooden handles to form effective implements. The main technological advantage of this period lies in the fact that a number of new combination of tools can be now prepared within a second by arranging the microliths on a suitable rod. Thus, few microliths can form a harpoon or an efficient arrow without much problem merely by selecting and arranging the microliths. Further, unlike the Palaeolithic age a tool in Mesolithic need not be discarded on being damaged. New microliths can be added in place of the damaged ones and the tool is again renewed for use.

Mesolithic culture in Europe shows a longer duration as one proceeds from East to West. The waves of change in the Middle East entered Central and Eastern Europe at a much earlier date than such Western European regions as Denmark, Netherlands or Northern England. Ecologic conditions made the people concentrate near coastal regions along river banks. He became almost semi-sedentary and this influenced his demographic picture. Smaller ban ds fishing and fowling did not have to be as mobile as the Palaeolithic large mammal hunters. With the increase of population density in these bands intergroup fighting broke out for possession of females or even for areas which are environmentally rich. Some Mesolithic cave paintings, depict these intergroup fights very vividly. Although still egalitarian in structure these bands became strongly organized for warfare. Cultural ramification into numerous regional bands with distinct socio-cultural characteristics is a direct outcome of this semi-sedentary pathway chosen by man. It is likely that the foundation of the cultural difference in modern Europe had a beginning traceable within the

Mesolithic period. When plant and animal domestication had started along the Euphrates and Tigris most of Europe was still continuing to survive as Mesolithic hunters and gatherers. It is important at this juncture to mention that the mere knowledge of botanical reproduction was not responsible for the onset of the Neolithic culture with agricultural economy. Agriculture is a labour intensive economy and its fruitful adaptation requires an entirely differently organized social structure. Social stratification and emergence of semi-professionals with a sort of leadership organizing the distribution of the product are some of the basic requirements of an agricultural society. In all probability organizing slave labour (found in the subsequent metal age) may have been conceived by the early agriculturalists. Pottery for the storing of surplus was another technological evolution which required professionals to process clay, cut fire wood and finish the product. In the Mesolithic tradition called Ertboel in Germany crude pottery types already make their appearance. This demonstrates that socio-culturally speaking Mesolithic was a more or less preparatory stage which finally culminated into a cultural form suitable enough to shift the basic economy of collecting into producing.

East Africa

In the tropical area a clear cut emergence of Mesolithic is not quite disernable. With the end of Pleistocene there was a period of extreme dryness and many of the deserts of the world were in the process of formation. Sea level increased and the rivers dried up into many fresh water pools. Man automatically shifted his exploitable environment to the water species and fishing and fowling emerged as the main economy like in Europe (although caused by a different kind of change in the environment).

This process of change must have been felt much earlier in the tropical and subtropical regions. We have seen how right in the late Palaeolithic the Capsian showed a distinct adaptation to microliths. During early Holocene this microlithic trend is further specialized into Elementeitan and *Wilton* in Kenya and *Magosan* and *Lupemban* in Uganda. The tools are mostly prepared on black obsidian and are accompanied by crudely baked hand-made pottery as well.

India

The microliths in Africa and also in India are found from late Palaeolithic to metal age. It is only the accompanying cultural indicators other than the microlithis which decide the finds as being from the Mesolithic, Neolithi or Chalcolithic age. Further, there are many sites where a purely Mesolithic culture is flourishing in the neighbourhood of an advanced tradition. Thus a chronological delimitation for the definition of this culture is not helpful.

Microliths have been noted in India and described from as early as 1863. Till the identification of this separate microlithic culture, the tools were variedly referred to as Proto-Neolithic depending on the collective character of the assemblage. A distinct microlithic site associated with shells were discovered from as far in the east as the Andmans. Microliths have been collected from almost all over India except the coastal stretch in kerala and parts of Punjab and Haryana. A very few of these microliths actually come out of stratigraphic layers. Whatever knowledge we have of Indian Mesolithic period it based only on the few excavated sites. The excavated sites at Birbhanpur in West Bengal, Teri sites in Tamil Nadu, Langhnaj in Gujarat, Bagor in Rajasthan, Bhimbethka and Adamgarh in M.P. and Sarai Nahar Rai in U.P. The basic informations gathered from the excavated sites may be summarized as follows :

1. Mesolithic people had not only achieved their special adaptation but also settled in artificially erected structures in as early as 8000 B.C. This, in other words, can be taken to indicate that the time of onset of this culture agrees with the same in both Europe and Africa. So far we have only one site with such an early date from India (Sarai Nahar Rai). The rest of the sites ranges from 5000 B.C. (Bagor) to 2000 B.C. (Langhnaj).
2. Most of these sites show total adaptation to microliths and do not contain any such heavy duty tools as picks or axes. Antlers or for that matter ivory are rarely used in Indian Mesolithic. Haematite with evidence of its having been rubbed, and spherical stone balls used as sling bolas are the other important features of the Mesolithic way of life and their hunting method. Some of the rock paintings discovered

from Mirzapur district in U.P. and B himbethka could be isolated from the large number of art executions as being of Mesolithic antiquity: All these show animal forms with isolated hunting and fishing scenes. The hunting implements are spears with multiple barbs apparently obtained easily by attaching microliths.

3. At Bhimbethka there is evidence of a special structure erected outside the cave mouth to act as a wind break. At Bagor natural concrete from river bed seems to have been specially transported to the living site to pave the living floor.
4. At Adamgarh, a large number of animal bones were found to be domesticated although associated finds were mainly suitable for hunting functions. The domesticated animals could not have been taken to indicate pastoral economy because there was about six varieties of mammals found in this deomsticated group. Further, Adamgarh is a cave site and pastorals cannot live in caves for longer duration. Apparently our information about this site is not quite complete. It may be representing a younger industry.
5. That intergroup fight or warfare is not merely a conjecture for this period is proved by the skeleton found at Sarai Nahar Rai with a microlith embedded into one of its ribs.

Neolithic Culture

Neolithic marks a cultural stage where man takes to production economy and evolves special tools to suit this economic behaviour. Along with these tools that he evolves he has to by necessity modify his social behaviour to large extent in order to suit the sedentism required when one has to wait for a harvest. Thus, a proper peasant community emerges by the time man settles down to a full blooded agriculture.

The tools he used were specially ground and polished dyke stones worked into sharp axes and adzes. These are also referred to by the general term celt. It is believed that these transverse edged hacking tools were specially evolved to cut trees and bushes in order to clear land for agricultural use. There are some ethnographic evidences available where a specially flattened and pointed variety of celt was found used also as a shoe of a plough or hoe. So it is likely that apart from clearing ground these tools were also directly used in ploughing. The other technological innovation he had to go for in order to make his new economy workable is to evolve pottery to store his harvest. That is, surplus is the key of the economy and the absence of proper storage of the surplus can reduce the entire benefit of this economy to cipher. Most of these ceramics in the initial period was hand made and then crudely fired. "Table wares", therefore, are not so much a need but a novelty which appear at a later date.

Earlier it was believed that agriculture developed first in the Middle East and then spread over the rest of the Old World and New World. Discovery of early agriculture, in the recent years, at more than one area spread over Middle East, South East Asia and Mexico has changed the problem totally. Some authorities went to the extent of hypothising at least a dozen centers where early agriculture might have been independently evolved. The story regarding domestication of animals to establish a livestock productive economy is equally hazy. In the following section, therefore, we will look at the main features of transformations at some early sites only, rather than doing a survey like in the earlier sections. Finally, we may hurriedly look into the features of the Indian finds during this stage.

It was generally an accepted view that plant domestication began in such areas where the wild ancestors of the domesticated species are abundant. It was surprising, therefore, to the scientists when they observed that wild wheat and barley rows over thousands of hectares in one specific region in Iran, and could have been easily harvested by a medium sized band without ever feeling the need of domesticating it. At a prehistoric site in T*ell Mureybad* on Europhrates in Syria the assumption was proved. Here a pre-ceramic cultural level with clay walled houses, grinding stones and roasting pits, and with a radio-carbon date of Circa 8000 B.C., large number of charred grains were recovered. None of these grains were found to be domesticated in variety. In other words, such archaeological indicators as grinding stones or the existence of crude ceramic technology need not always be taken as diagnostic evidence of the existence of productive economy.

It will appear that, Mesopotamian plains and the Zagros mountains produced a number of contrasting environments within a limited geographic area. Evidence of the earliest prehistoric occupation in the area seem to last until around 10,000-8,000 B.C. Culturally this period shows an adaptation to a seminomadic hunting and gathering economy. The second period of occupation, which lasted till about 5,500 B.C. marks the beginning of early dry farming along with goat and sheep domestication. Permanent villages with mud plastered houses also appear in this period. It is in the third phase, which lasted till 3000 B.C. that a large variety of domesticates appear. These include wheat, barley, lentils, grass peas and linseed besides cattle, pigs and dogs in addition to the sheep and goat. It is argued that the gatherers, because of the security of supply at the nucleus zone (where wild crops grow), slowly increased in population. This, by necessity, required periodic migrations of "daughter" bands from the nucleus zones to marginal areas. In the marginal areas the new arrivals tried to recreate the same crops which they have earlier harvested in the wild. The earliest cultivation as such occurs in areas where wild varieties are unknown. Since dry farming does not always provide a security because of the possibility of rain failure, these early cultivators also took to a simultaneous occupation of animal raising. That is, plant cultivation and animal herding need not be always two separate subsistence activities. The later was a "banking" mechanism for the farmers. In years of bumper harvest the surplus is converted into cereals by exchange with suitable areas. Irrigation as a technology takes away this load of uncertainity. This form of agriculture is always associated with advanced beaureaucracy. Land laws, revenue, distribution and of course a ramiflcation in the professional classes emerges. This stage was once thought to be so closely related to irrigation that many social historians labeled these cultures as *Hydraulic societies.*

With the relatively recent discovery of Non Nok Tha and other evidences of early cultivation from Thailand a new problem of agricultural origin has now been added. It appears that small groups of wandering populations of Burma and Thailand had already domesticated varieties of bananas, taro, sugarcane and coconut in as early a period as sixth millennium B.C. Unlike the situation in Mesopotamia tropical rain forests are areas with more than 200 cm. yearly rainfall and a humidity of over 95 per cent through out the year. These forests maintain a very high degree of floristic diversity. Man had to only manipulate the environment to be able to domesticate plants. This is merely a 'lateral' change in contrast to the 'vertical' change necessary in seed agriculture. Here only branches of plants exploited (non flowering) need to be planted near the home base and you have a productive economy without any trouble of storing the surplus or distributing it. This variety of production strategy can survive comfortably within a society adjusted to hunting-gathering. This type of "vegeculture" stage is comparable to the stage of wild seed collection in Mesopotamia. This may have finally led to shifting to seed culture in a later date.

Recently some authorities have challenged the above view of the birth of agriculture. Climate change and/or population increase in isolation, according to this view, does not convincingly demonstrate this shift. It is proposed that resource diversification through time progressively shifted towards small and short maturation species and this had led to a true seed agriculture. It is an interesting possibility which may not have been acting in isolation but in combination with the already discussed dispersion process from wild seed growing areas.

In Mexico, where a similar early centre of agriculture is recorded, the situation had been almost comparable to the micro-climatic zones in Mesopotamia. The species adopted at this area, however, seem to be quite different.

Europe

Neolithic culture in Europe is first recorded along the river valleys in Balkans around 7000 B.C. Further east the well known occupation is Jarmo in Zagros foothills of Jordan where cluster of mud houses and direct evidence of cereal agriculture has been recorded. In the immediate neighbourhood Catal Huyuk inTurkey also yields evidences of a rapidly transforming Neolithic character almost within the same chronological period. Argissa – Meghula is a village in Greek Thessaly with a carbon 14 date of 7000 B.C. Here evidences of emmer wheat and barely has been found as cultivated cereal along with domesticated cattle, sheep and pig as live stock. These early Neolithic settlements are in the form of compact villages. The dwellings are one room units built of baked mud plastered on poles and wicker. The *Starcevo* site near Belgrade yields this classic succession of the earliest Neolithic settlements in the Balkans. These are usually referred to as *Karanovo* culture. Here a series of continued occupation shows how livestock economy was successfully combined with agriculture. Ill fired thick pottery or mud plastered baskets were used to store the harvest. These village clusters continue to flourish until about the arrival of metal.

Around 5500 B.C. the Danubian coasts and the loessic zones of Germany, Czechoslovakia, Austria and Hungary gets occupied by a new farming population. Probably these were the pre existing Mesolithic folk who were in contact with Balkan Neolithic group. Here they develop distinct cultural features and are commonly referred to as *Danubian* culture. The ceremics associated with these sites have characteristic incised decoration and hence the culture is also called *Linear band Keramic* or linear banded culture. By about 4000 B.C. they expand over numerous other river valleys along the entire mid-latitude of temperate Europe. Their expansion extended from southern Holland in the west to Dniestr valley in Ukrania in the east. Naturally in course of time the Danubian culture can be seen to develop some regional features at places.

The Danubians made round based vessels with lines and spirals incised on the clay. These are hand made ill fired pottery mostly in the shape of bowls with slightly converging rim. They cultivated barely, einkorn, emmer wheat and some minor crops like flax. The latter was grown to make garments. It is believed that they practiced shifting agriculture and lived in large rectangular houses with a number of segmented rooms in them. The houses measure 20 to 50 meters in length and 7 to 10 meters in breadth. These were constructed with timber and thatch. Probably even livestock used to also sleep within these structures along with their owners.

Population increase may have cause some fissions in these groups who might have shifted to fresh areas. We find around 4000 B.C. a series of farming villages appear on the shores of the Swiss lakes. These were occupied by cattle owning farmers who cultivated barley and wheat as well as many minor crops. The houses were built on damp ground between the lake reed beds and the scrub brush of the valley behind. The rectangular huts were replaced by two-room structures built on specially erected thick log piles. Apparently ladders must have been provided to get into these houses. It is also possible that floats or boats were used to approach these ladders. Although very inconvenient, these dwellings can provide security from wild animals and also a complete right to fishing in the waters.

There was yet another group found spread all along the Mediterranean coasts as well as the west European Atlantic and British coasts. This culture, usually referred to as the *Megalithic* group is known from Italy Spain, France, Scandinavia, Britain and Ireland. They are first recorded around 4000 B.C. and continues to survive in some parts up to 2500 B.C. The Megaliths are characterized by large communal tombs of stone with buried chambers and large stones erected as memorial. Pottery with distinctive scalloped incised decoration referred to as cardium shell impressed pottery characterize this culture. Growing of cereal crops, grazing of stock, sizeable settlements of rectangular houses and forests cleared with polished axes and/or firing along with the communal tombs distinguish this group. Extensive bartering networks from one end of Mediterranean to the other exchanged sea shells, obsidian, exotic stones and later on copper ore.

Africa

One of the earliest evidence of farming and live stock raising comes from upper Nile valley, where in all probability microlith using part time farming communities can be traced well within the Pleistocene period. Fishing and hunting continued as an important subsidiary economy during these early settlements. The Fayum region shows the emergence of *Merimde* culture around 5000 B.C. with reed shelters or crude mat houses. Wheat and barley was cultivated along with sheep, goat, pigs, dogs and cattle. Baskets or crudely fired pots were used to store the harvest. In a slightly later period (4000 B.C.) the *Badarian* culture flourished in the upper Nile region. Emmer wheat and barley was cultivated and cattle formed a large percentage of live stock. House structures were transient in nature. The Badarian pottery appears relatively more progressed than the Merimde forms. The dead were buried with linen shrouds and skin covers. The women wore ivory combs and plaited their hair. By 3100 B.C. an unified state of Egypt emerges and a complex system of economy and trade develops. Gradually metals like copper, bronze and gold start appearing with increasing frequency.

The Sahara region was a grassland from early Holocene to 3000 B.C. Cattle, sheep and goat owning nomads are known from sites dating 4600 B.C. It is believed that millets and sorghum was grown by these nomads.

In the sub-Saharan Africa fishing and vegeculture develops as a dominent economy and hence a proper Neolithic village does not develop until about 1000 B.C. when iron appears.

India

India like Africa also maintains extremely diverse eco-zones. Further, the rivers in the northern latitudes offered large areas of fertile alluvial plains which attracted settling populations from across the borders. While settled communities using intensive gathering of wild cereals are recorded from as early as 5600 B.C. at Mehrgarh (in Baluchistan); rice cultivation along riverine lakes must have established at Koldiwaha (Allahabad) around 5000 B.C. It is interesting to note that while Mehrgarh develops a village structure even before a full blown farming is adopted as an economy. In contrast to this the evidences known from Koldiwaha although having yielded domesticated cereals does not show a comparable phenomenon although this is a riverine site. When one compares the latter with other Neolithic sites like Burzahom (2300 B.C.) in Kashmir and Chirand (2000 B.C.) in north Bihar one is left with no doubt that hunting and gathering continues to play a fairly dominent role in all early Neolithic sites. Furthermore this early phase continues till fairly late at some suitable eco-zones. In fact these continue to survive when well developed urban chalcolithic centers are known from immediate neighbourhood.

In the east Meghalaya has yielded numerous sites with shouldered celts and basket impressed crudely fired pottery. Of these Daojali Harding is one site which was also excavated. Like in the west where population movement from Iran, Iraq and Afghanisthan can not bedenied, these eastern evidences can also be taken to indicate population movement from south China, Thailand and Burma.

In the Malwa regions and regions further south in the peninsular extension Neolith appears in a village like settlement, although probably a couple of centuries later than in the north. Millets gain a popularity as one moves south and this is coupled with cattle keeping as a dominent component of economy. Since all these settlements spread basically during the second millennium B.C. when Indus Valley was not only in its peak but also spread into Rajasthan and Gujrat the effect of it can be seen also in the Central Indian, Deccan Neolithic settlements. For instance, pottern in these sites start being prepared on wheels with distinct decorations and occasionally small metal objects, beads and terra-cotta objects start occurring within otherwise purely Neolithic villages. This led Sankalia to call them as Deccan Neolithic or Neo-Chalcolithic of India.

VI. CHALCOLITHIC CULTURE

One of the earliest evidence of copper extraction is seen in the Zagros mountains in Iraq around 6000 B.C. These scattered settlements of metal users come down to the Euphrates and Tigris delta by 5000 B.C. The area between these two rivers occupying nearly 400,000 square kilometers is the cradle of the rise of the Sumerian civilization. Beginning at 4000 B.C. this area seems to have been continuously occupied until about 1000 B.C. when the Assyrian empire is established.

At a slightly later date the Nile valley in Africa and the Indus Valley in the Indo-Pakistan region show a similar development of the rise of an urban civilization. The highest form of socio-cultural development in these three polar regions led Gorden Childe to hypothise the concept of 'Urban Revolution'. A closer look can, however, show the concept of 'Urban Revolution'. A closer look can, however, show distinct variation in the character of these three centers of culture. Metallurgy, writing and unifying religious force was taken as the prerequisites of the definition of a civilization. The Nile center does have a script and also a centralise religion but it hardly develops an urban center like one can see in Indus Valley. Again the Sumerian center develops script and religion but not many citizens dwellings instead the centre of power gets fortified with heavy emphasis on military culture. Consequently, it will appear that no universal definition of urban culture should be attempted.

When the first farmers moved to the delta region of the two rivers, ditches had to be dug and clogged channels had to be cleared for more effective adaptation of agriculture within this otherwise climatically harsh environment. With the onset of Chalcolithic even irrigation channels had to be dug out.

With the increase of food surplus as specialized agriculture became successful, trade network was an established activity. The village of *Ubaid* developed within this socio-economic back drop. Huts made of mud brick and reeds were clustered together during the *Ubaid* period. The economy basically depended on cereal crops which were harvested with clay sickles fitted with microliths. Goats, sheep and some cattle were herded on the flood plain. Abundant fish and water fowl were caught and fruits of date palm collected to support the agriculture. The pottery consists of brilliantly painted bowls, dishes and flasks. The *Eridu* temple, which was also constructed entirely by mud brick occurring around 4750 B.C. is an evidence of a much organized and regulated society.

The settlement of Uruk and Ur nearly 120 Km apart, show the rise of an entirely theocratic state with temples shaped in the manner of Ziggurat housing the surplus and organizing the redistribution. Highly hierarchical in structure these city structure were fortified and had separate quarters for the craftsmen. From 3000 to 2000 B.C. the Sumerians ruled over a large number of sattelite villages and their agricultural products.

The break of the central control and trade caused fissions in the larger Sumerian city state in the latter half of the second millennium B.C. The *Elamites* appears around 1600 B.C. and finally even they are eliminated when the Assyrian empire is established.

Europe

Unlike the earlier held views when the origin of both agriculture and metallurgy was sought from the middle-east, archaeologists now are willing to accept that copper work was developed independently in south-eastern Europe.

Between 4680 to 4200 B.C. occurs the *Varna* cemetery, in Bulgarian Black Sea coasts. This site has yielded 130 richly decorated graves with numerous fine gold and copper tools. The burials offer striking evidence for differential wealth. In the eastern Europe settled farming societies had lived on the edge of the huge Russian steppe land for hundreds of years and in all probability had contacts with both the Bulgarian and South Russian groups. This group in south Russia are called the *Kurgan culture.* These represent a wide spread copper using agriculturalists who lived in rectangular thatched huts, cultivated many crops and also domesticated animals which probably included the horse. They even used wheeled vehicles and made copper as well as stone battle axes. These widely dispersed south Russian Chalcolithic folks reached as far in the west as Holland around 3000 B.C. Their peculiarity in the west is designated by ceramics with cord impression on them. These globular bowls are, as such, called *corded ware.*

In central and northern Europe, they are described as *Battle Axe,* or *Corded Ware Culture.* These replaced the Danubians of the Neolithic period. At many Megalithic sites one can see the *Corded* group co-existing for a while and then totally replacing the former. Many linguists believe that the corded ware culture brought Indo-European language in Europe.

Between 2700 to 2000 B.C. a much widely distributed culture with characteristic bell shaped beakers as their pottery spread all over the southern and coastal regions of Europe. Thus, like corded in the north the Bell beaker culture brings metals to the southern regions. Around 2500 B.C. tin is seen as being used to form an alloy with copper to form bronze. It is first recorded in Chechoslovakia and then it does not take much time to spread over the entire western Europe. Once this technology takes root numerous weapons and ornaments made in cast metal start appearing.

Amber trade, inroduction of plough for more intensive production and extensive stock breeding formes the most vibrant Bronze Age culture of central and western Europe. Between 1200-800 B.C. the east Hungarian *Urnfield* culture takes over. This new group is named so because they started cremating their deads and burying the ashes in urns. Urnfield people began to make full use of horse drawn vehicles and lived in fortified villages. Sheet metal helmets, shields and slashing swords distinctly indicate the warfare culture that was adopted by them.

Arrival of iron and then the scythians completely changed the political enclaves of Europe and probably marked the beginning of numerous principalities which the Romans encountered in later centuries.

Africa

Metal age in Africa is almost entirely dominated by the Egyptian civilization. Although metal reaches most of the other regions of Africa by 1000 B.C. but this does not bring about substancial change in their highly organized pastoral or hunting-gathering economy.

Beginning of Christian era sees the appearance of the Bantus involved in iron working. Copper and bronze does not appear to have any impact on the pre-existing populace in the entire continent, although feudal states of kinship based kind may have started forming in Western Africa by the beginning of the first millennium B.C.

The Nile valley polarize the microlith using *Badarian* farmers till about 3600 B.C. The *Amratian* of upperEgypt represent a farther polarization of scattered farmers under a more organized society. Elegant stone vessels in alabaster and basalt start appearing along with the usual ceramic types. Magnificent flint knives and daggers also start appearing. These were taken to indicate the gradual rise of eliticism in the culture. No wonder, this phase is also referred to as *Pre-Dynastic* phase in Egyptian Chalcolithic.

Between 3100 to 2181 B.C. the Old Kingdom grew and is best exemplified at Giza. Some of the pyramids built during this period are as high as 480 ft and spread over nearly 13 acres area. The rise of a pictorial language system helped the Egyptian dynasties to develop scribes and train them to maintain administrative law, trade and other details. This period maintained an entirely despotic relation with the primary producers. During 2000 B.C. a less despotic dynasty began at Thebes in upper Egypt, and this continued till 1786 B.C. This period is referred to as Middle Kingdom. Finally the New Kingdom appeared and flourished between 1567 to 1085 B.C. when the rule of the Pharoes could expand as far east as Nubia and Palestine.

Civilization in Egypt all these two thousand years does not lead to any urban settlement. It is true that during the later periods some clustered quarters of workers have been found but these defy the characters known from other urban centers. Material culture and primary production base are also little known because of the fact that most of our knowledge of Egyptian Chalcolithic is based on royal tombs and tombs of other important members of the ruling clan. It would appear from these grave goods that heavy trading of exotic stones, gold bronze and finished objects were maintained on the basis of a surplus which was collected directly from the producers scattered all along the Nile. Warfare objects are far less conspicuous when one compares these with the Sumerians.

India

Chalcolithic India produces two distinctly different features. While the west shows a spread of 1 million square kilometer area of a very distinct urban growth from around 2700 – 1600 B.C.; the rest of India shows variegated village structures along with copper,bronze and even iron during 2300 B.C. to 1100 B.C. There is no uniformity in these village cultures and only for convenience they are grouped into the eastern zone, the central and western zone and the southern zone.

The west shows large settlement sites from Mehrgarh and Quetta valley from as early as 5600 B.C. There is no doubt that Mehrgarh because of its strategic position and also because of its knowledge of cotton could easily enter into extensive trade with centers of higher culture further west. There must have been numerous similar scattered sites in the hills towards Afganisthan along suitable water holes all along 4000 B.C. Such settlements soon had to move to areas of more adequate water supply and sites like Kot Diji show the evidence of such attempts. The Indus and its tributaries get finally occupied under a consolidated group which had to organize a great deal of labour. The evidence of Jodhpura and Ganeshwar in Rajasthan with copper tools at 2880 B.C. having fair indication of Pre-Harappan features known from Kalibangan (Rajasthan) would tend to indicate that colonization of the Indus was contributed by communities lying east of Indus as well. Forests had to be cut and enormous amount of fire wood had to be logged to fire tons of bricks of same size to create sprawling city centers. The character of these laid out cities are so uniform that many believe that the various Indus city centers were linked by a federal system. The individual metropolitan centers were probably headed by clan heads of the same ruling lineage. Huge grainaries and baths adjoining to them were taken as indicating 'Priest-Kings' organizing the collection and redistribution of produce. Objects of art, game, measures and deluxe pottery from this grainary complex – usually referred to as the Citadel, more or less prove them to be the quarters of the ruler.

The lower city shows rows of dwelling structures almost in the plan of the modern blocks of any planned city. Wells and toilets in some houses and absence of them or even the occurrence of smaller number of rooms in others have led many to interpret a stratified society among the Harappans.

While the identical structures were not found in Haryana and Saurashtra but the expansion of the Harappans over these regions can be simply proved by the occurrence of the Indus Valley material cultural objects all over these regions.

South-east Rajasthan shows another kind of a village culture developing their distinct pottery with inverted firing and decoration with streaks of white colour. These are usually referred to as Black-and-Red ware pottery. Terra Cotta spindles, bangles and toys are other distinctive features of this cluster. These sites are known from the Banas valley at *Ahar, Balathal* and *Gilund.* (2600-2150 B.C.).

Bihar, Orissa and West Bengal has another group of copper age village sites where tiny celts, microliths and wheel made Black-and-Red ware pottery is found with copper. *Chirand* in Chhapra district and *Pandu Rajar Dhipi* are two important sites of this zone (1755 B.C.) *Kayatha, Eran Nagda* and *Navdatoli* are the heavily occupied village from the central Indian zone which is believed to have had the flourishing around 1600 B.C. These occurrences are grouped together as *Malwa* culture. Some authors believe that the area had already received metal around 2000 B.C. from a group who had links with the Harappans. This is identified as the Savalda culture. Around 1300 B.C. the Malwa occupations decline and southward movement towards the various tributaries of Godavari in Maharashtra is discernable *Inhamgaon* represents one such migrated group. The pottery of these people is distinct in shape, fabric and decoration and is usually referred to as the *Jorwe* culture on the basis of this pottery type. Cultivation of millet appears to take up the dominent subsistence base.

Further south along the tributaries of Krishna, and also along the adjoining mountains occur the Deccan Chalcolithic sites. These were essentially hill dwellers who had peripheral cultivation of Ragi and Hulgi the two common millets of this zone. They buried their dead under the floor of their dwelling places and created huge urns to bury their dead in some cases. Some times they have executed art on the rocks outside their dwellings. These are in the form of puched dots and depicts human figures as well as horse driven carts. Pottery basically remain black in colour with very little decoration. But all these evidences show no trace of urbanization.

A second urbanization is visible only during iron age in the Gangetic region. Even these urban centers remain fairly limited in distribution and can hardly be compared with the Harappan expansion.

GLOSSARY

Abbevillian	Oldest industry of the European Paleolithic named by abbe H. Breuil after the type site Abbeville on the Somme River in North France where it was first discovered. It is characterized by crude, massive hand axes. These are prepared by stone hammer technique and usually carry very few or no secondary flaking.
Acheulian	This term was adopted from St. Acheul on the Somme where a characteristic lower Palaeolithic form was first described. It is characterized by medium sized handaxes and cleavers. This is believed to have been directly evolved out of the Abbevillian and hence the total cultural phase is also referred to as Abbevillian-Acheulian. Cylinder hammer technique used for final shaping acts diagnostic for the Acheulian.
Aggradation	The phase in the rivers when heavy material can be transported. Such phases are usually connected with the wet phase and hence pluviation.
Agricultural Revolution	Emergence of economy which are able to rely on domesticated plant and animal resources, the management of these economics is carried out

	by such a mechanism that enables production and storage of surplus without social conflict.
Alluvium	Sediments deposted by a river. These can be constituted by both big boulders and gravesl and also by fine clay. The former is taken to interpret a very wet climate while the latter indicates a relatively dry phase.
Anthropomorphic	Representation of human forms.
Archaeology	It basically means the study of antiquities. In an extended sense, the study of archaeology means the construction of the history of a region. The process of socio-cultural change through time, however, does not interest a classical archaeologist.
Archaeomagnetism	Measurement of magnetism in ancient objects.
Archean	Relating to the earlier part of the Pre-Cambrian era, characterized by the absence of life.
Artifact	Any object made and used by humans. Also spelt as artifact. Literally means an object artificially created. In an extended sense, artifact acts as the basic clue to understanding group behaviour.
Assemblage	The total cultural left over found at an archaeological site which belongs to the same level or time.
Aurigancian	An Upper Palaeolithic culture of Europe named after Aurignac, a cave site in southern France. This culture which follows the Perigordian has been dated between 39000 and 20000 B.C.
Australopithicus	Pre-hominid primate.
Autochthonous	Indigenous, native.
Awl	Pointed tool of stone, bone or metal.
Band	It is the name given to the simplest form of organization which is identified among the apes. The duties and obligations between the members of a band are limited to group protection and mating code alone. Often a leader emerges on the basis of physical power.

Biface	This is a name suggested by Franco Bordes in order to bring hadn axes and cleavers under a single tool type category. By definition, these are core tools flaked from both sides but do not include flakes which are bifacially worked like the leaf-points. But then neither are the bifacially worked discoid cores or discs customarily considered a biface. Thus, it is safe to consider it as merely a synonym of hand axes and cleavers.
Bifacial	Flaked on both faces.
Bi-polar technique	In this technique a pebble or a lump of stone is placed on an anvil or a slab of rock and then hit by a stone hammer. As a result the flakes so removed bears two bulbs of percussion one at each end. The bulb a the lower end will be caused due to the rebound blow from the underlying anvil or slab rock whereas that at the upper end will be produced by the stone-hammer. This technique is reminiscent of the simple method of craking arecanut with a stone or a pebble.
Black and Red ware	A specific kind of ceramic which is burnt black from the inside and is read on the outside. Usually limited to bowls and dishes and with a very little decoration done with white paint. It is distributed al over India. In western India, this ware occurs earliest in association with the late Neo-Chalcolithic. In Southern India, it occurs yet another 500 years later in association with iron and Megalithic burials.
Black on Red ware	Red pottery with paintings in black.
Blades	This term can be used for any flake which has a length equal to or more than twice its breadth. In practice the term refers to flakes which have parallel borders and uniform thickness along their length. Thus the blade technology would indicate a spcific development which is often taken to mark the emergence of the last lap of the palaeolithic or the upper palaeolithic.

Blank — A term used both for flake and a blade.

Borer — Awl

Brachiation — Locomotion by swinging from branch to branch with the arms over head. As opposed to this, ground living required a large degree of modification in the skeleton itself which released the hands for the function for which the hands were created. The origin of culture is linked with the stage where hands are freed from the functions of locomotion.

Bulb of percussion — A small elevated portion formed at the point of impact near the striking platform formed on the undersurface of a flake when detached from a core.

Burin — Pointed tool in stone or other material.

Burnisher — Tool used to provide lustrous finish to pottery.

Cairn circle — Mound of rough stones built as a land mark or memorial.

Calibration — Method to calculate dates.

Carbon 14 dating — A scientific method of dating (radiocarbon dating).

Celt — Axe or adze of stone, bronze or iron.

Charnokites — A kind of rock.

Chellean — Derives its name from Chelles-su-marne near Paris. The tool industries now known as early acheulian were termed by V. Commont as Chellean after the above mentioned site and those of Abbevillian as pre-chellean.

Chiefdom — A cultural system which resolves contradictions of a pure domestic mode of production by ensuring a reciprocal movement of surplus goods with services within the community. This is operationalized by the chief with help of retainers. Some chiefdoms can specialize to such an extend as to maintain full time professionals for the community.

Chopper — Early Stone Age pebble tool. This tool has usually a round, semi-oval or almost straight cutting edge. The edge is formed by removal of flakes from only the upper surface of the implement. The cutting edge may either be along the side or across the end of the specimen. A chopper is thus a unifacial tool, worked on one side only and hence some scholars designate it as a unifacial chopper. It is made on a peeble or a lump of stone or a thick flake.

Chopper/chopping tools — Usually prepared on a pebble. Few primary and secondary flakings are done to prepare a transverse working edge. When unifacial it is called a chopper and when bifacial, a chopping tool.

Chromlechs — A type of Megalithic burial.

Clacton Culture — Named after the site Clacton-on-sea (Essex, South Britain). The Clactonian industry fifers from the Abbevillian and Acheulian in that it does not contain handaxes and cleavers. It is basically a flake industry. Thus, it is a non-handaxe Lower Palaeolithic industry. It belongs to the initial Middle Pleistocene age.

Cleaver — Early Stone Age tool with a chisel edge.

Colluvium — Material washed down the hill usually angular in nature.

Conglomerate — Consolidated or cemented mass of boulders or pebbles or gravel known as boulder conglomerate, pebble conglomerate and gravel conglomerate, respectively.

Controlled flaking — A type of flaking in which the stroke is given against the thickness of the specimen. This blow does not go deep but causes an abrupt splitting of a tiny flake leaving a 'step' at the flaked portion. This kind of flaking was mainly used in secondary flaking or retouch, particularly for shaping or re-sharpening of tools.

Gopper hordes — Group or hoards of copper tools.

Core — A pebble or a lump of stone from which flakes are struck.

Cortex — A natural surface of a stone usually with a crust.

Cultural Area — The term was originally used by the German Human Geographers of the last century (Kulturkreis). Clarf Wissler used it to analyse cultural metamorphosis. It means a geographic area inhabited by people sharing a similar culture.

Culture — A term which is usually applied when describing a number of industries of the same type and of which the distribution is not of local nature.

Debitage — Chipping waste resulting from the manufacture of stone tools. Usually, these include various forms of cores, flakes and chips.

Delta — Fane shaped alluvial tract formed at the mouth of a river.

Detritus — When primary laterite is washed by seasonal rains and slits and gravel from it gets stained red, such deposits are referred to as secondary laterite or detritus.

Diffusion — A common English word meaning 'spread'. In Anthropology, this term is used as one of the several approaches to express the process of culture change. Contact through trade, population migration, invasion or even matrimonial exchange can be counted as modes of diffusion.

Discoids — 'Discular' stone tools.

Domestic mode of production — A type of economy that is characteristic in the Palaeolithic hunting and gathering band. It can create serious redistribution problems which may be solved by transition to chiefdom. When economies are organized by domestic groups and kinship relations, it creates centripetal force with in a domestic group and centrifugal force between families within a band.

Econiche — Environmental zones or niches that exhibit specific and constant clusters of plant and animal species with equally specific climatic conditions.

End flake	A flake struck laterally from the core and if the bulb lies on the shorter side such a flake is called a end-flake.
Eolith	A very early roughly broken artifact.
Erratic	A stone or boulder carried by ice (Glacier) to a place where the local rock formation is entirely different in composition.
Escarpment	A long sleep slope at the edge of a plateau.
Ethonography	Documentation of cultural patterns, which include basic information about peoples technology, subsistence system, social organization, ideology and language.
Flake scar	A scare or a depression on a core resulted from the removal of a flake.
Flake tools	Any specific type of border working which is visible on a flake and which is identically repeated on several other flakes. It is demonstrated that flake tools can yield more than ten times the amount of working border possible from raw material converted into a core tool.
Fluvial deposit.	Deposits formed by river action.
Fossil	A relic, remnant or representatio of a plant or animal that existed in the past, occurring in forms of materialized bones, shells, wood etc.
Glaciation	Cold climatic ages when glaciers covered large parts of the earth.
Glaciers	Great sheets of ice, some times over 300m thick, which move slowly over the land under the influence of gravity. They are found in the areas where there is abundant snowfall, cold temperature and a low rate of summer melting of snow.
Halophytic zones	Mangrove forested areas.
Harpoon	Missile of bone or metal, comprising of a barbed, pointed head and a barbet shaft.
Holocene	Geological period flowing the Pleistocene and extending upto the present.

Home erectus — The second level in human evolution. It was first recorded from Cheswanja in East Africa. This generalized human face had a brain size which was about 2/3rd of the modern human brain size. It is believed to have lived for the longest duration of period in the evolutionary history of man. Hand axes, cleavers, clactonian and levalloise flakes are the main tool types typically evolved and perfected by them.

Homo sapiens — It is the earliest form of a full man. At certain places, it is found in an over specialized form at its initial stages. This over specialized form is called the Neanderthal. Both the middle and the upper palaeolithic culture are the result of this form.

Human cranium — Human skull.

Hydraulic Society — In 1995, Karl A. Wittfogel argues that cultural societies change towards statehood when irrigation is managed by a centralized political system. He named these societies as hydraulic societies. He further argued that this kind of social formation seems to be more evidenced towards and in the east of European countries and to suit his thesis, coined the term 'Oriental Despotism' for them. The concept has since then been challenged by many experts on rather substantive grounds.

Ideology — Since, culture is the set behviour common to a group of people, that this commonality must have shared beief structure is but logical. Thus ideology refers to the ideas and beliefs that a group shares in order to behave and act in a 'common way'.

Igneous rock — The rocks which have been formed by the solidification of the magma or lava.

In situu — In its original position.

Industry — This usually refers to the collection of similar assemblages. The similarity is normally of the raw material, so that we have such expressions as Stone industry or bone industry.

Interglacial — It is the warm period between two glacials. Usually, this is marked by the proliferation of plant and animal types.

Interpluvials — It is the relatively drier climate between two pluvials.

Interstadials — Periods of relative warmth during the presence of the glacial. Fauna and flora can develop during these stages but they are usually the cold loving varieties.

Khondalite — A type of stone.

Late Stone Age — This is the same as Mesolithic in Europe.

Laterite — A thick reddish crust found in tropical mountains. These crusts are rich in iron and aluminum oxides. These are caused by heavy rain in the past. These weathered red rocks are referred to as primary laterite.

Levallois — A stone tool technique named after the site levallois-perret, a suburb of Paris.

Levalloise Flake — It demonstrates the human planning for obtaining a desired flake. Since thinning a normal flake, always result in its breaking, to counter act which, it appears, man prepared a desired dorsal surface on the core from which he could finally detach the flake. It is known to occur from the time of late Acheulian period and continues to occur even in the Mesolithic phase. A levalloise flake, being consistent in its techno-morphological features, is not counted as a mere artifact, but also as a tool bank. When retouched into a type, it gets the status of being a tool type.

Libation vessels — Vessels used in ritual offerings.

Littoral — On the sea coast.

Loessq — Fine clay like silt deposited by winds is referred to as loess. Usually the glaciated regions exhibit huge deposits of loess.

Magdalenian — It is an Upper Paloeolithic culture of France. It takes its name from the rock-shelter La

Madeleina near Tursoc (Dordogne), S.W. France. It dates between 15000 and 9000 B.C.

Maxilla — The jaw or jaw bone, especially the upper jaw in most vertebrates.

Megaliths — Funerary or commemorative monuments characterized y the use of large stones.

Mesolithic — This literally means 'middle stone age' (not to be confused with the term Middle Stone Age in India). The gap occurring between the cultures following the Pleistocene and the onset of agriculture is called the Mesolithic. Usually, microlithic tools occur during this stage.

Metamorphic rocks — The rocks which have undergone change in their nature, being acted by heat and pressure, but with out fusion.

Microchrome — Single colour.

Microliths — Small tools made on fine-grained stone.

Microlunate — Microlith shaped like a half moon.

Middle Stone Age — In India and Africa, th Late Palaeolithic culture is termed as the Middle stone age. In European terms, it includes both middle and the upper Palaeolithic cultures.

Miliolite — These are a kind of limestone, popularly known as porbander limestone. It occurs on the western coast of Saurashtra. There are two views about its mode of formation. According to one, it is thought to be of Aeolian origin and according to another, a shallow water marine deposit. Now a days, oyster beds, dead coral reefs and coral reefs and coast-fringing rocks are also included in the term miliolite.

Molluscs — Soft-bodied animals with hard shells such as oysters, mussels and snals.

Moraines — These are accumulations of detritus taken up, transported and laid down by glaciers. That derived from scoring of the sides of the valleys and carried down along the sides of the glaciers and deposited on their either sides form the lateral morines. When two glaciers meet, a lateral morine of one glacier unites with a lateral morine of the other forming a medial morine. When glaier melts at its termination all the material is dropped in a crescentic shape its termination all the material is dropped in a crescentic shape across the valley. This is called terminal morine.

Mousterian culture — It is named after a type site La Moustier on the river Vezer in the Dordogne district of France. Mousterian is a middle Palaeolithic culture of Europe, Western Asia and North Africa, its authos being the Neanderthal race. Diferent groups of Mousterian industries have been recognized, such as Mousterian of Acheulian Tradition, Typical Mousterian, Denticulate Mousterian, Quina Mousterian and so on.

Neolithic — The term literally means New Stone Age. Culturally, this marks the beginning of productive economy and precedes the discovery of metal. In practice, plished celts, ring stones, grinders, pottery, domesticated cereals or animal remains and settled village sites-indications of which found in combination or individually, are taken as archaeological evidence of the Neolithic.

Northern Black Polished Ware — A distinctive pottery with a highly lustrous red and black surface.

Ochre Colour Ware — Orange to deep red pottery.

Painted Grey Ware — Iron in North India appears with a very fine fabric of ceramics which has been fired at such a high temperature that it turns grey in colour. Some decorations in thick black paint is done on them. The shapes in this fabric is limited to dishes and bowls only.

Palaeolithic — This literally means the Old Stone Age and in practice includes the cultures occurring during the Pleistocene period. From the time man appears on the scene to almost 15000 years from today forms the duration of the composite culture. Since it spans a period of almost 1.6 million years, it is divided into three sub-periods as follows:

(a) Lower Palaeolithic chopping tools : (1.8 M.Y. – 200,000 Y). Constituting hand axes, cleavers and chopper

(b) Middle Palaeolithic : (200,000 – 36000 Y) constituting such medium sized flake tools as side scrappers and points.

(c) Upper Palaeolithic : (36,000-8000 Y) constituting blade and bone tools.

Patina — A thin film occurring on the surface of stone due to chemical weathering.

Periglacial zone — An area adjacent to the borders of the Pleistocene ice sheets.

Perigordian — An earlier Upper Palaeolithic culture of Europe which derives its name from Perigord region in south-west France. This has been dated to 33000 B.C.

Petroglyph — Prehistoric rock carving, bruising or pecking.

Pit Dwelling — In the area of extreme cold, dwelling structures at some places were constructed by digging a pit in the ground. The mouth of the pit used to be covered by a thatched structure. At Burzahom, steps are cut out to descend below. In many of the pits, steps stop before reaching the floor. It is argued that a movable ladder used to be attached to this gap for going and coming freely. At night these ladders could be removed so that an easy access to the lower floor was ruled out.

Pleistocene — The geological period corresponding with the last ice age. The period between 4 million years to 10,000 B.P. is covered by the term Pleistocene. It marks the evolution of apes and man. The last third of this period is also marked by a series of climatic extremes which occur as glaciations in the temperate regions and as pluviation in the tropical regions.

Pluvials	Extreme wet phases when the rivers and lakes were filled to the brim is called the period of pluviation. The power of carrying load by the rivers, more than it would be able to carry normally increased and hence boulder and gravel deposits are taken to represent such a period.
Pollen analysis	A scientific analysis of pollen used to establish relative chronology.
Polychrome	Multi colour.
Porthole cist	An aperture in a coffin or Megalithic burial chamber.
Potwar	It is an elevated plateau of folded siwalik deposits. T is roughly bounded by the Indus in the west, the Jhelum and Poonch rivers in the east, the Pir Panjal foothills in the north and the Salt Range in the south. The region (now in Pakistan) includes the Rawalpindi and other districts of west Punjab.
Prehistory	It literally means the era preceding the phenomenon of the emergence of writing (which marks the beginning of history). In practice, a Pre-historian is more interested in economy, social organization and the process of culture change than an archaeologist. The latter has more of a historian's approach while the former prefers to use models of cultural Anthropology.
Primate	Member of the highest order of mammals, including humans, apes and monkeys.
Prismatic Core Scrappers	A type of stone tool.
Protohistoric	This term describes people in past history who remained without writing and yet demonstrate (with the literate group), a well developed settled life.
Quern	Mill for grinding grain, typically consisting of two stones.
Radiometric	It is the method of measuring age by the estimation of the decay rate in unstable isotopes.

Rift valley	A valley which has been formed by the sinking of land between two roughly parallel faults, that is fractures in the earths crust along which movement has taken place.
Rouletted Ware	Pottery characterized by concentric dotted bans produced with the help of a roulette (a toothed wheel).
Scrapper	A type of artifact made of stone, bone or metal.
Sedimentary rocks	Rocks which are formed from the decomposed or weathering of pre-existing rocks or by chemical or organic agency.
Sepulcher	A tomb especially cut in rock or built of stone or brick; a burial vault or cave.
Seriation	The process of ordering a series of artifacts in terms of relative similarity, with the most unlike placed farthest apart. Thus the degree of techno-morphological gradation can be taken to ascertain the relative age of a given object.
Settlement Pattern	This term can be described as the distribution of different areas of human activities. (eg. Village site, factory site, kill site etc.)
Shingle bed	Formation of pebbles and rocks along the course of a river.
Side-flake	A flake struck laterally from the core so that its bulb of precussion lies on the longer side of the flake removed instead of at the shorter side.
Site	It is a basic unit of space investigated by an archaeologist. Often the site can extend much beyond the region investigated by any one archaeologist. When another archaeologist discovers sites from the extended region, such sites are referred to as localities. Thus one can have several localities of a site.
Slip	Liquid clay coating on pottery.
Social Formation	A concept used y Marxian sociologists to indicate a modes of production defined as a specific configuration of forces of production and relations of production and their condition of existence and reproduction.

Social Organisation — The term describes the pattern in which all the members of the society are organized in terms of duties and obligations. This enables people to satisfy their biological and cultural needs without creating conflict. Every generation of the community reproduces the parental organization by the inbuilt mechanism of enculturation.

State — Monopoly of power at the disposal of any government in a class stratified society. Usually the various social strata found in a statehood are – (a) Primary Producers (b) Professionals (c) Military and (d) Bureaucracy.

Step flaking/Resolved-flaking/ — It is a layer or deposit which is bereft of any cultural material.

Sterile layer — The presence of such a deposit or layer between two cultural horizons indicates a cultural gap or time-gap between the end of the lower and the beginning of the upper.

Stratigraphy — The study of the order and the relative position of strata for historical interpretation.

Striking platform Technology — I the area on the core surface which is struck for detaching a flake. This term describes the means of improving the methods of the retrieval of resources. Normally, this involves shaping and assembling of natural resources/objects for the satisfaction of human needs.

Terrace — These are the bench like features left along the valley sides. Usually these are caused by the down cutting of the river which flows at the bottom of the valley. Since each of the terraces represents the earlier bottoms of the river, the topmost terrace is the oldest as far as the date of its formation is concerned.

Terracotta — Clay that has been baked but not glazed; the term connotes statuettes and figurines made of baked clay.

Thermo-luminiscene — A type of scientific dating used especially to date potsherds etc. (TL)

Tradition — When similar archaeological material occurs over a reasonable area through a reasonable period of time, such a group can be taken to indicate a tradition. Thus we can have a core tool tradition or a blade tool tradition.

Triangles — Of the three varieties of triangles, the isosceles triangle has two equal adjacent sides each making angle of 60° or 30 ° with the third side. In the scalene variety of triangle none of the sides is equal and not two angles are equal. All the three sides o an equilateral triangle are equal. This last one is very rarely found, the first two being the most common. The obliquely blunted blades and points are morphologically similar to the triangles as well as the pen-knife blades. There are also some tools which are intermediate between a triangle and a true lunate. Because, in some of the lunates the back shows a slight angularity. In such cases, it becomes difficult to separate triangles from angular lunates. Morphologically a scalene triangle is similar to a crescentic point and both could serve as barbs of hunting tools. From the functional point of view the isosceles triangles and a crescent or lunate could have been used as barbs for arrow and harpoons or as components of a composite tool like sickle.

Tribe — When a number of bands organize themselves on the basis of geographic proximity to increase survival potentiality, they give rise to a tribe. Modes of production need not change although a broad spectrum exploitation becomes easy.

Unifacial — Artifact flaked on one face only.

Vall Technique — This is a technique of finishing a hand axe in such a manner that the ventral surface et a flat scar which renders a v-shaped cross section to the tools. It was first described from sites around the vall river in South Africa. Bordes felt that since this requires the prior preparation of a

	biface and then the delivering of the tranchet blow from one of the surfaces, it should be considered as a precursor of the Levalloise technique. Hence he called this a 'para Levalloise technique'. In Bhimbetka (India), the technique is commonly recorded.
Victoria West	This is a term to explain massive hand axes prepared by bold flaking from the under surface in order to converge into a keel like feature on the dorsal surface. The under surface may be formed by a single hollow scar or even the original cortex. A large number of these hand axes are found in Attirampakkam region.
Ware	Any specific kind of poattery, also used to denote the fabric.

SELECT BIBLIOGRAPHY

Acharya, P., 1930, In "History of Orissa", R.D. Banerjee, Vol. I, Calcutta, R. Chaterjee, pp. 39-40.

Agarwal, D.P., 1982, "The Archaeology of India", Scandinavia Institute of Asian Studies Monograph Series, No. 46, London, Curzon Press.

Allchin, R., 1995, "The Archaeology of Early Histric South East Asia", Cambridge, Cambride University Press.

Ball, V., 1876, "On the Stone Implements found in the tributary States of Orissa", Proceedings of the Asiatic Society of Bengal, 120-121.

Banerjee, R.D., 1930, History of Orissa, Vol. I, Calcutta, R. Chaterjee, pp. 39-40.

Basa, K.K. 1992, "Ethnoarchaeology of Orrisa : A Review". Main in Society – p. 79-106.

Basa, K.K., 1997, "Archaeological Heritage", P.K. Mishra (ed.) "Comprehensive History and Culture of Orissa".

Basa, K.K., 1999, "Neolithic And Post-Neolithic Cultures of Orissa", in S. Pradhan, (ed.), "Orissan History, Cultue and Archaeology", N. Delhi, pp. 9-32.

Basa, K.K; Mohanty, P., (Ed.), 2000 "Archaeology of Orissa".

Basa, K.K., Das, T.K., Mohanty, B.K., 2000, "Neolithic Cultures of Pallahara, Central Orissa" Basa (ed.) "Archaeology of Orissa", pp. 264-84.

Behera, P.K., 1989, "Archaeology of Sundargarh district, with special reference to the Brahmani Valley, Orissa", Unpublished Ph. D. Thesis, Banaras Hindu University, Varanasi.

Behera, P.K., 1992a. "The Pebble Tool Component of the Banaigarh Neolithic Complex, Orissa", Man and Environment, XII (2) : 57-63.

Behera, P.K., 1992b. "Sulabhdihi : A Neolithic Celt Manufacturing Centre in Orissa", Puratattva 22, p. 124-32.

Behera, P.K., 1992, "Prehistoric Rock Art Painting of Fertility Cult and other subjects of Orissa", Pragdhara, 2, 1991, 92:7-17.

Behera, P.K., Panda & N. Thakur, 1996, "Techno-typological analysis of little artifacts, from the Pari-Dungari Acheulian sites, Sambalpur district, Orissa". Man & Environment 21 (2), p. 13-26.

Behera, P.K., 2000, "Neolithic Culture Complex of Bonaigarh, Orissa". Basa (ed.) "Archaeology of Orissa", pp. 222-263.

Bose, N.K., D., Sen and G.S. Ray, 1958, "Geological and Cultural Evidences of the Stone Age in Mayurbhanj, Man in India, 38, p. 49-55.

Bose, N.K., and D. Sen, 1948, "Excavations in Mayurbhanj", Calcutta University.

Cammade, L.A. and Burkitt, M.C. (1930), "Fresh Light on the Stone Ages in Southeast India", Ant. 4 (No. 15), pp. 327-39.

Chakarbarti, S. and Chottapadhaya, 1988, "A Note on the Lithic Industries in Mayurbhanj and Keonjhar, Orissa. Man and Environment 12, p. 203-08.

Chakarbati, S., 1990, "The Stone Age Prehistory of Khiching, Orissa, Man and Environment, XV, p. 13-21.

Chakarbarti, S., "Kalapathara : An Upper Palaeolithic Site from Mayurbhanj", (In Press).

Chakladar, H.C., 1952, "The Prehistoric Culture of Bengal", Man in India, Ranchi, Vol. XXXI, pp. 124-64.

Chanda, R.P., 1930, "Exploration in Orissa", Calcutta, Memoir of the Archaeological Survey of India.

Cockburn, J., 1883, "On the recent existence of Rhinocerosondicus in the north western provinces and a description of a tracing of an archaic rock painting from Mirzapore representing the hunting of this animal". Journal of the Asiatic Society of Bengal, Vol. 52, No. 2, 56-64.

Corvinus, G.K., 1968, "An Acheulian Occupation Floor at Chirki – on – Pravara, India", CAG, Nos. 9, Nos. 2 & 3, 216-18.

Corvinus, G.K., 1973, "Excavations at an Acheulean site at Chirki – on – Pravara in India". In South Asian Archaeology, pp. 13-28.

Dash, R.N., 1986, "Sankerjang : A Chalcolithic Site in Orissa" Orissa Historical Research Journal, 32, pp. 99-125.

Das, R.N., 1987, "Neolithic of Orissa". Unpublished thesis, Utkal University, Bhubaneswar.

Dash, R.N., 1987-88, "Neolithic of Orissa – A Study on Late Stone Age", Unpublished PhD Thesis, Utkal University, Bhubaneswar.

Dash, R. N., 1990-93, "Orissa Neoliths : A typo-technological Study", Manav, Pp. 127-47.

Dhavalakar, M.K., 1997, "Indian Protohistory", Books and Books, Delhi.

De Terra, H., and T.T. Paerson, 1939, "Studies on the Ice Age in India and Associated Human Cultures", Washington, D.C., Carnegic Institute. p. 315

Duff, R., 1970, Crist Church, "Stone Adzes of Southeast Asia, Canterbury Museum, Bulletin, No. 3.

Erwin, N., 1992, "Rock Picture in Orissa, Puratattva, 22.

Ghosh A.K., Ranjan Ray, Panchu Chaterjee, Paresh Nanda and Peter Bellwood, 1984. "Archaeological Reconaissance in the Sanjay Valley, Singhbhum District, Bihar", Bulletin of the Indo-Pacific Prehistoric Association No. 5:24-28.

Ghosh, A., 1989, Vol. I, "Encyclopedia of Indian Archaeology", pp. 110.

Gordon, D.H., 1950, "Stone Industries of the Holocene in India and Pakistain", Ancient Incida 6:64-90.

Haimendorf. F.C. Von, 1943, "Megalithic Ritual among the Gadabas and Bondas of Orissa", Journal of the Royal Asiatic Society of Bengal 9(10 : 143-178.

Henwood, W.S., 1856, "Megalithic Cultures at Devidhoora in Almora", Edinburgh, New Philosphical Journal (New Series), Edinburg, 204-5.

Indian Archaeology : A Review : 1964-65.

Indian Archaeology : A Review : 1956-57:31.

Indian Archaeology : A Review : 1959, p. 38.

Indian Archaeology : A Review : 1976-77.

Indian Archaeology : A Review : 1988-89:65-66.

Indian Archaeology : A Review : 1989-90:77-80.

Jayswal, K.P., 1935, "Th Vikramkhol Inscription, Sambalpur District", The Indian Antiquary, Vol. 62, 58-60.

Jayaswal, V., 1978, "Palaeohistory of India", Agam Kala Prakashan, Delhi, p. 1-2.

Joshi, R.V. 1955, "Pleistocene Studies in the Malaprabha Basin", p. 49.

Joshi, R.V., 1978, "Stone Age Cultures of Central India", Poona, deccam College Post Graduate and Research Institute.

Kar, S.K., 2000, "Gopalpur : A Neolithic Chalcolithic site in Coastal Orissa", Basa (ed.) "Archaeology of Orissa", pp. 368-391.

Kumar, G. and G. Narvare, 1984, "Ostric Egg Shells and Early Rock Paintings in India", In K.K. Chakarvarty (ed.), Rock Art of India, New Delhi.

Lal, B.B., 1949, "Sisupal Garh 1948 : An Early Historical Fort in Eastern India", Ancient India, No. 9, pp. 98.

Mathpal, Y., 1984, "Prehistoric Rock Paintings of Bhimbetka", Abhinav Publications, New Delhi.

Mishra, V.N., Y. Mathpal and M. Nagar, 1977, "Bimbetka" Poona, Deccan College, Post Graduate and Research Institute.

Mitra, D., 1956-57, "Excavations at Jaugara in the District of Janjam", Indian Archaeology – A Review, 1956-57, pp. 30-31.

Mohanty, P. 1988-89, "Mesolithic Culture of Keonjhar, Orissa, with special reference to the Heavy-duty tool components : A Functional Interpretation. Bullitin of the Deccan College Research Institute, Pune, p. 47-48, p. 227-237.

Mohanty, P., 1989, "Mesolithic Settlement System of the Keonjhar District, Orissa", Unpublished Ph.D. Thesis, University of Pune.

Mohanty, P., 1992, "Stone Age Research in Orissa : An Overview", Man in India, 72, p. 207-232.

Mohanty, P., 1993, "Mesolithic Hunter-Gatherers of Konjher, Orissa", Asian Perspective 32, p. 85-104.

Mohanty, P., K. K., Basa and B. Tripathy, 1997, "Stone Age Cultures of Mayurbhanj District, Orissa", Man in India.

Mohapatra, G.C., 1962, "The Stone Age Cultures in Orissa", Decan College, Poona.

Nanda, S.C., 1984, "Stone Age Cultures of the Indravati Basin, Koraput District, Orissa", Unpublished Ph.D. Thesis, University of Poona.

Nanda, S.C., 2000, "The Upper Palaeolithic and Mesolithic cultures of the Indravati Valley, South Orissa : An Ethnoarchaeological Study", Ed Basa, K.K., pp. 151-172.

Narasimhai, B., 1980, "Neolithic and Megalithic Cultures in Tamil Nadu", New Delhi, Sandeep Prakashan.

Neumayer, 1983, "Prehistoric Indian Rock Paintings", Oxford University Press, New Delhi.

Neumayer, E., 1992, "Rock Pictures in Orissa", Puratattva, 1991, 22, 13-24.

Neumayer, 1993, "Lines on Stone, the Preshitoric Rock Art of India", Manohar Publisher and Distributors, New Delhi.

Ota, S.B., 1986, "Mesolithic Cultures of the Phulbani District, Orissa, with special reference to the Heavy-Duty Tool Component", Bulletin of the Dcan College Post-Graduate and Research Institute, Poona 45, p. 47-56.

Paddaya, 1994, "Investigations of Man-Environment Relationship in Indan Archaeology : Some Theoretical Considerations", Man and Environment, XIX : 12.

Patal, A., 1974, "History of Orissa", M.Phil Thesis, Unpublished.

Pradhan, S., 1994, "Painted Rock Shelters of Orissa : A Case Study of Manikmoda", The Orissan Historical Research Journal, XXXIX, 1-4 : p. 40-45.

Pradhan, S., 1999, "Chalcolithic Cultures of Orissa", S. Pradhan (ed.) "Orissa History, Culture and Archaeology", New Delhi, pp. 33-38.

Pradhan, S., 2001, "Rock Art in Orissa" Aryan Books International, New Delhi.

Pradhan. S; Barik.K. B & Garnayak. D.B.,. 2006. Discovery of New Rock Art Sites In Orissa. "The Journal of Orissa History. Vol. XIX. Pp. 236-240.

Rajguru, S.N., 1950, Journal of the Kalinga Historical Research Society, p. 245.

Ray Ranjan (1993) "Discovery of a Chalcolithic site near the source of River Baitarani, Orissa", Journal of the Indian Anthropological Soviety 28(1) : 97-102.

Rath, B.K., Nath, A., 1985-86, "Indian Archaeology – A Review, 1985-86, p. 65.

Rath. S.N. and D.K. Bhattacharya, 1988, "Lower Paleolithic from Kuchinda (Orissa)." Men & Environment 12, pp. 23—28.

Sahoo, D., 2000, "Preshistory of Darpankhas (Dist. Jajpur), Coastal Orissa", K.K. Basa (ed.) "Archaeology of Orissa", pp. 173-200.

Sankalia, H.D. 1946, "Investigations into the Pre-historic Archaeology of Gujarat.

Sankalia, H.D., 1979, "Indian Archaeology Today", p. 26.

Senapati, N. (ed.), 1971, Orissa District Gazetteer, Sambalpur, Cuttack.

Senapati, N. (ed.), 1975, Orissa District Gazetteer, Sundargarh, Cuttack.

Sinha, B.K., 1993, "Excavation at Golabai Sasan". Dist. Puri, Orissa Puratattva – 23, p. 40-50.

Sinha, B.K., 1996, "Excavation at Golabai Sasan, District Khurda, Orissa", C. Margabandhu and K.S. Ramachandran, (ed.) Delhi.

Sharma, H.C., 1994, "Palaeolithic Finds around Burla, District Sambalpur, Orissa", Man and Environment XIV (1-2) : p. 285-290.

Singh Deo, J.P., 1976, "Prehistoric Cave Painting of Joghimath Donger", The Orissa Historical Research Journal, Vol. XXII, NO. 2, 21-22.

Singh Deo Jitamitra Prasad, 2000, "Archaeology of Kalahandi and Nuapada District, Orissa", Basa (ed.) "Archaeology of Orissa", pp. 418-430.

Singh, P.K., 2000, "Stone Age Cultures of Central Orissa, K.K. Basa. Edited "Archaeology of Orissa", pp. 102-113.

Sinha, B.N., 1971, "Geography of Orissa", National Book Trust, New Delhi.

Tiwari, R., 1990, "Rock Paintings of Mirzapur", Lucknow.

Thapar, B.K., 1961, Indian Archaeology –A Review, pp. 35-36.

Thapar, B.K., 1985, "Recent Archaeological Discoveries in India", UNESCO.

Todd, K.R.U., 1939, "Palaeolithic Industries of Bombay" JR Anth. 169, Pt 2, pp. 257-72.

Tripathy, K.C., 1966, "A Metric Study of the Neolithic Celts of Mayurbhanj, Orissa", Historical Research Journal, Vol. 14, No. 2, 13-20.

Tripathy, K.C., 1970, "Microlithic Industry of Bhubaneswar", Prakruti 7(1) : pp. 77-92.

Tripathy, K.C., 1972, "Lithic Industries of South Western Orissa", Unpublished Ph.D Thesis Utkal University, Orissa.

Tripathy K.C. & Kar S.K., 1993, "Microlithic Industry of Tangi, Orissa", Manav, 4, pp.151-155.

Wheeler, M., 1948, "Excavation at Chandravali and Brahmagiri", *Ancient India,* Vol IV, pp. 180-310.

Yule P., B.K. Rath and K. Hojgaard, 1987, 1990, "Sankarjang – A Metal Period Burial Site in the Dhenkanal Uplands of Orissa", in M. Taddei (ed.), South Asian Archaeology, Rome, pp. 581-84.

Zeuner, F.E., 1950, "Stone Age and Plestocens Chronology in Gujarat", p. 23.

INDEX

A

B

C

D

E

F

G

H

I

J

K

L

M

O

P

Q

R

S

T

U

V

W

Y

Z

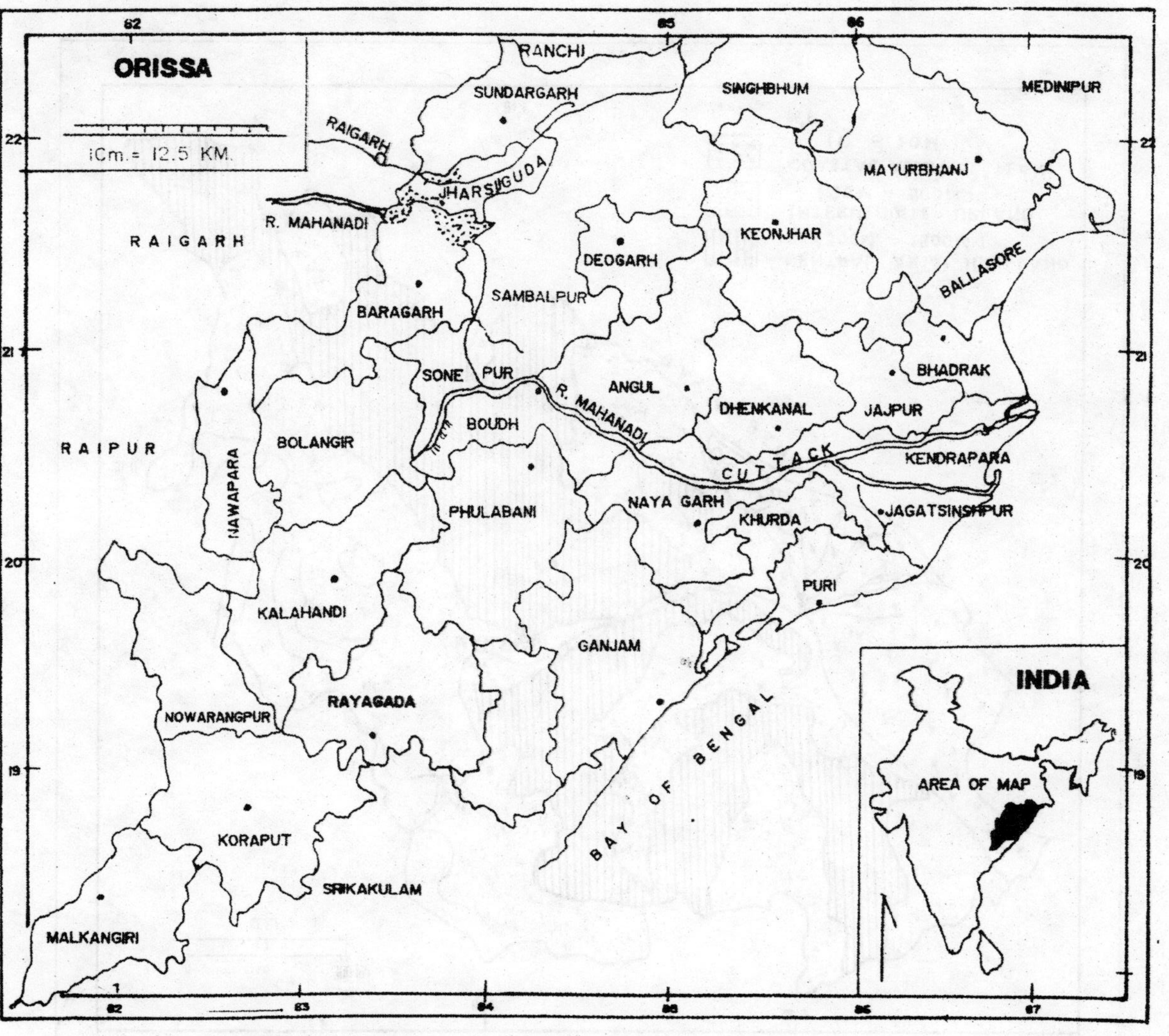

Fig. 1: Political map of Orissa

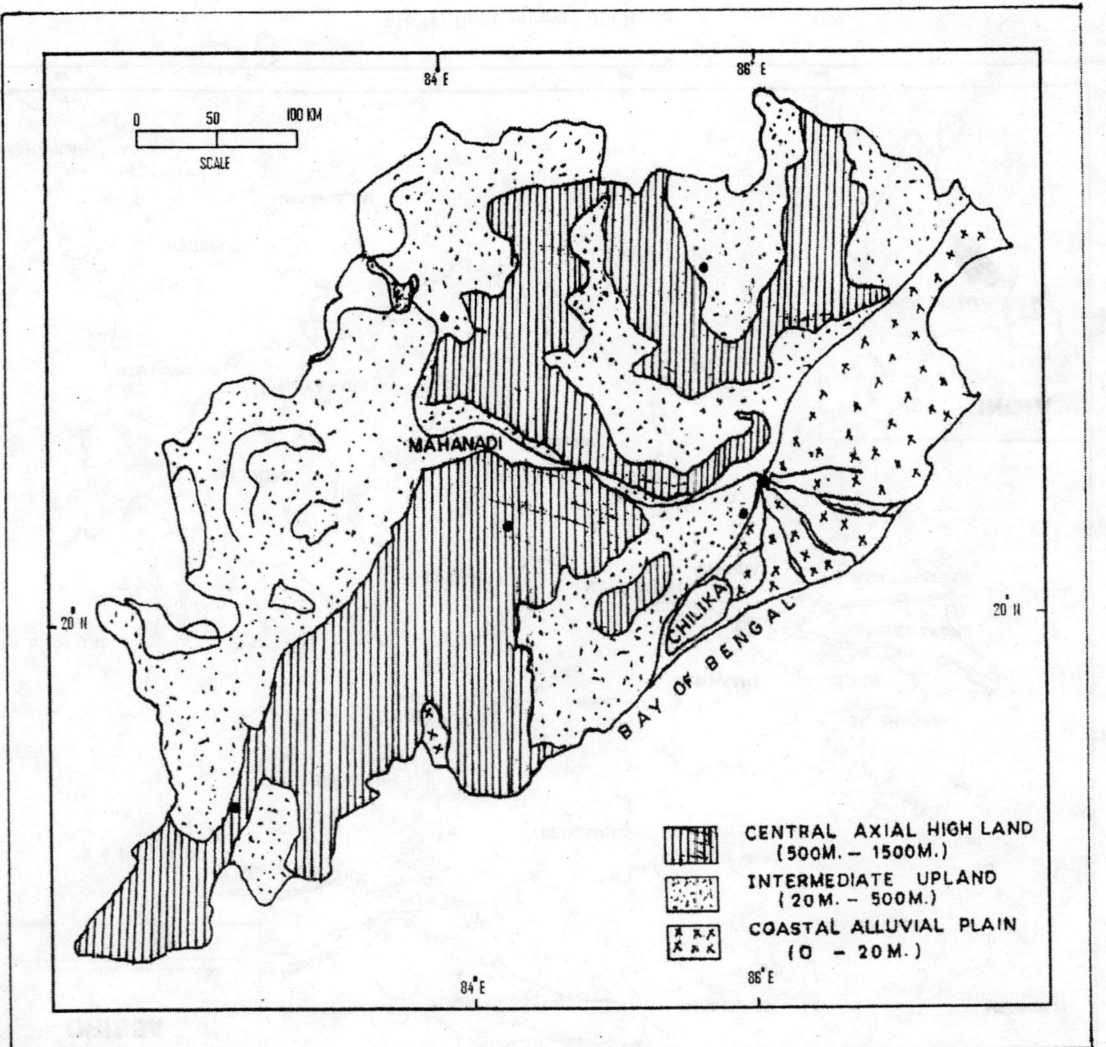

Fig. 2 : Map showing Geographical divisions of Orissa. (After N.K. Mahalik)

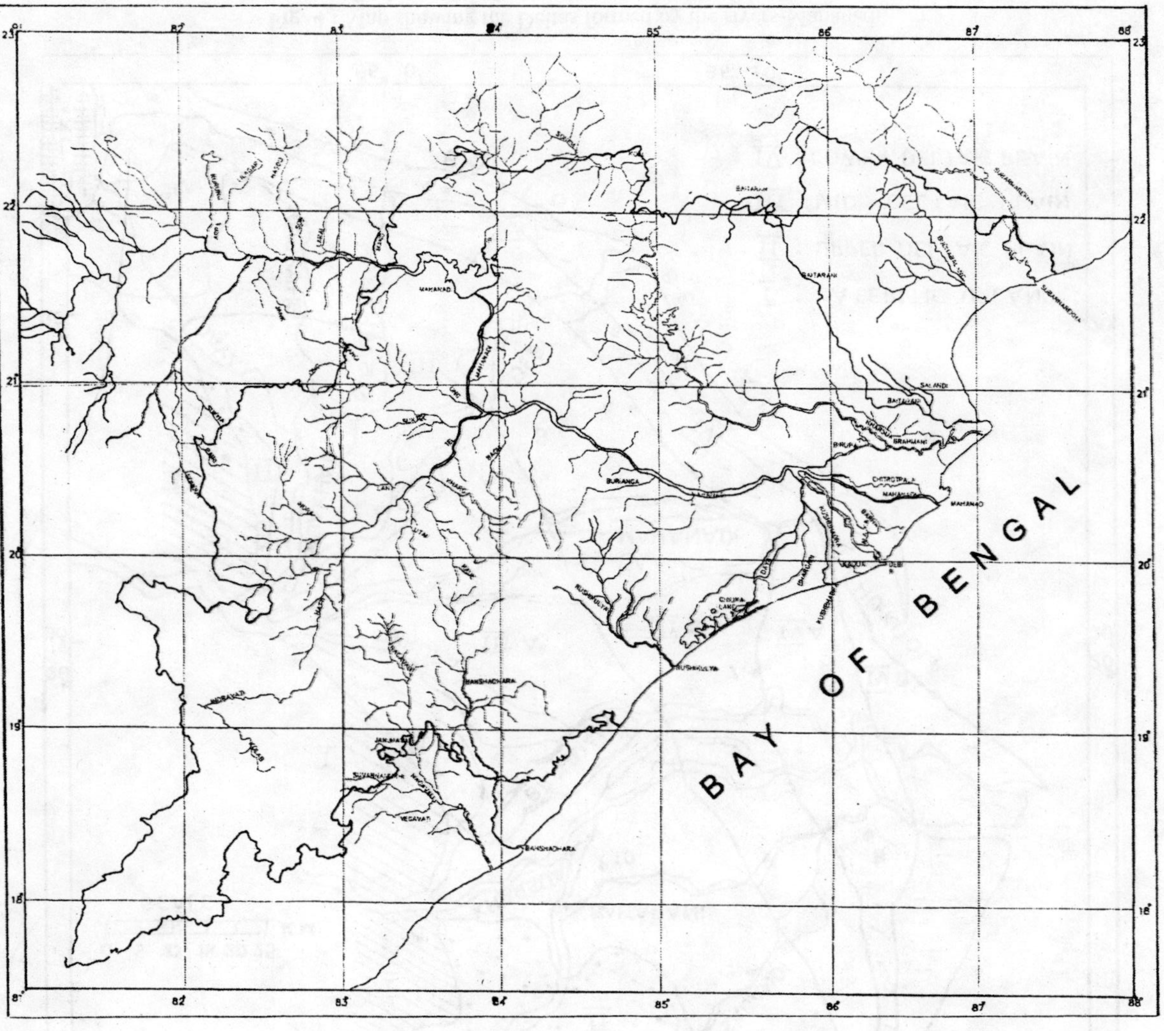

Fig. 3 : Map showing drainage system of Orissa.

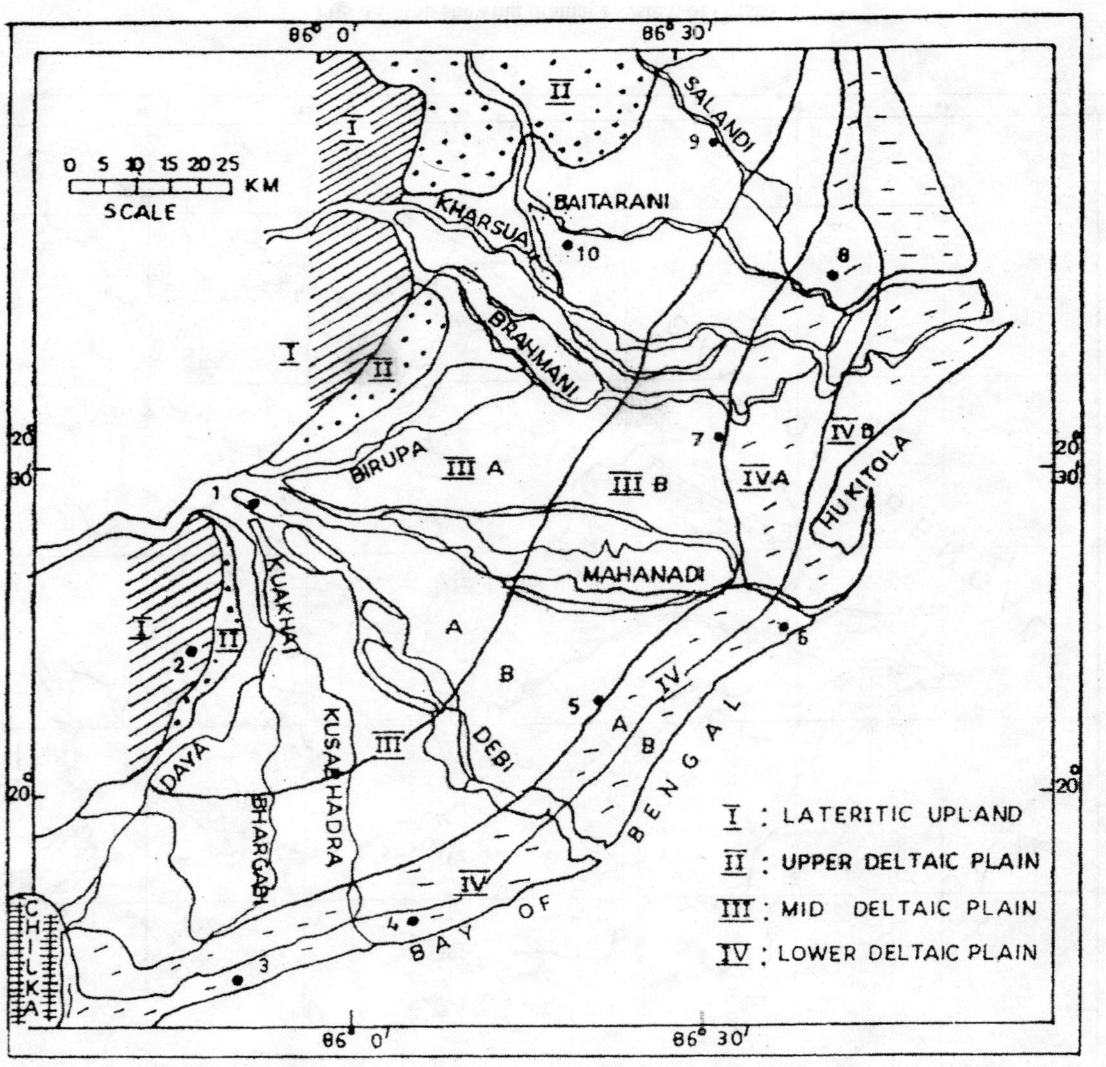

Fig. 4 : Map showing the Deltas formed by the rivers-Mahanadi, Brahmani and Baitarani. (After N. K. Mahalik)

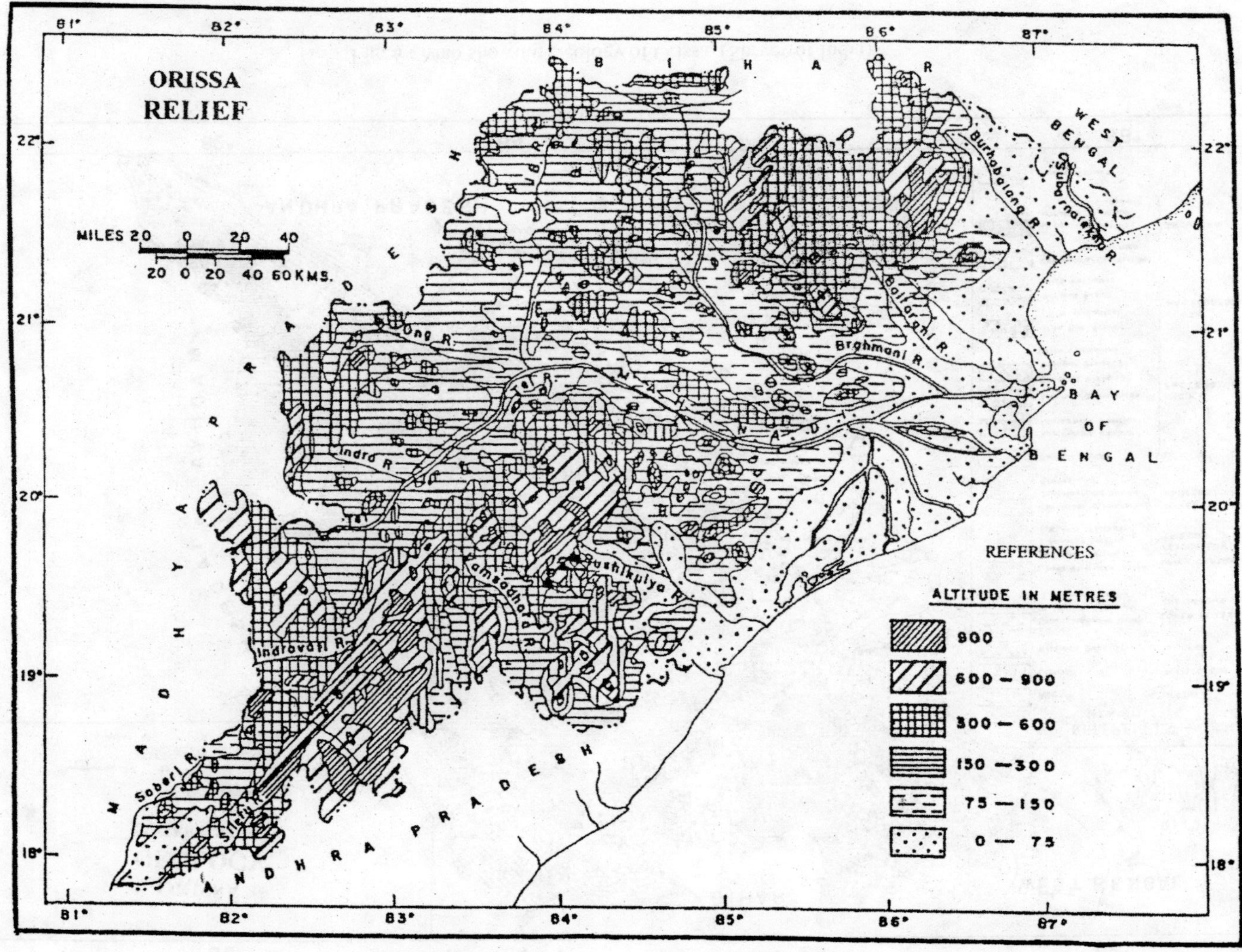

Fig. 5 : Map of Orissa showing the Relief Features.
(Survey of India)

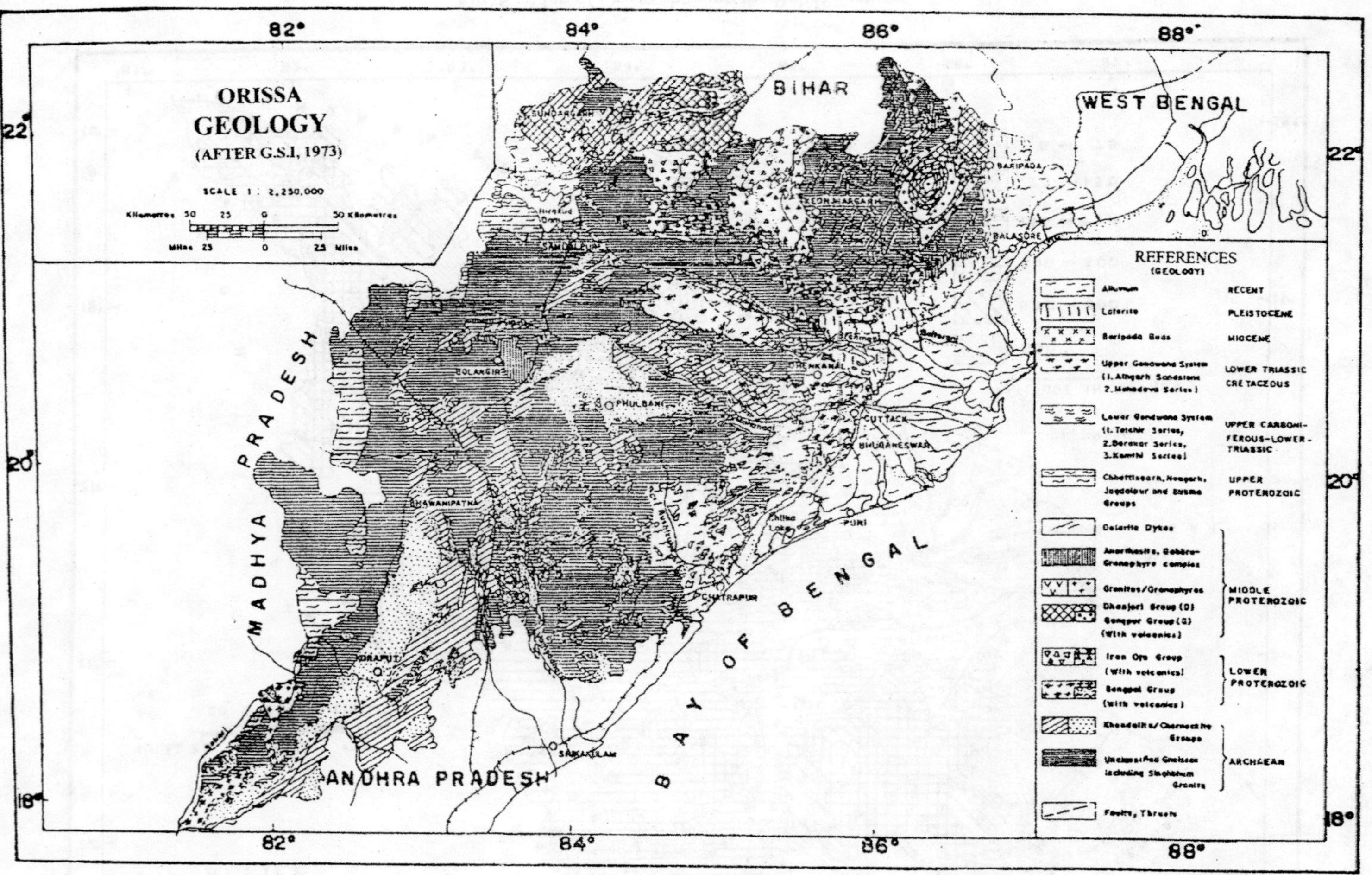

Fig. 6 : Map showing Geology of Orissa. (Survey of India)

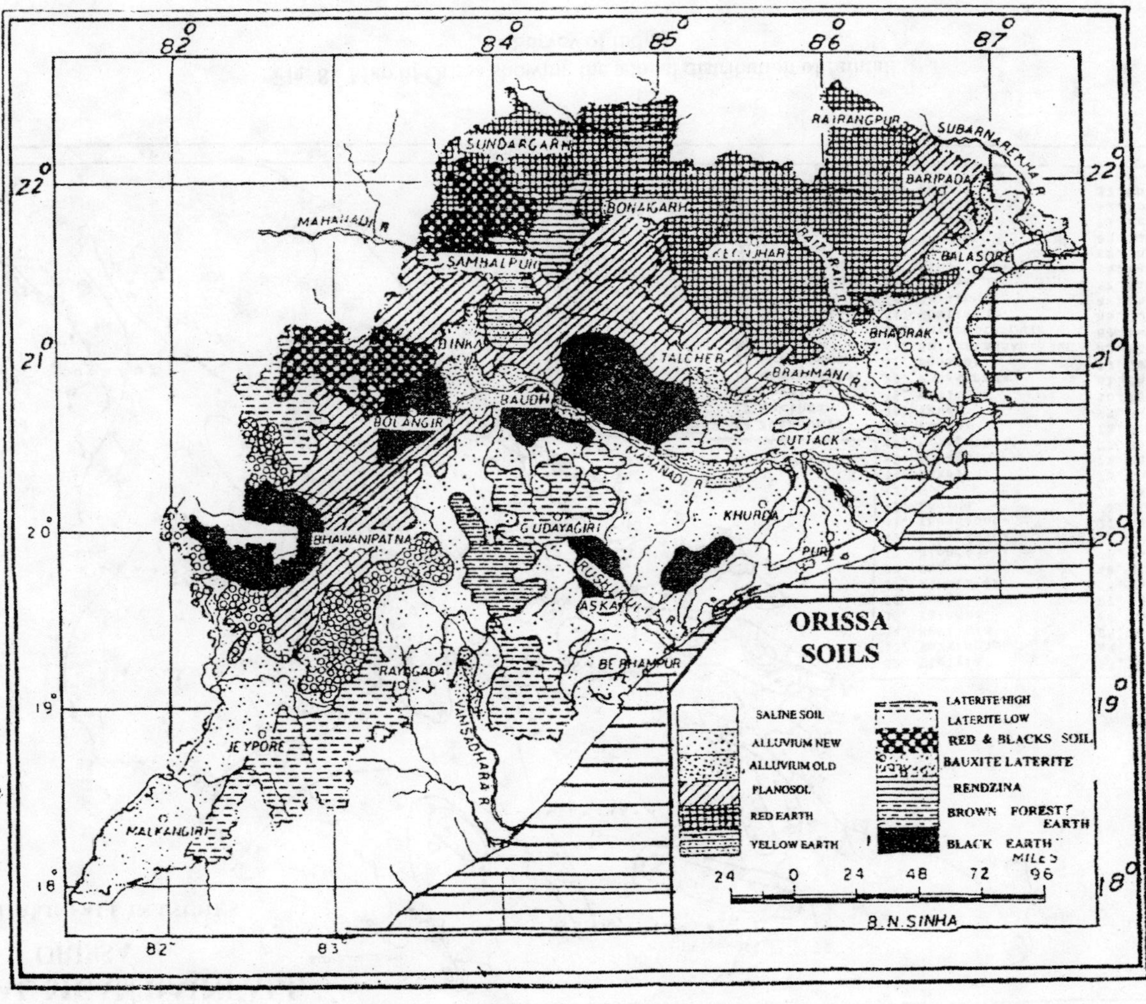

Fig. 7 : Map of Orissa showing the distribution of soil.
(Survey of India)

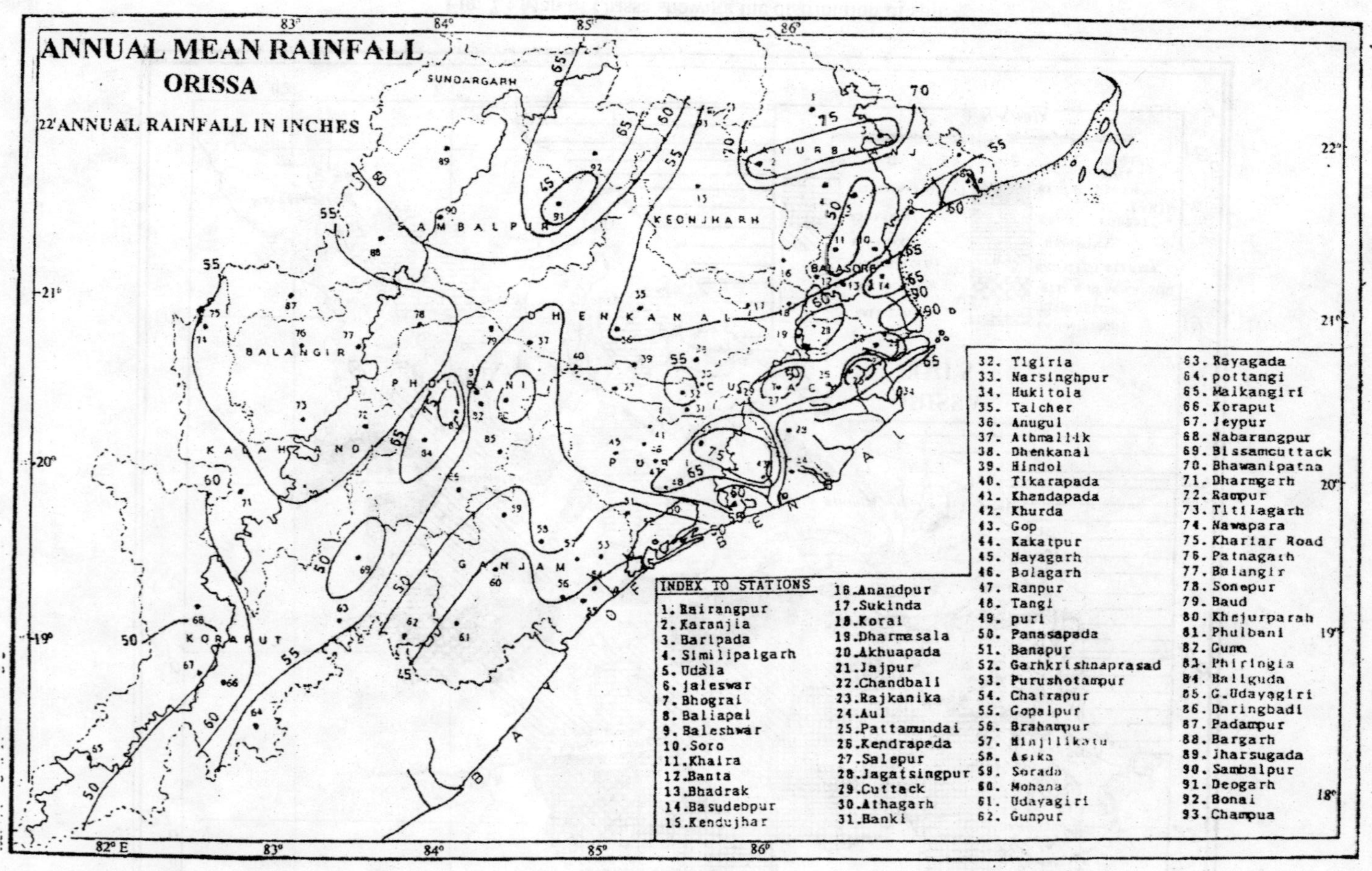

Fig. 8 : Map of Orissa showing the annual distribution of rainfall.
(Survey of India)

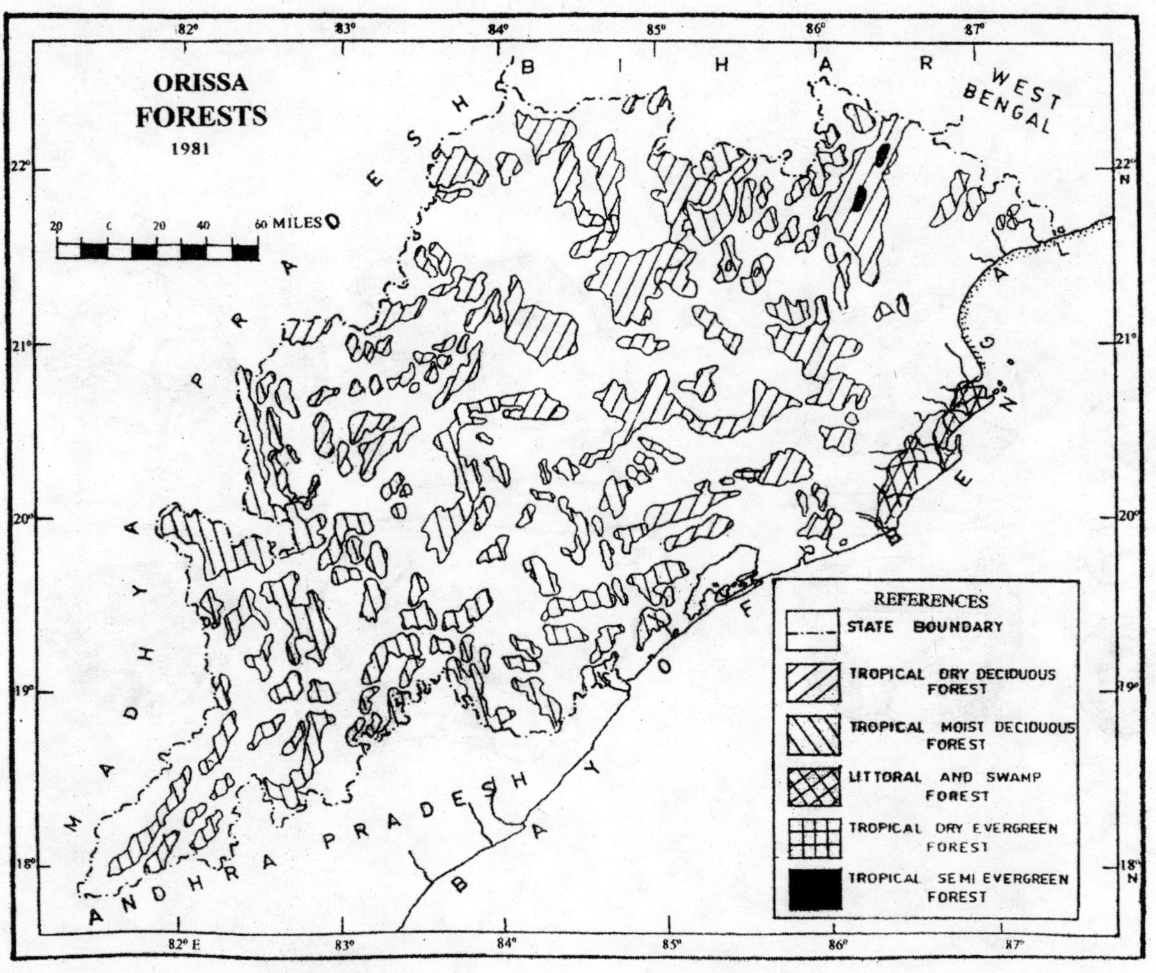

Fig. 9 : Map of Orissa showing the distribution of Forests.
(Survey of India)

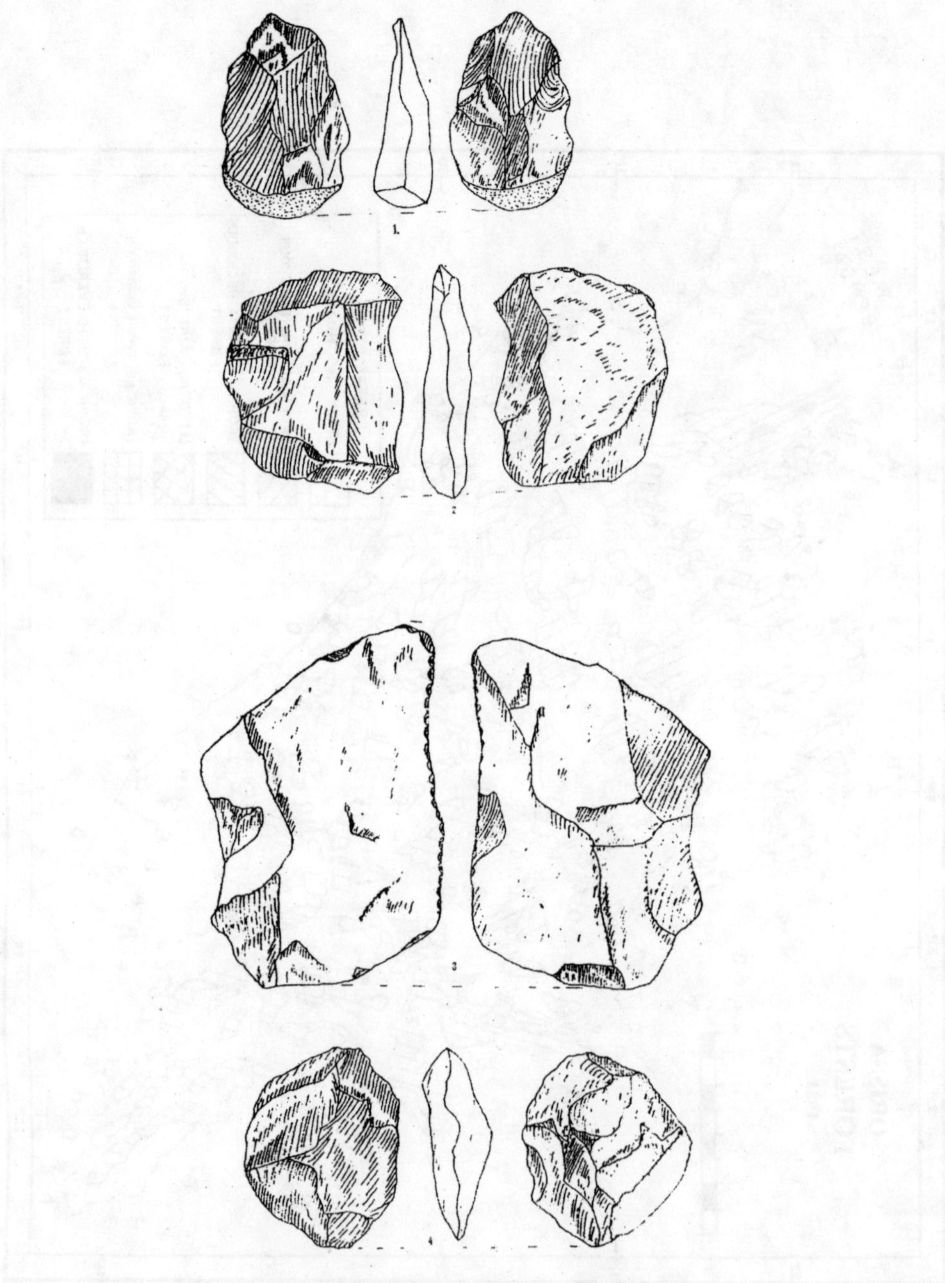

Fig.10 : Lower Palaeolithic tools from Sandim.
1. Handaxe, 2-3.Cleaver, 4 Small Ovate.
(After S. Chakrabarti)

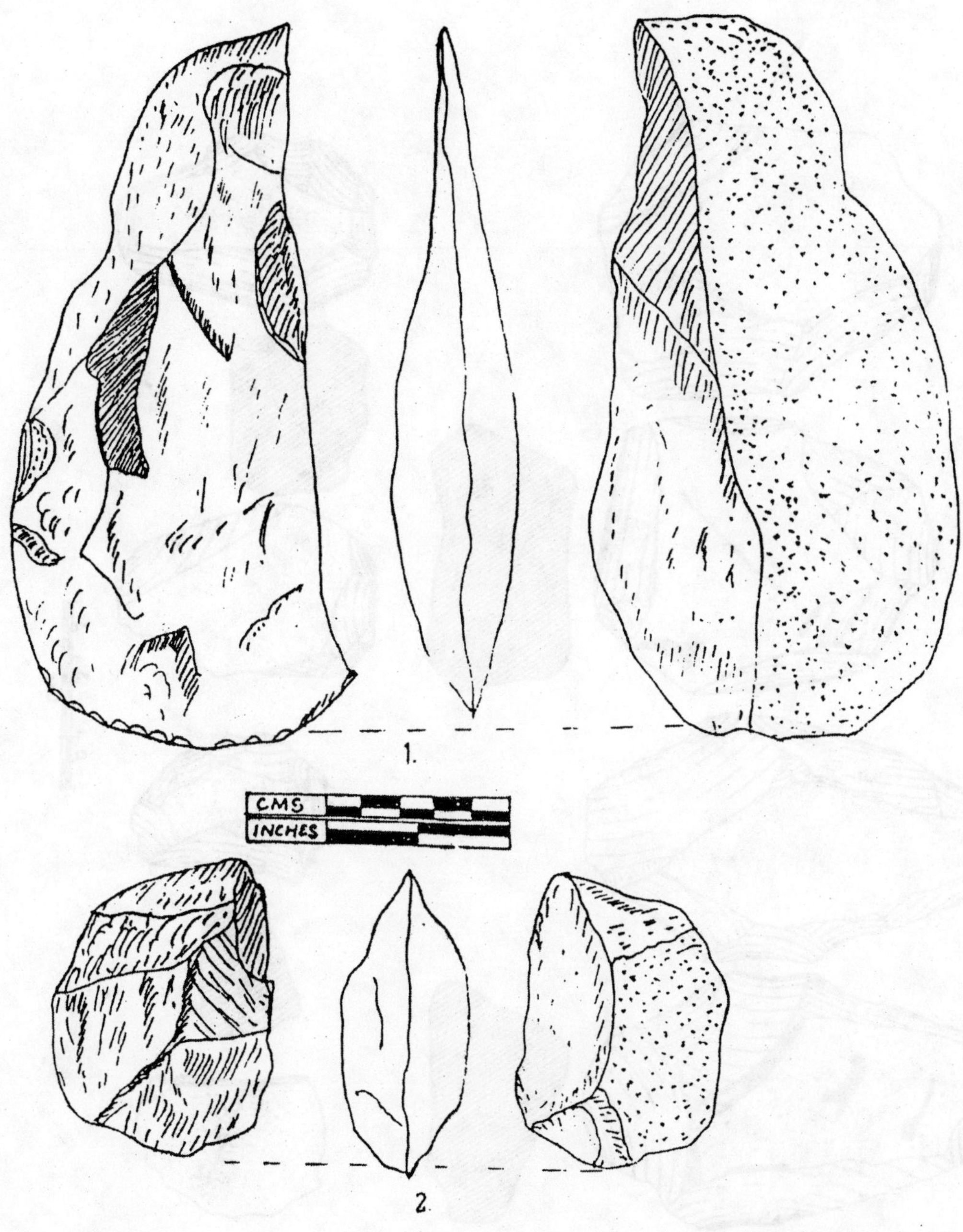

Fig. 11 : Lower Palaeolithic tools from Kamata.
1, knife; 2, small pick. (After S. Chakrabarti)

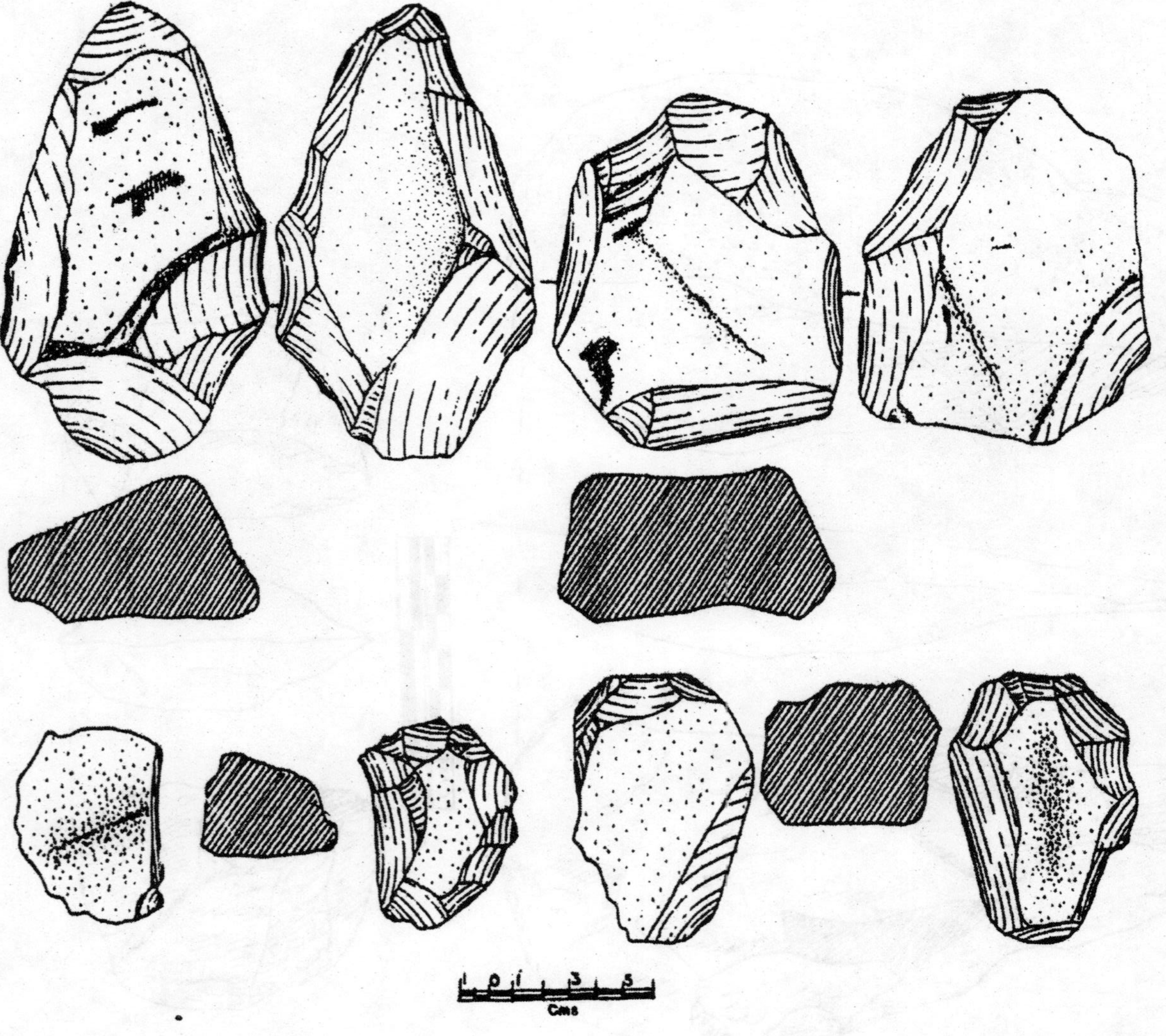

Fig. 12 : Lower Palaeolithic tools from Khiching Area.

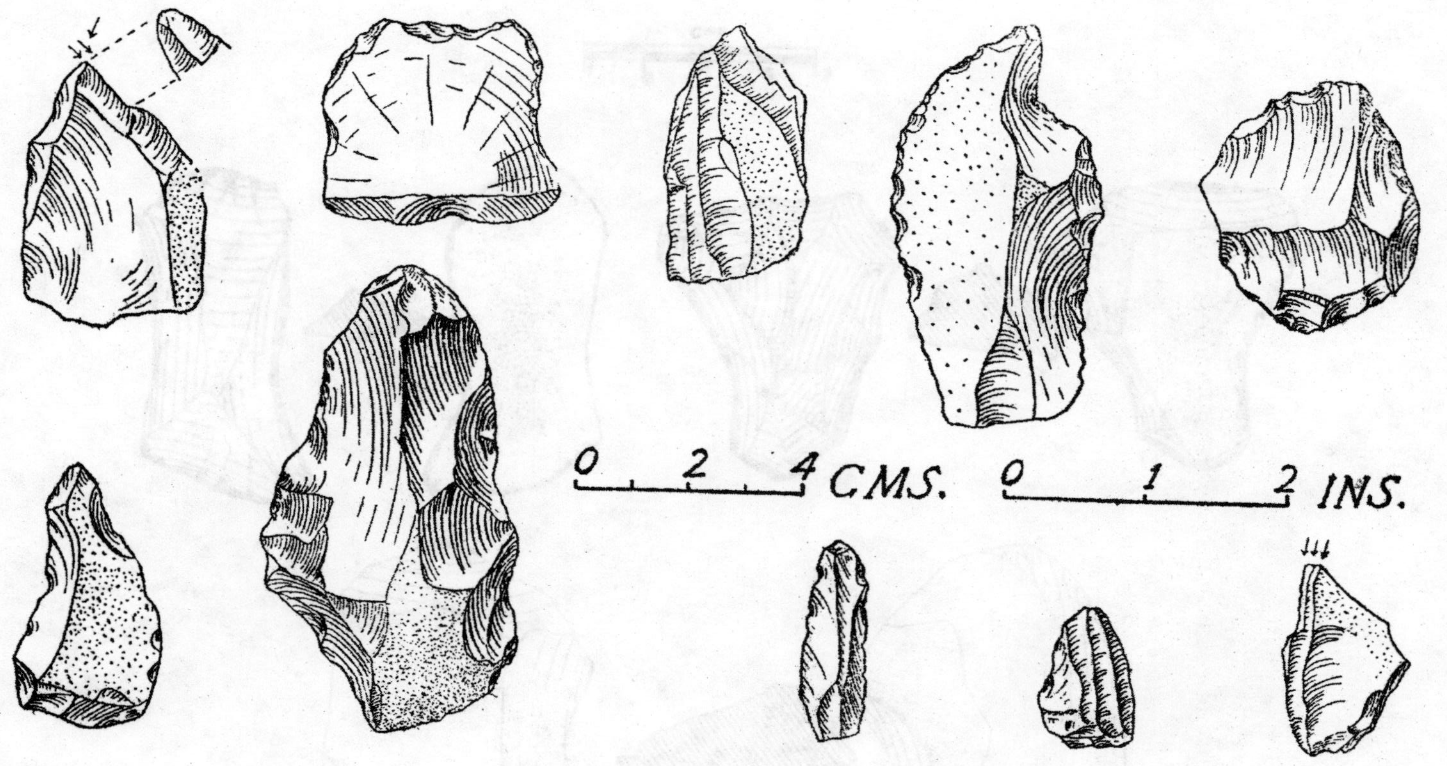

Fig. 13 : Middle Palaeolithic tools from Mayurbhanj.
(IAR: 1958-59, Fig. 16)

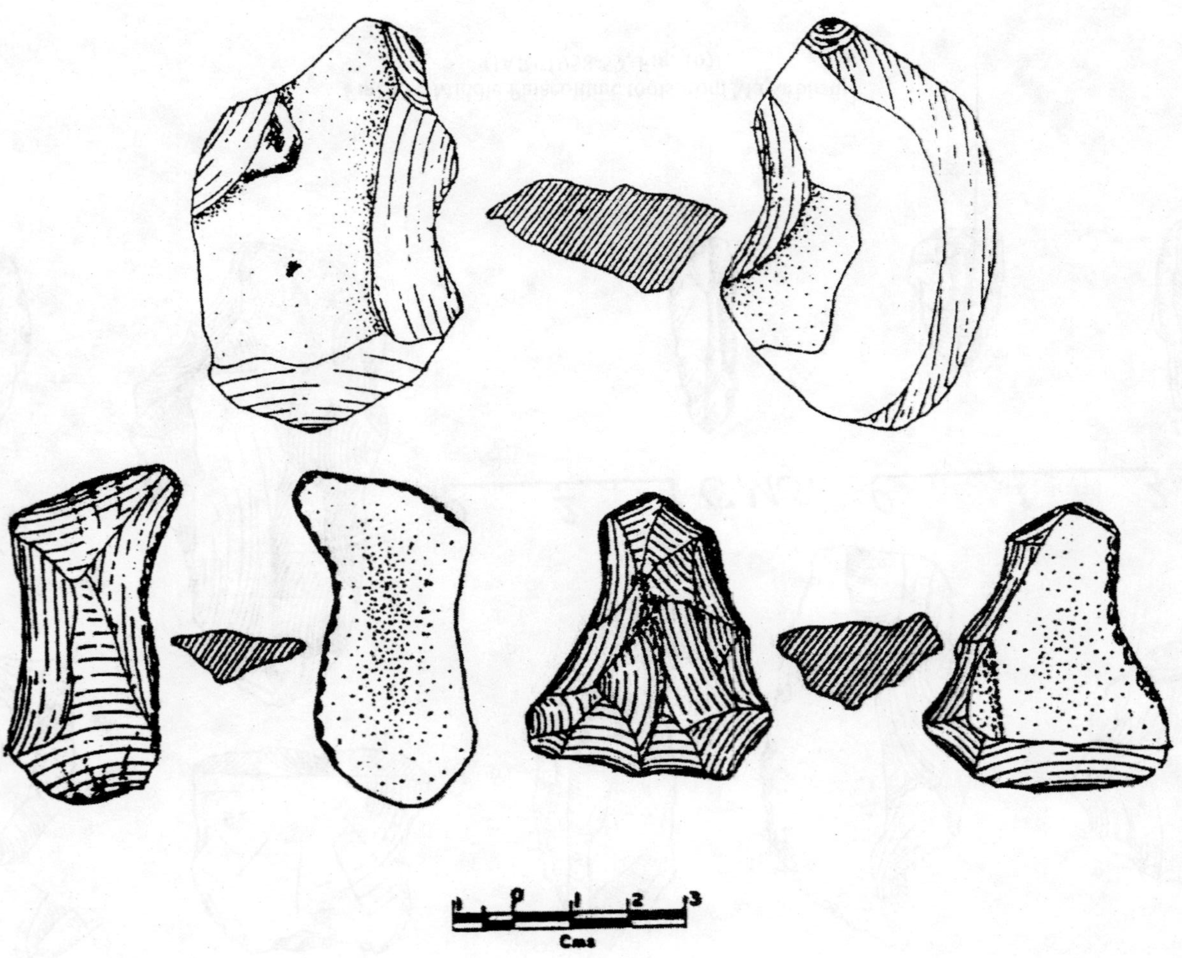

Fig. 14 : Middle Palaeolithic tools from Khiching area.
(After S. Chakrabarti)

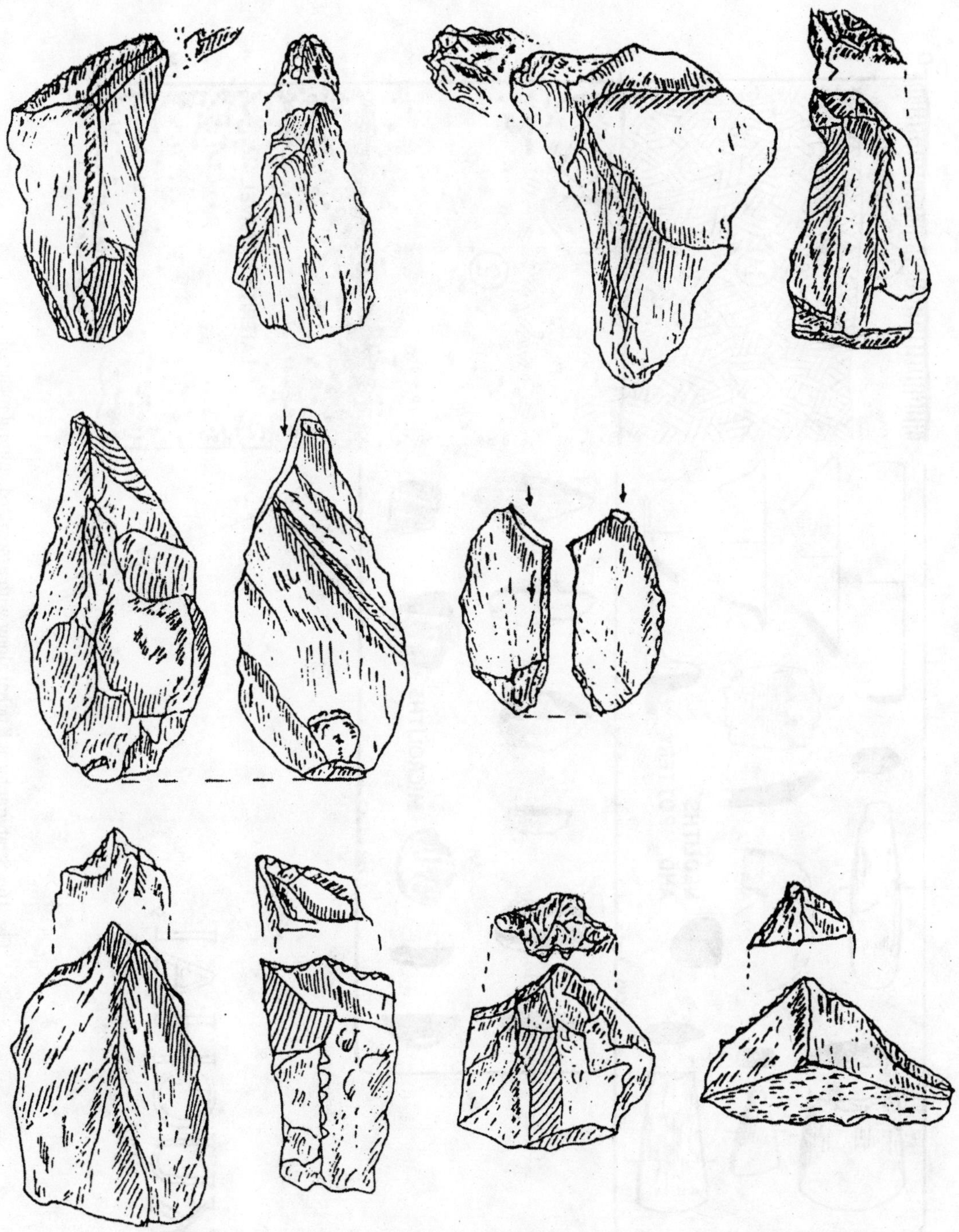

Fig. 15 : Upper Palaeolithic tools from Kalapathara.
(After S. Chakrabarti,2000)

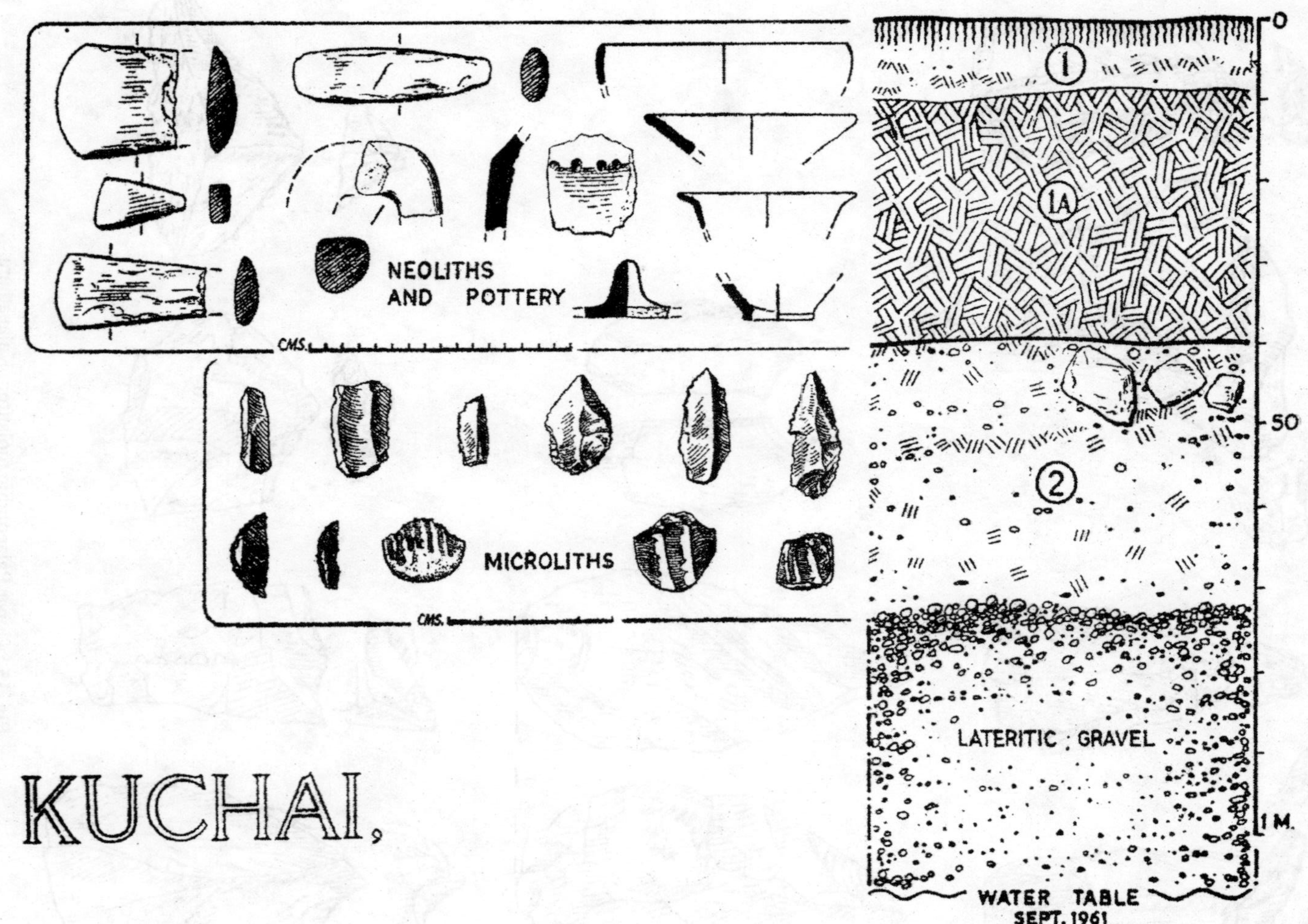

Fig. 16 : Stratigraphy at Kuchai along with associated cultural material.
(IAR: 1961-62, Fig.11)

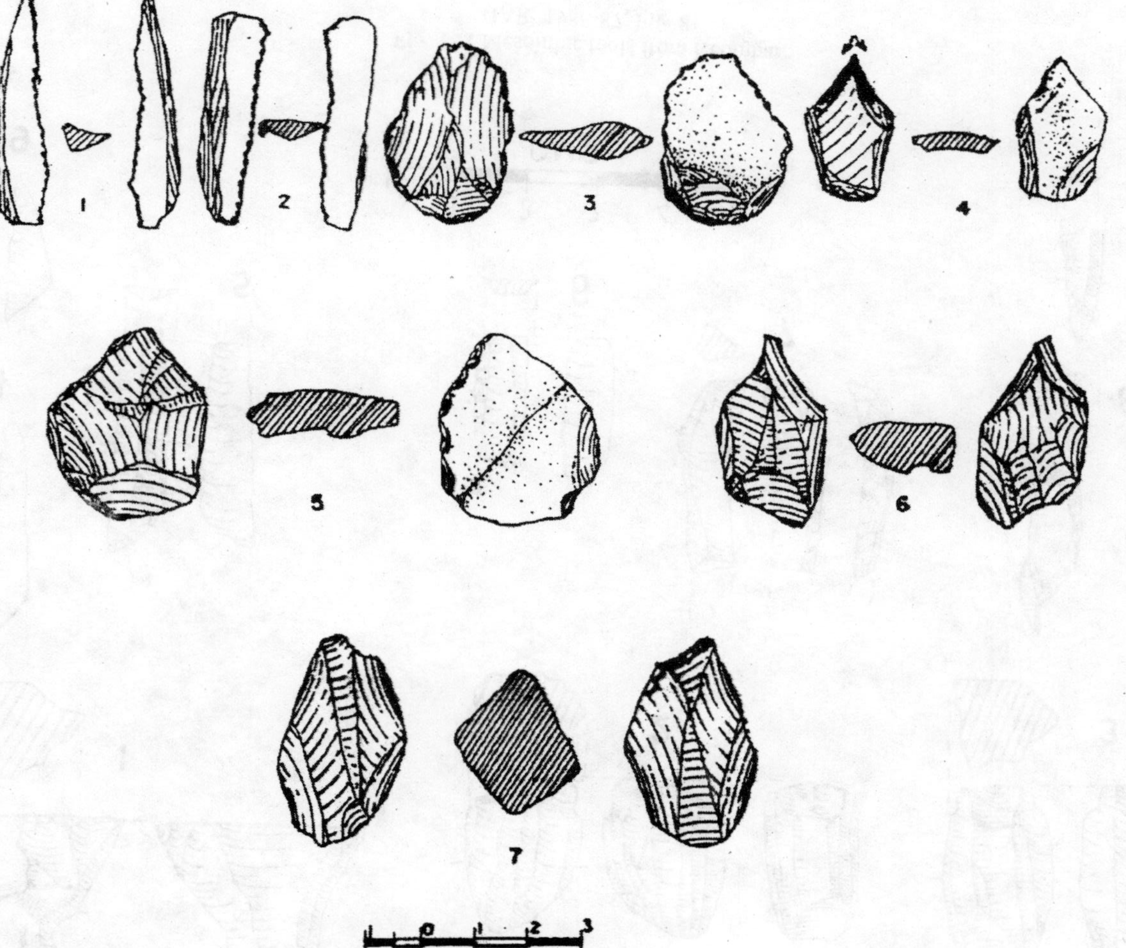

Fig. 17 : Mesolithic tools from Khiching area.
(After Chakrabarti)

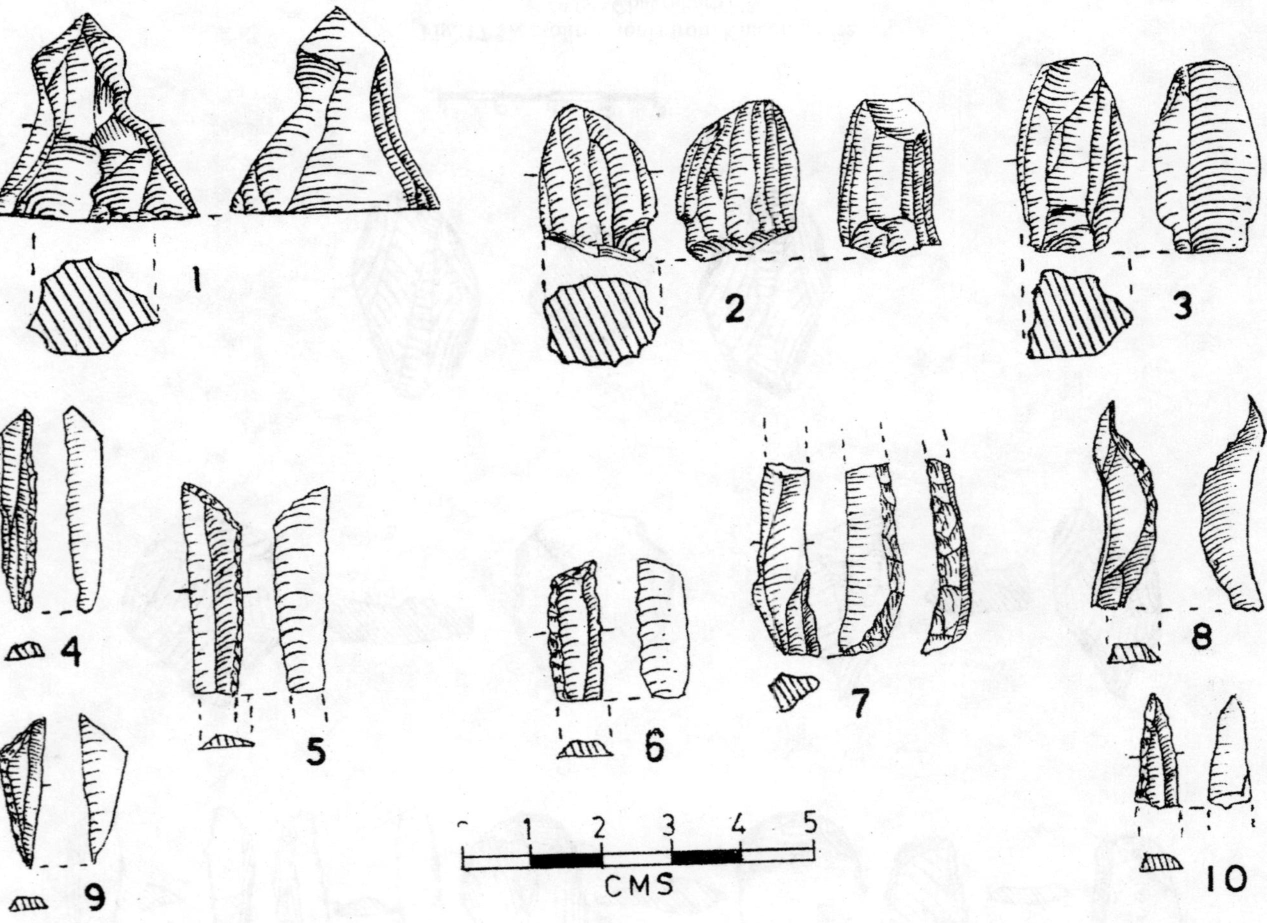

Fig. 18 : Mesolithic tools from Keonjhar.
(IAR: 1986-87, Fig. 8)

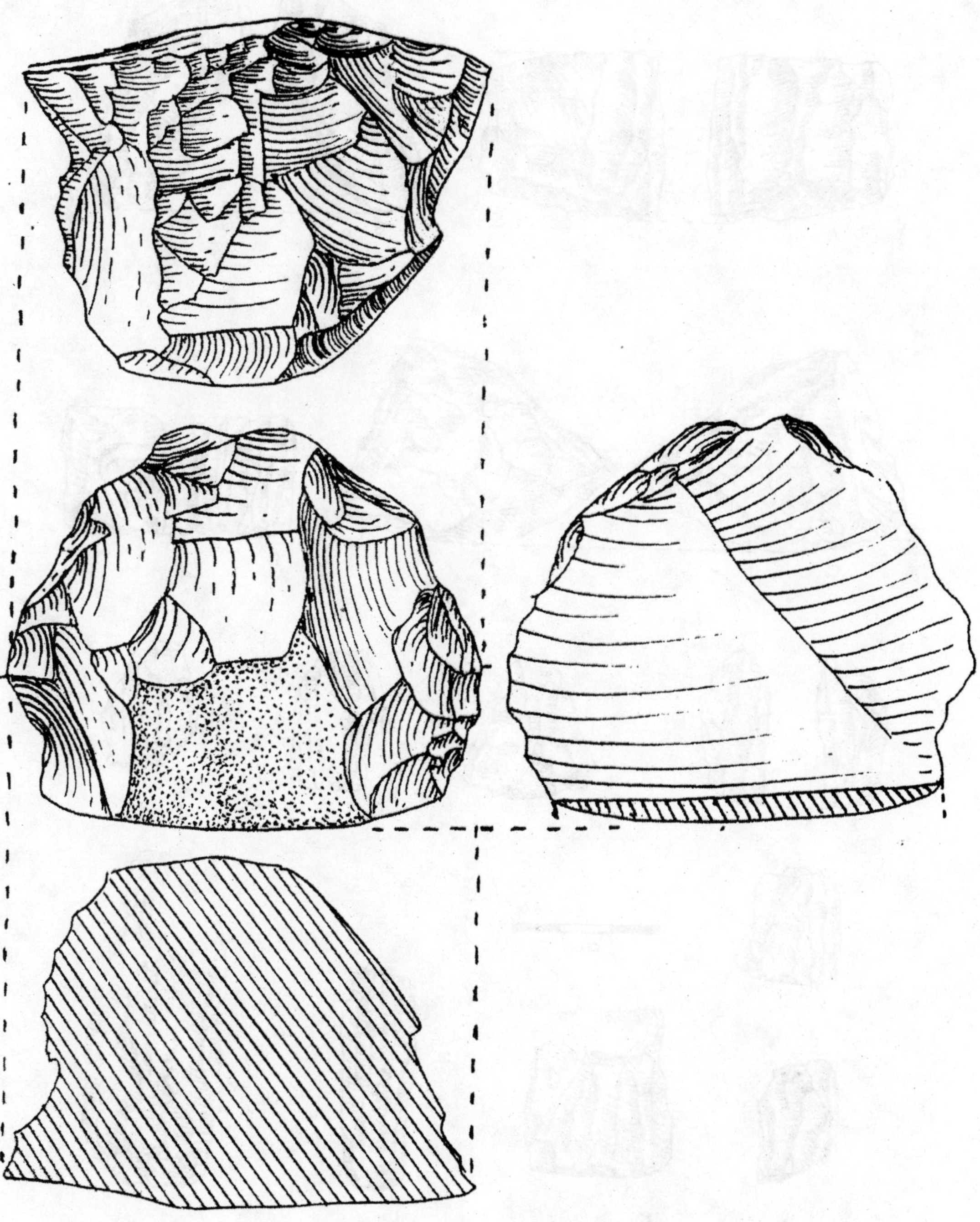

Fig. 19 : Heavy duty tools from Keonjhar (Horse-hoof Scraper).(IAR: 1986-87, Fig. 9)

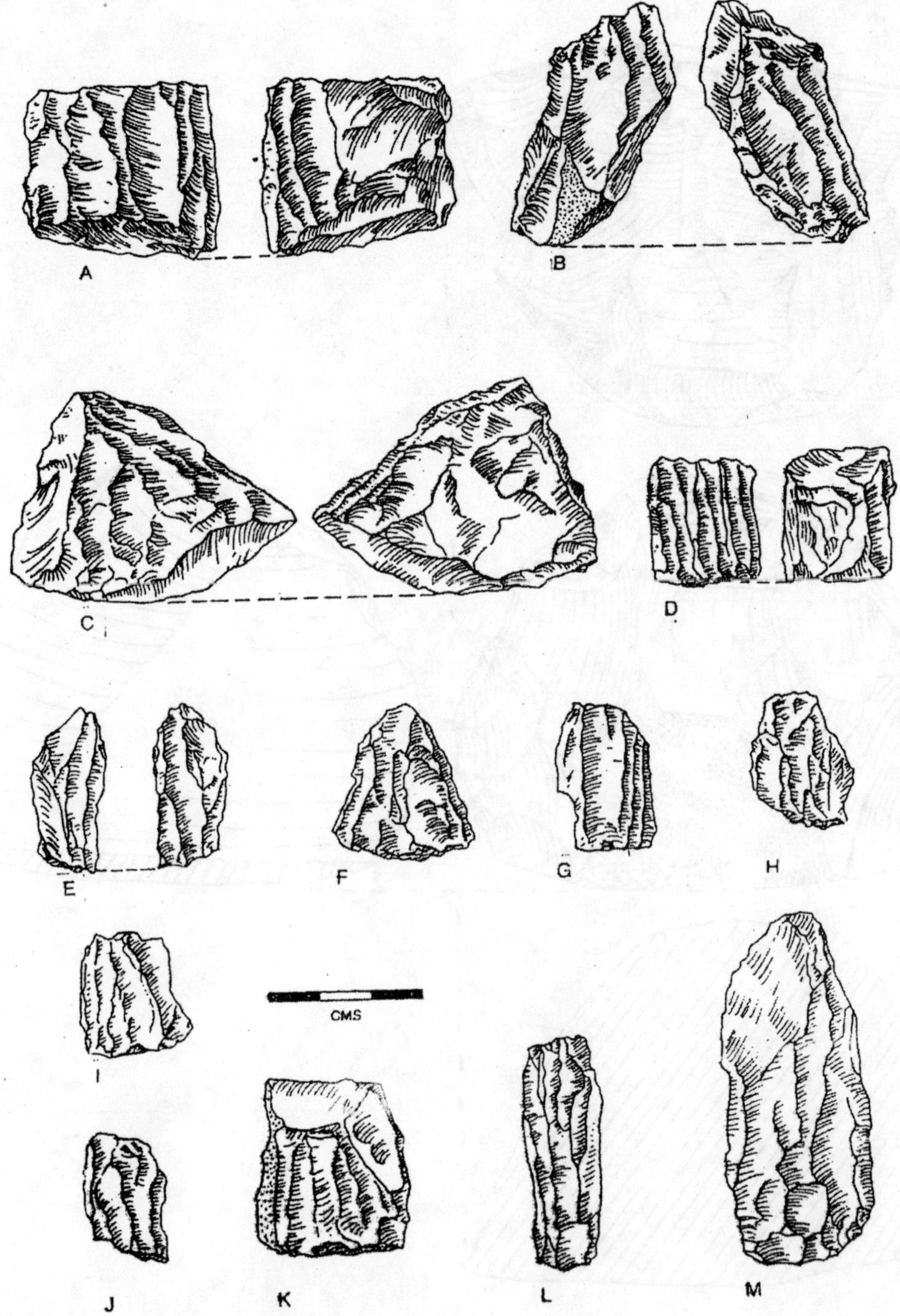

Fig. 20 : Blade cores (A-M) from Mesolithic sites in Keonjhar.
(After P. Mohanty)

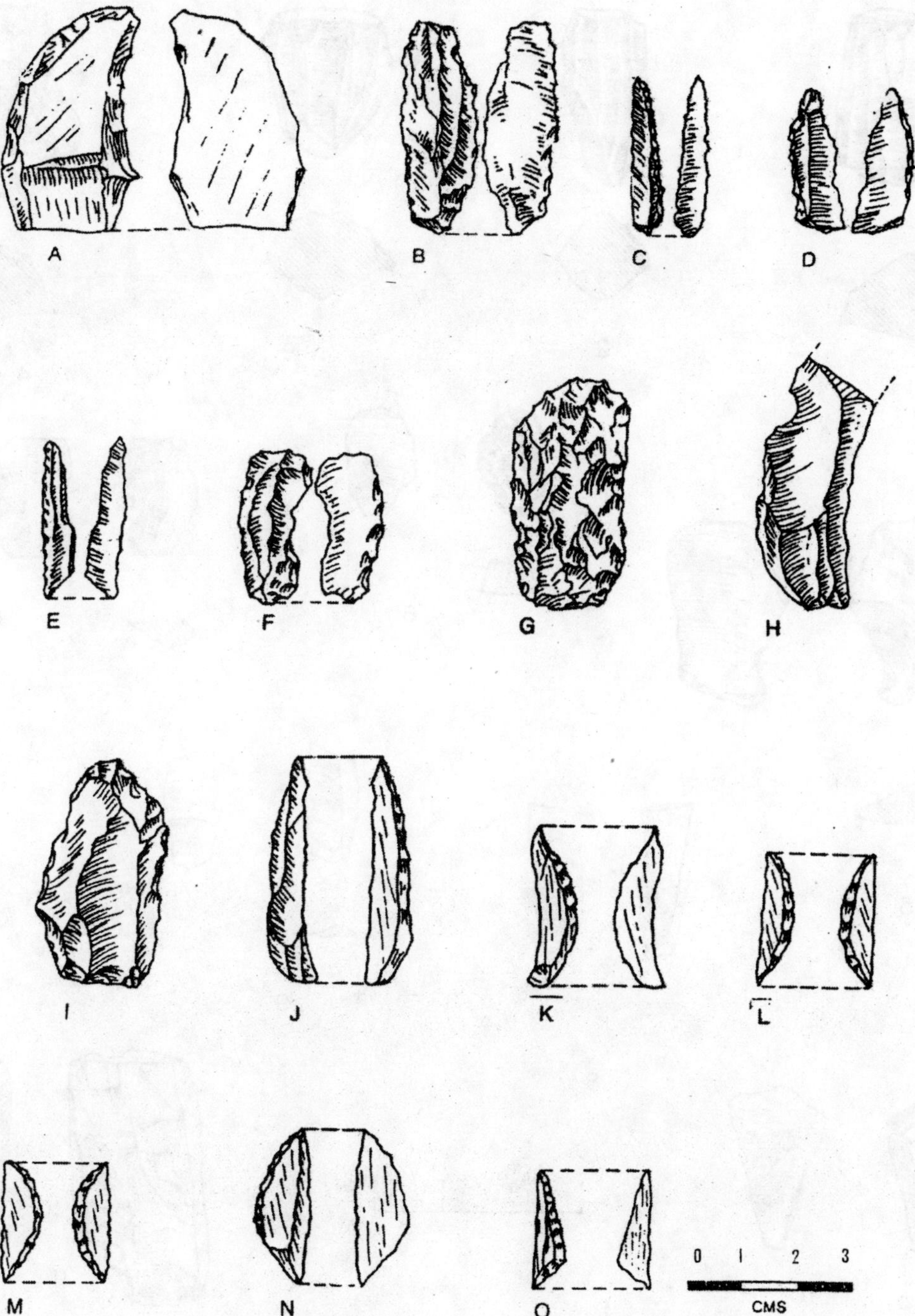

Fig. 21 : Microlithic blades (B,D,F,K,O); Points (C,E); Lunates (L, M, N); Triangle (A) from Keonjhar. (After P. Mohanty)

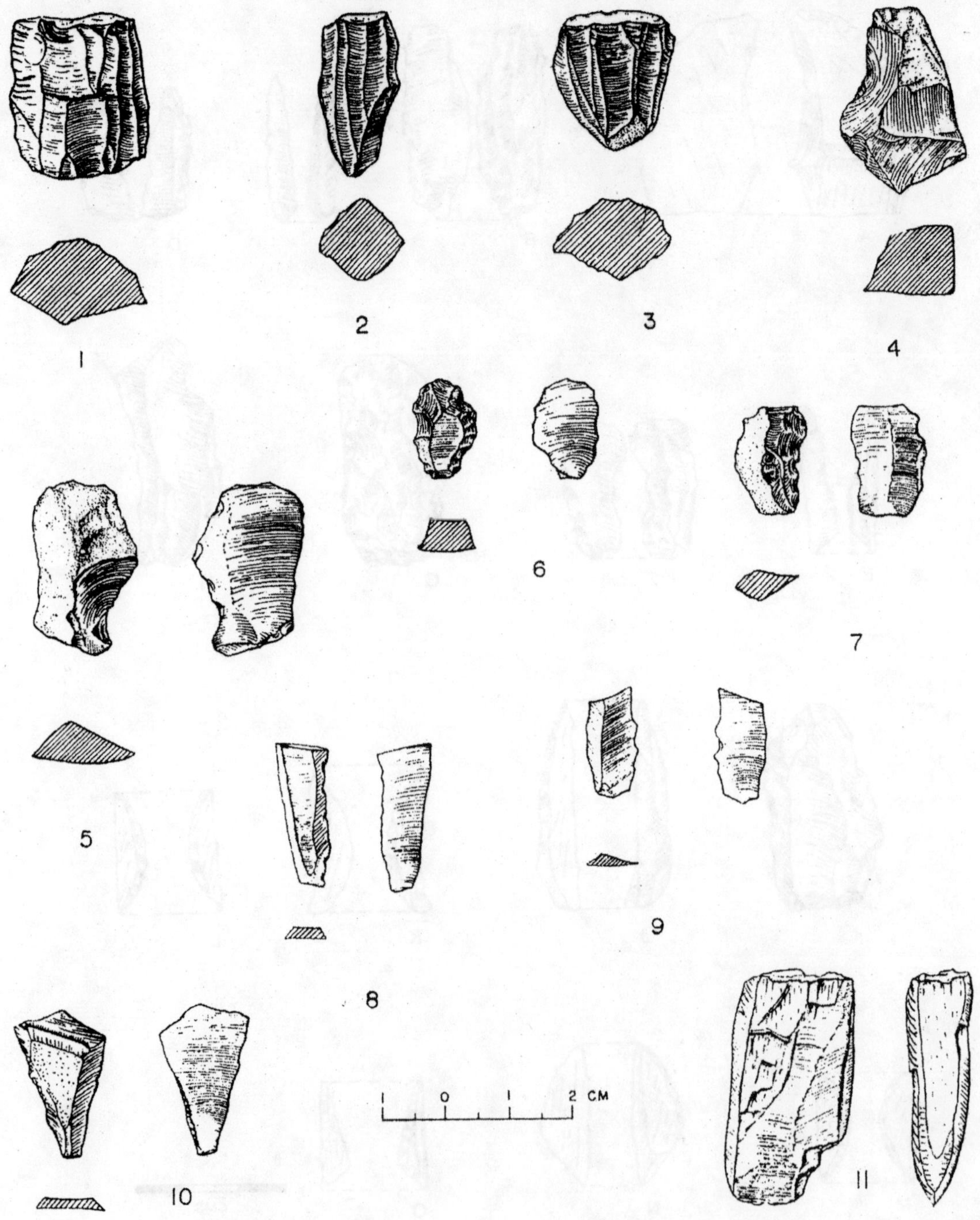

Fig. 22 : Manikmunda: Microliths. 1, blade core; 2-3, blade core; 4, flake core; 5&7, end flake; 6, round scraper; 8, blade; 9, blade; 10, end flake; 11, edge polished chisel. (IAR: 1988-89, Fig. 16)

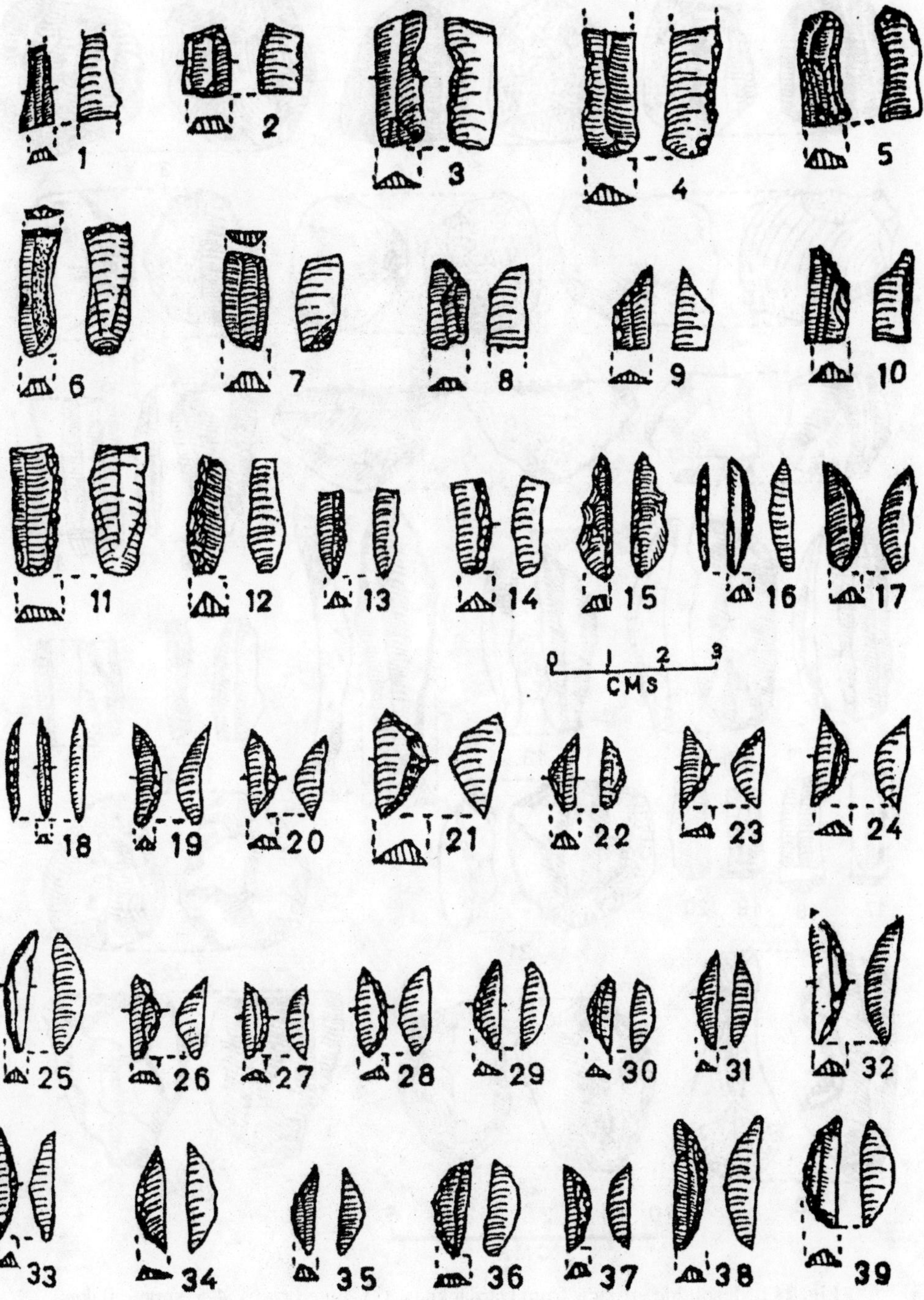

Fig. 23 : Microliths from Excavation at Girla.
(After S. C. Nanda)

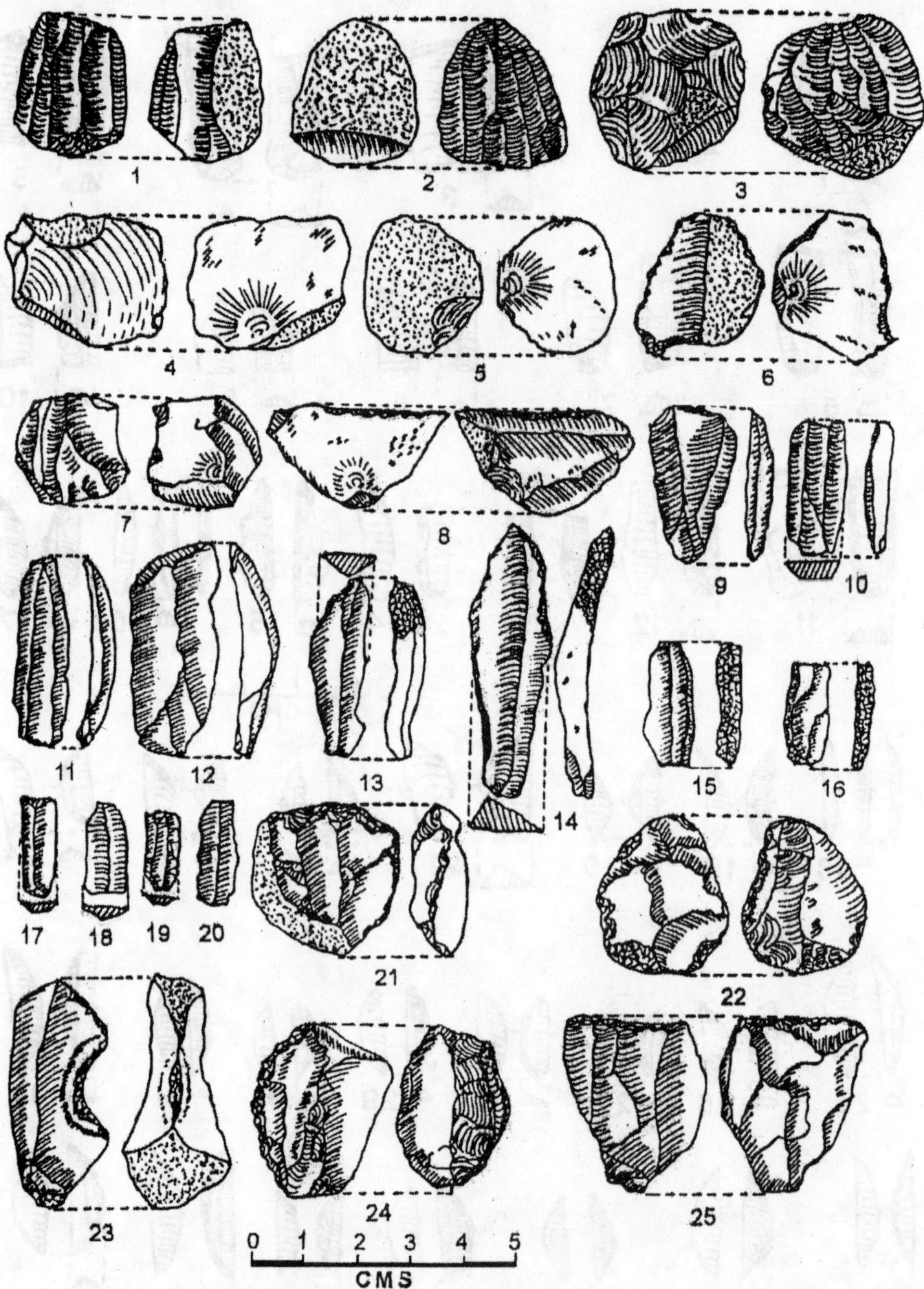

Fig. 24 : Mesolithic artifacts from Darpankhas, 1-3, fluted cores; 4-5, simple flakes; 6&8,utilised flakes; 7, fluted flakes; 9, simple blades; 10-12, parallel blades; 13&14, penknife blades; 15&16, backed blades; 17-20, microblades; 21&25, end scrapers; 22, round scraper; 23, notched scraper; 24, side scraper. (After D. Sahoo 2000)

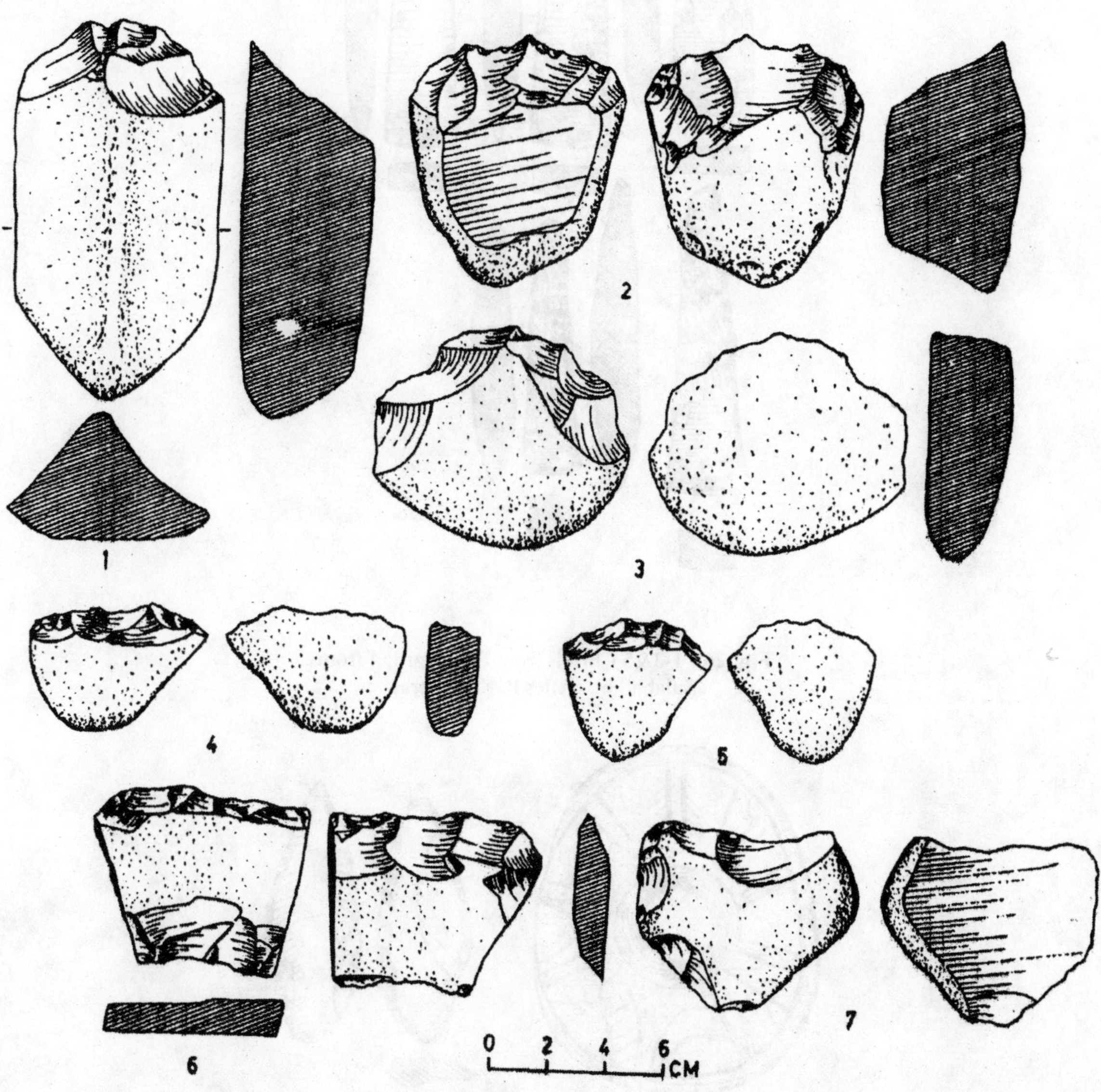

Fig. 25 : Bonaigarh, Chopper-chopping tools from minor workshop sites. (After P. K. Behera)

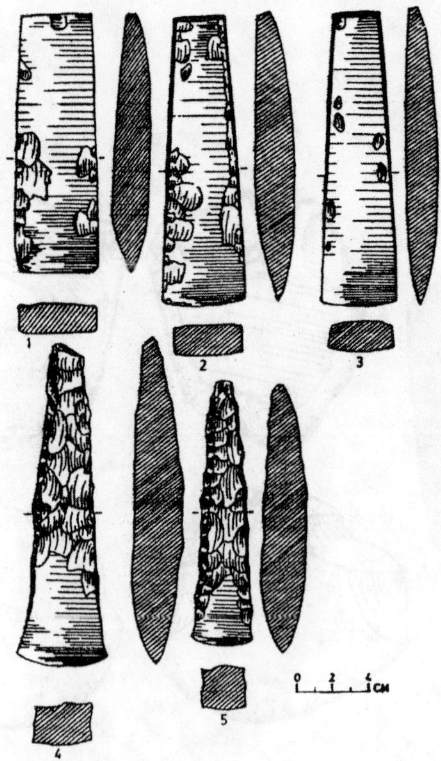

Fig. 26 : 1-3&5 Chisels from Bonaigarh; 4 from Sulabhdihi. (After P. K. Behera)

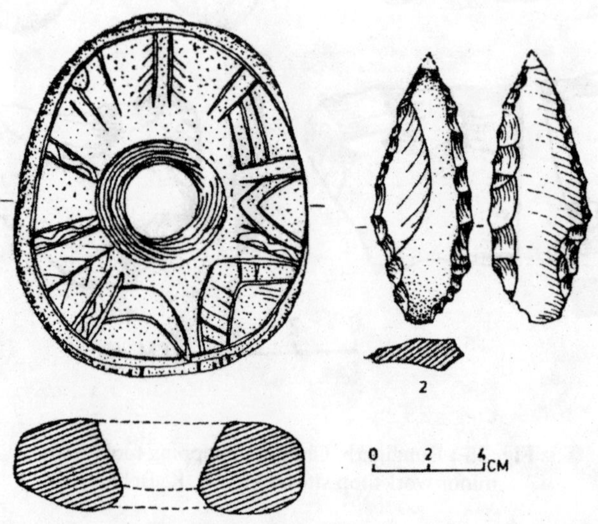

Fig. 27 : Bonaigarh, 1, Engraved bored-stone; 2, leaf-shaped spear-head. (After P. K. Behera)

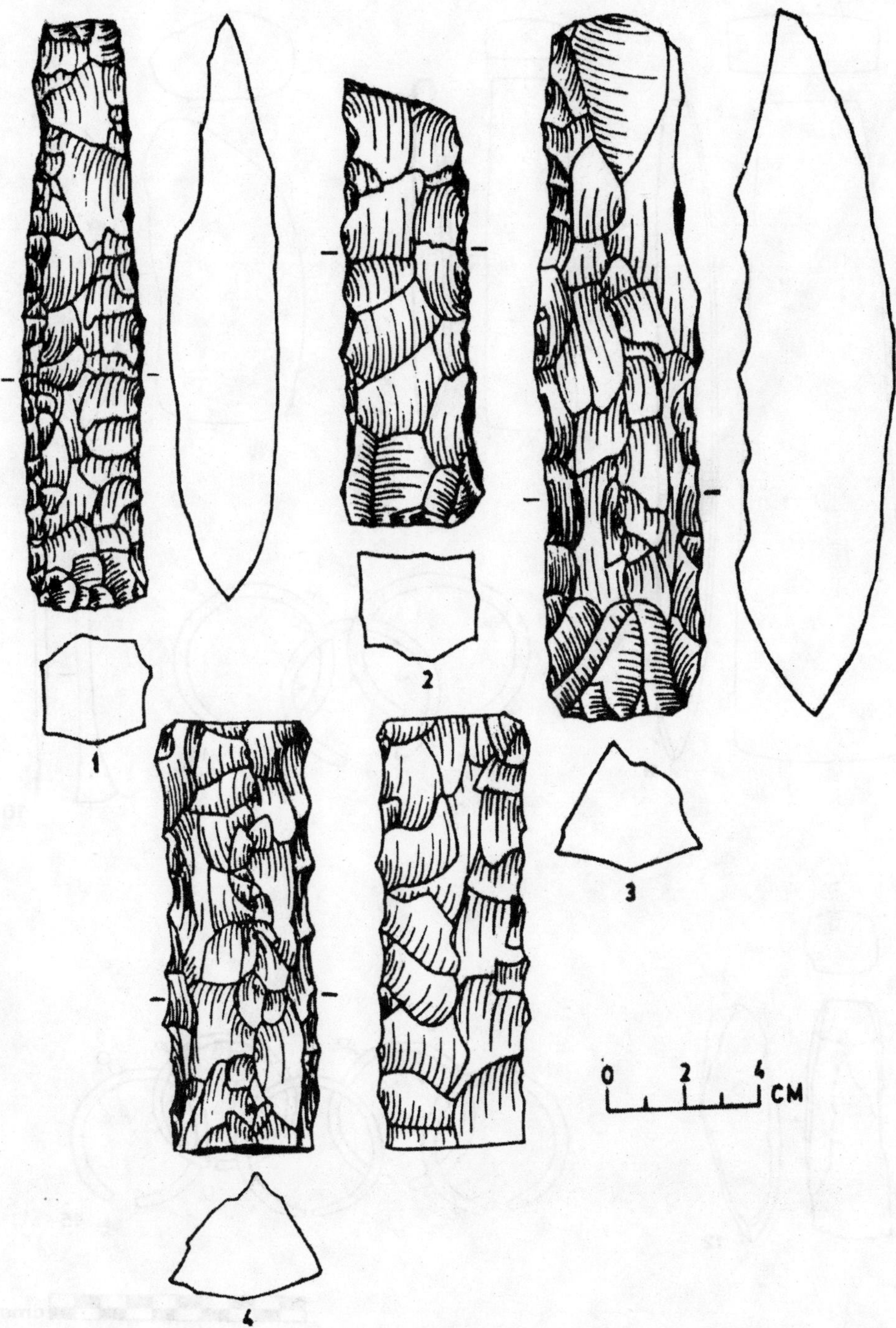

Fig. 28 : Chisels from sulabhdihi.
(After P. K. Behera)

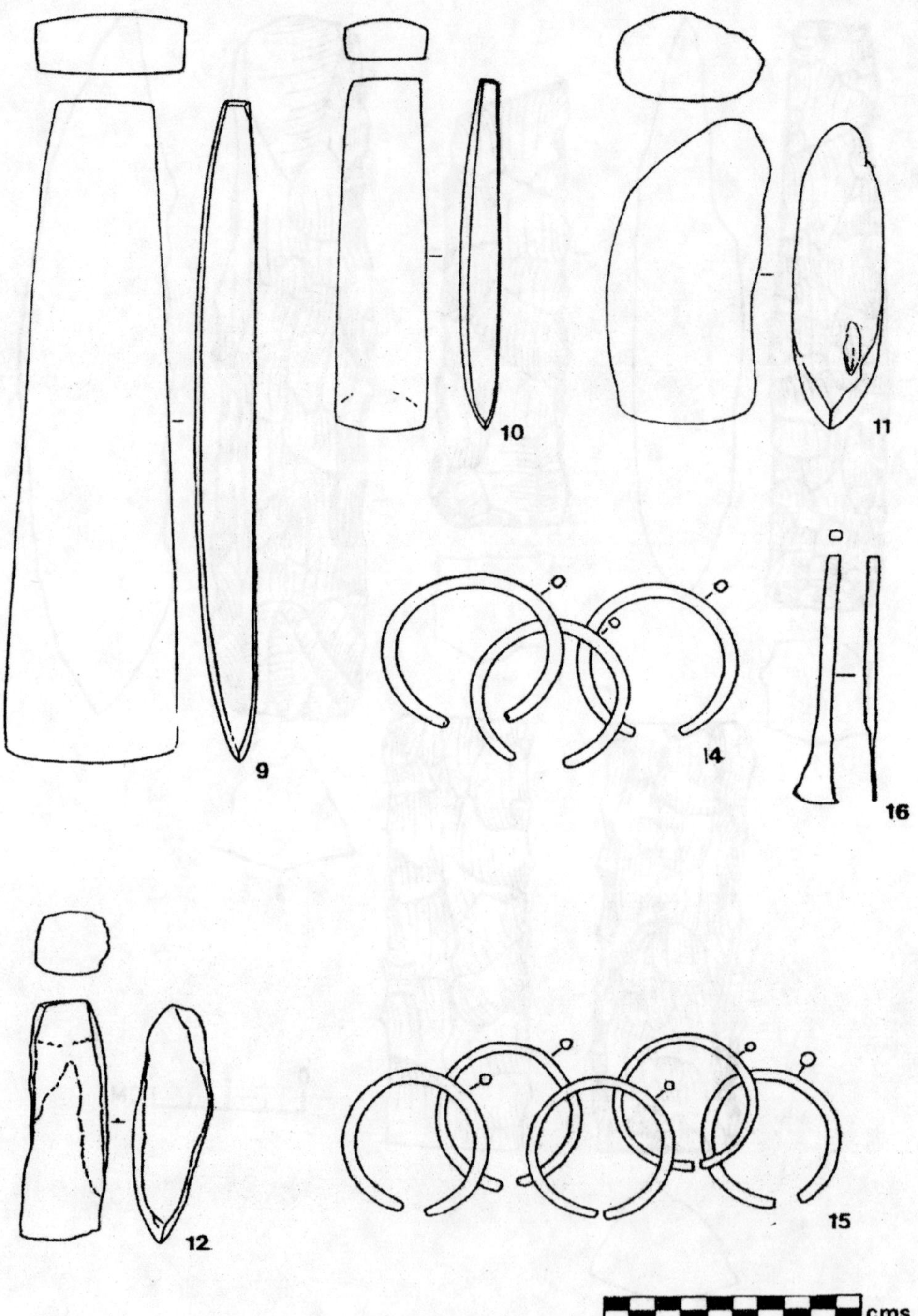

Fig. 29 : 1-5 Adzes/Axes; 6-7, Bangles of copper wire.
(After P. Yule and B. K. Rath)

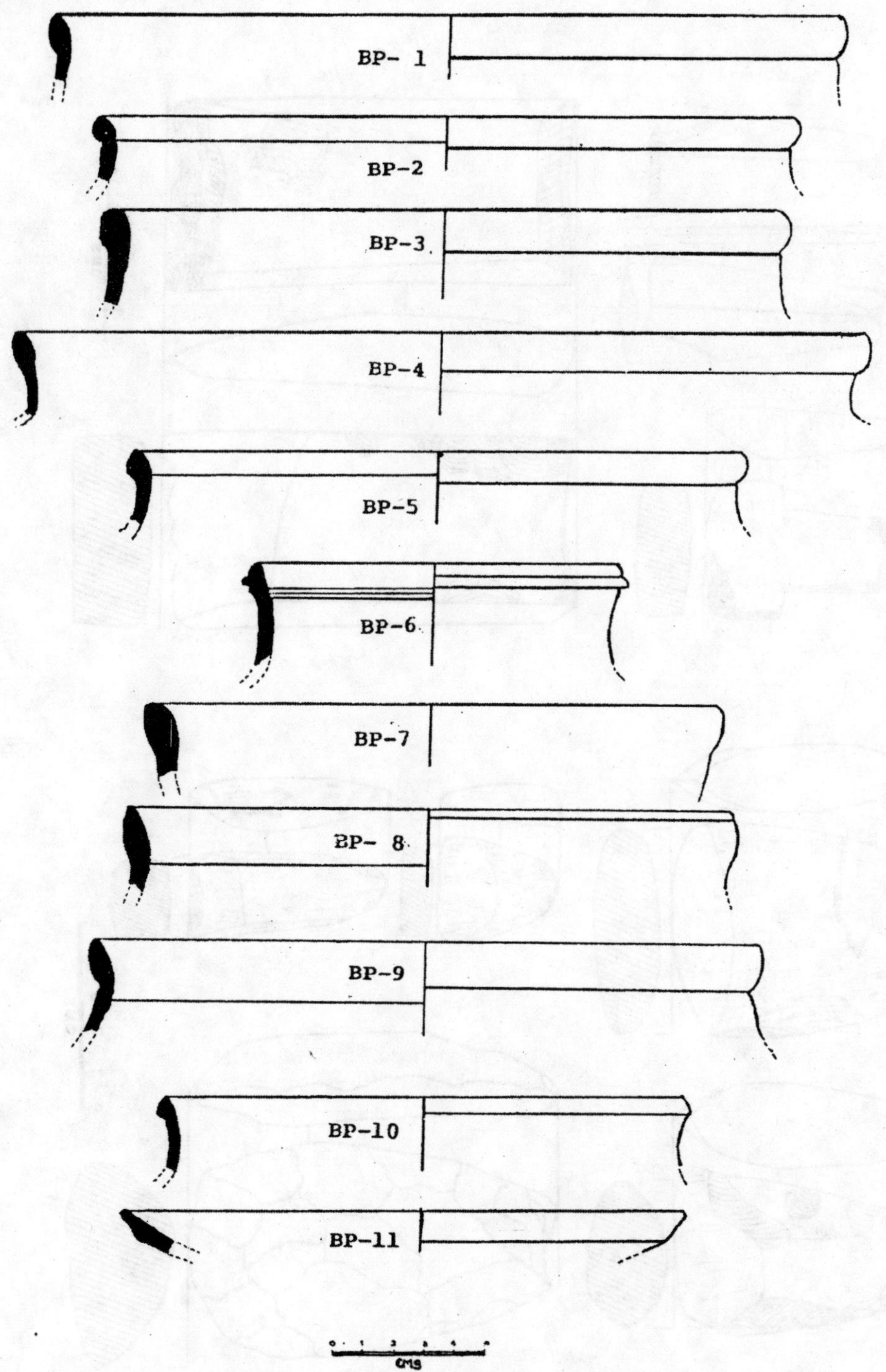

Fig. 30 : Coarse Red Ware, Neolithic Pottery from Bajpur.
(After Basa et al, 2000)

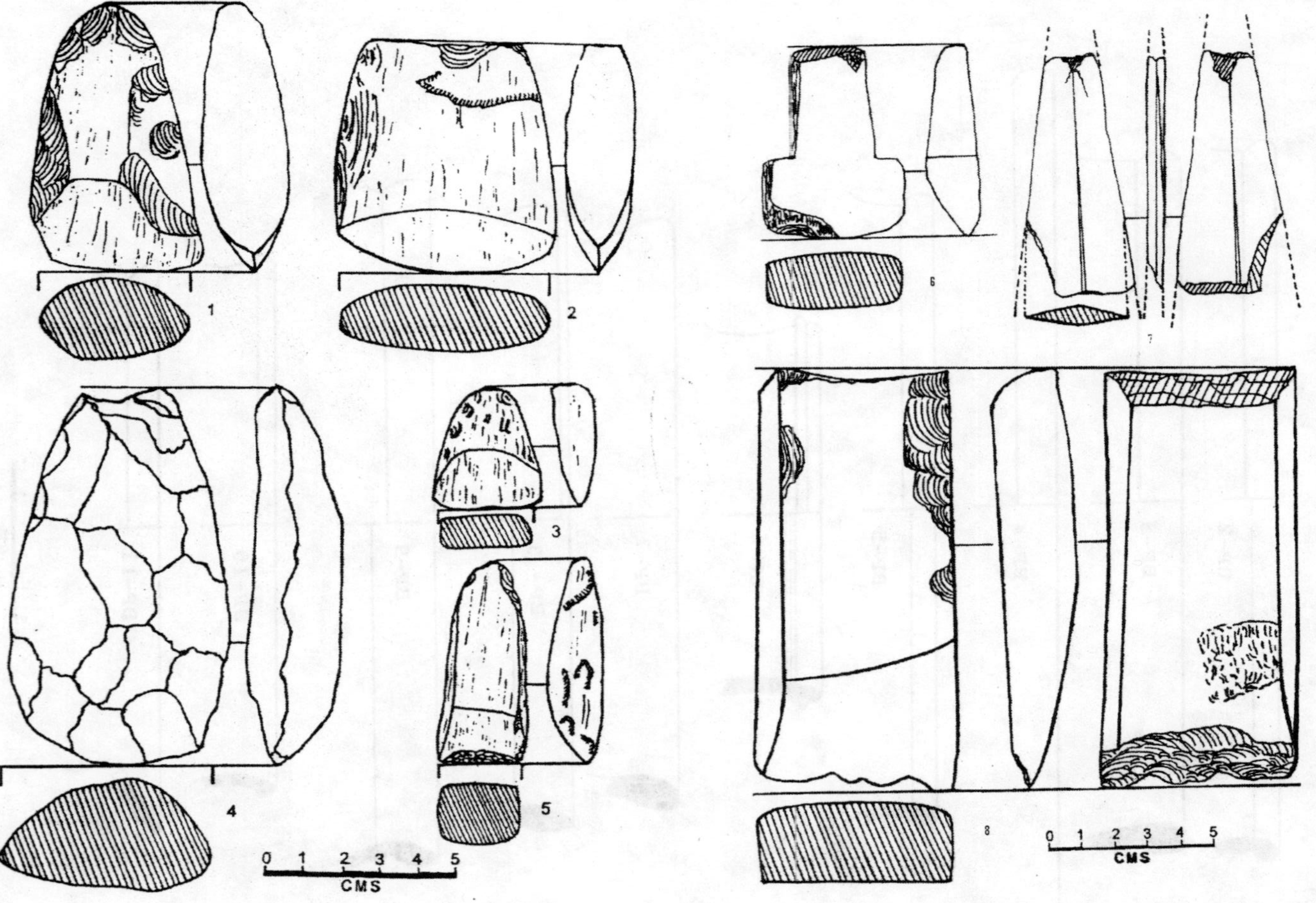

Fig.31 : Neolithic tools from Darpankhas. (After D. Sahoo)

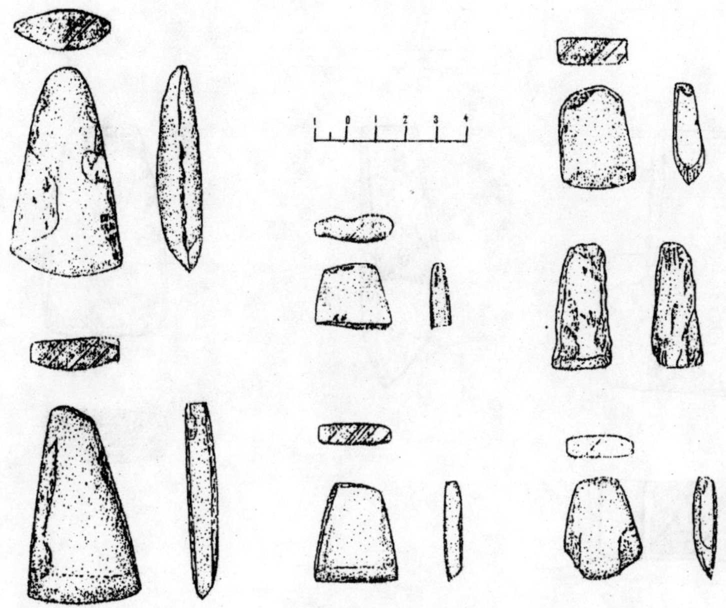

Fig. 32 : Celts from Jagati Mound. (After S. K. Kar)

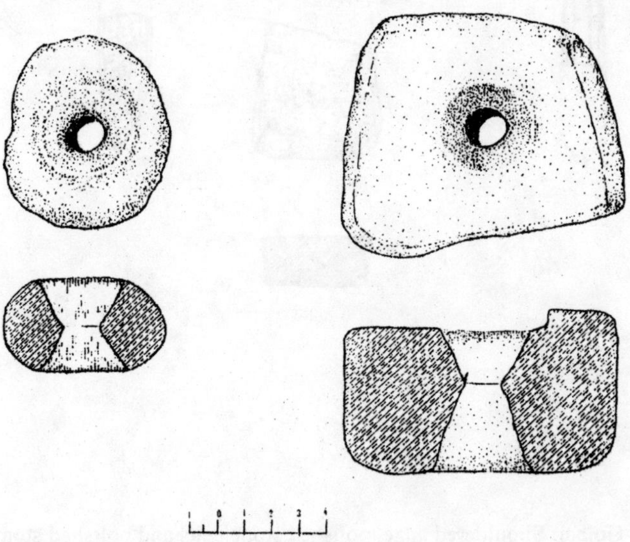

Fig. 33 : Perforated stones from Jagati mound.
(After S. K. Kar)

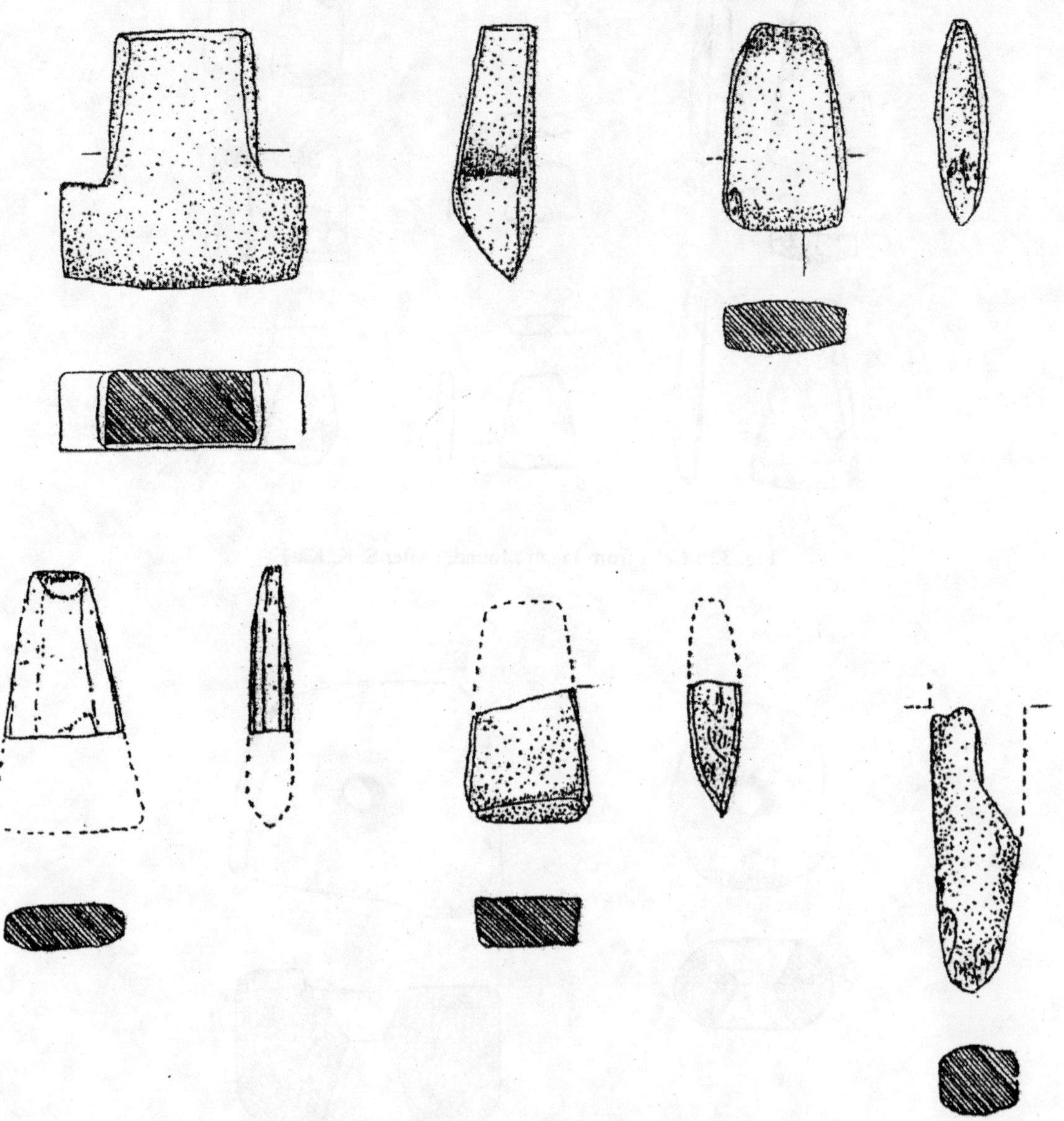

Fig. 34 : Golbai: Shouldered adze, polished stone celts and polished stone adze, Period IIa. (After B. K. Sinha)

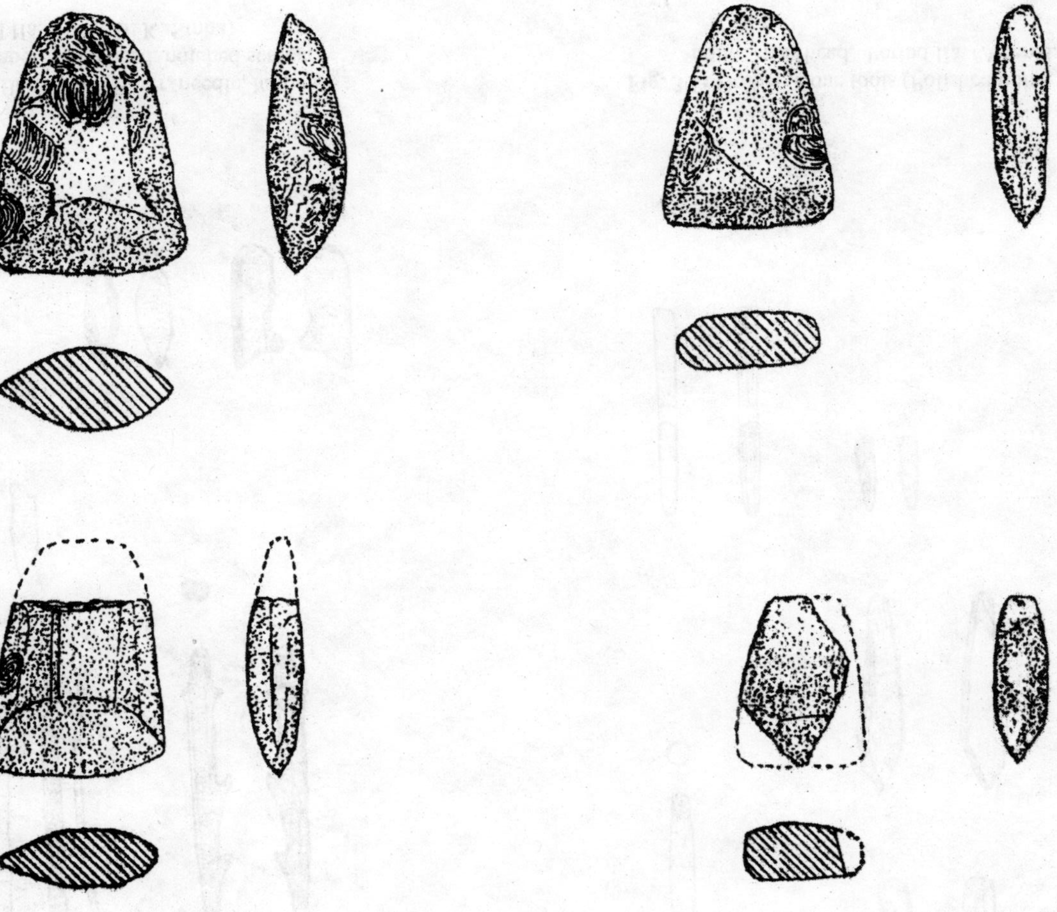

Fig. 35 : Golbai: Polished stone tools, Period IIa.
(After B. K. Sinha)

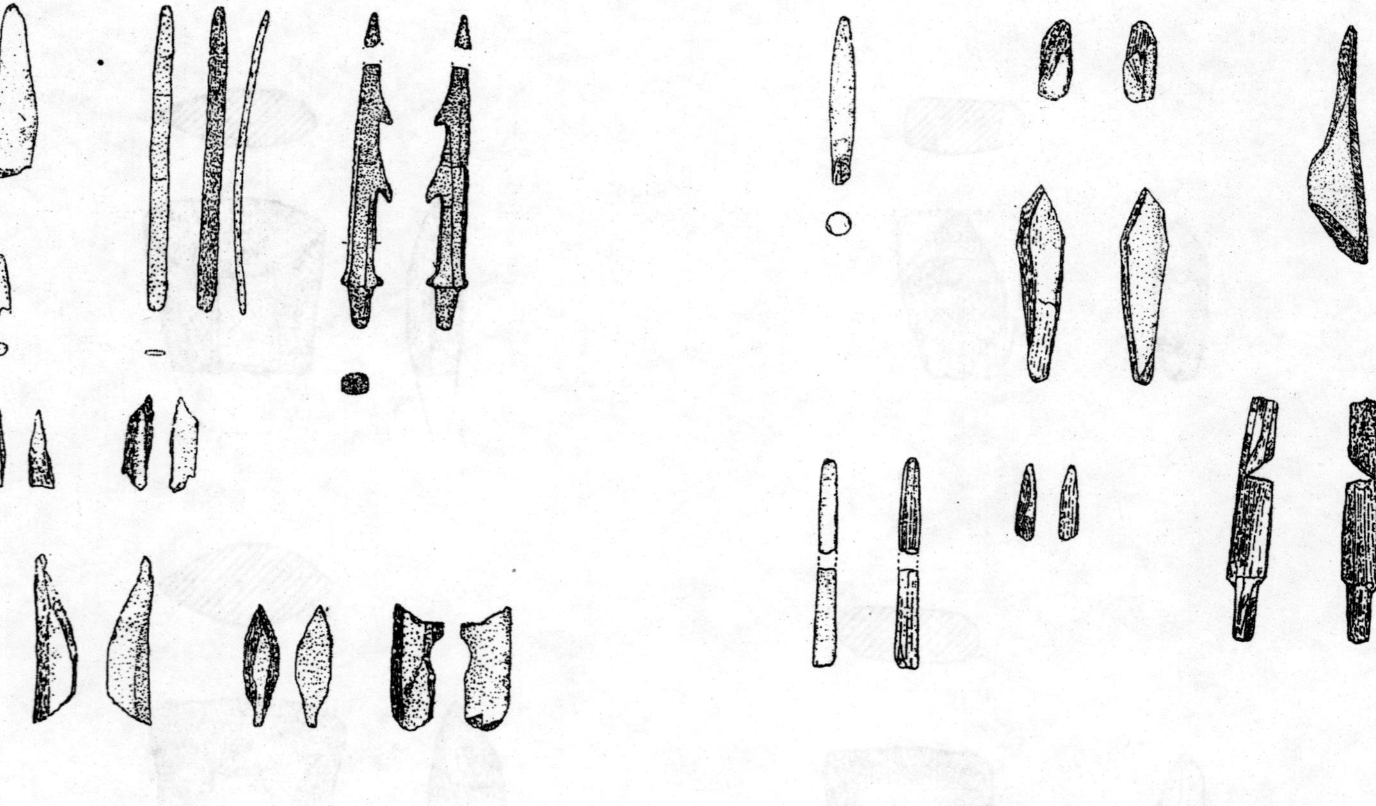

Fig. 36 : Golbai:Bone tools(Borer, needle, harpoon, point burin,Scraper, arrowhead, notched scraper. Period IIa. (After B. K. Sinha)

Fig. 37 : Golbai: Bone tools (Polished point, end scraper, awl, point, spearhead, Period IIa. (After B. K. Sinha)

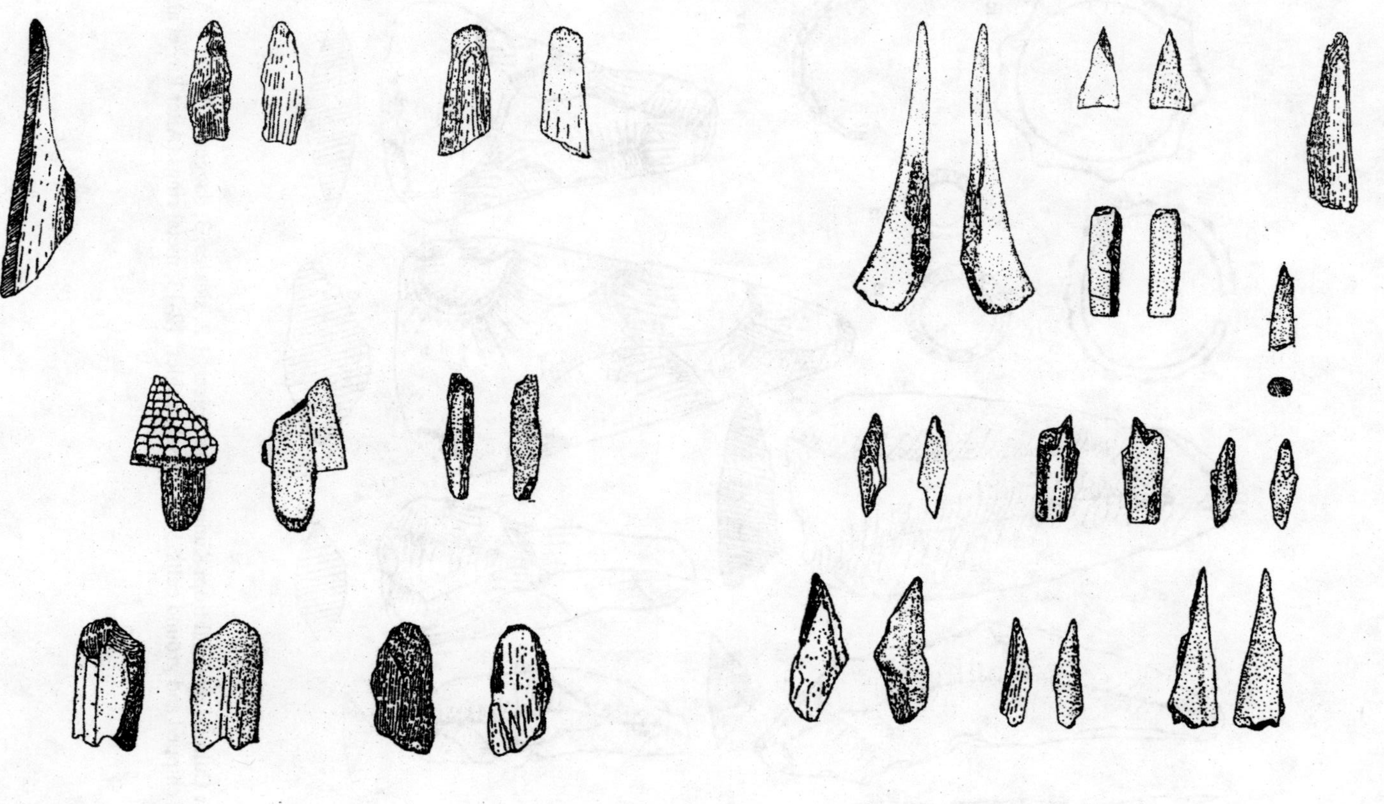

Fig. 38 : Golbai: Bone tools(Alw, point, burin, end scraper), Period IIa. (After B. K. Sinha)

Fig. 39 : Golbai: Bone tools(Awl, point, burin, borer), Period IIa, (After B. K. Sinha)

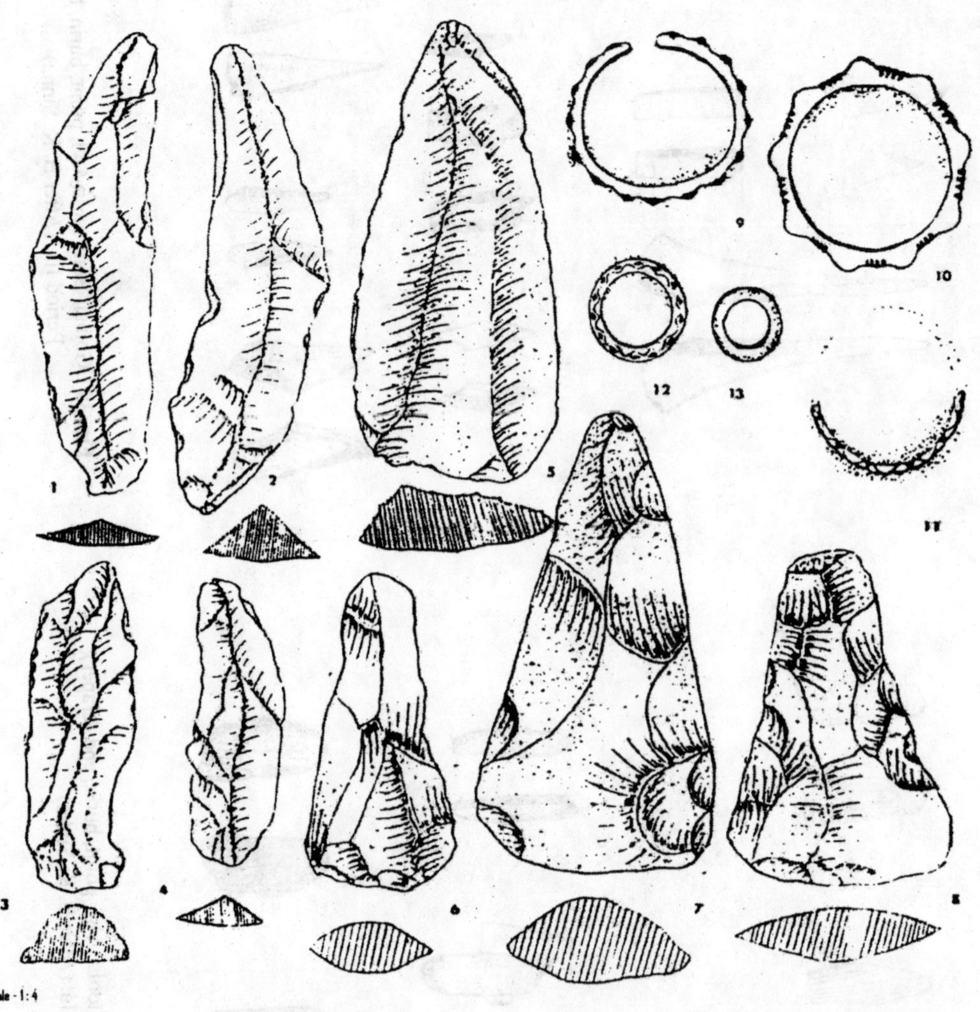

Fig. 40 : Cultural material from Kunar. Stone objects 1-2, sickles; 3, dagger; 4, knife; 5, celt of flake; 6-8, chipped and ground celts; 9-11, metal bangles; 12-13, metal rings.(After Ray et al, 2000)

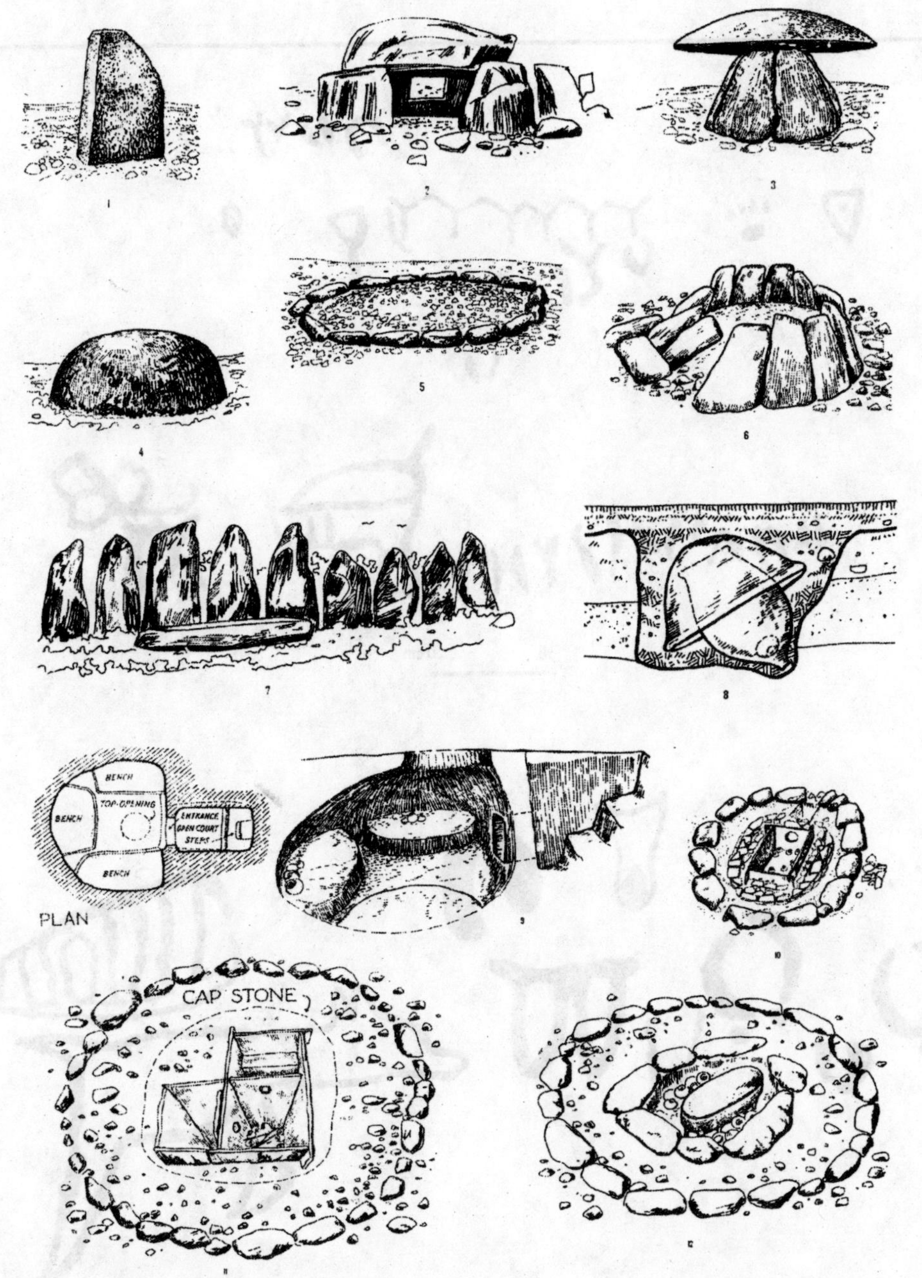

Fig. 41: Megalithic types: 1, menhir-Kerala; 2, dolmenoid cist-Tamil Nadu; 3, topi-kal; 4, Kundan-kudai(or hood stone)- Kerala; 5, cairn-circle-Tamil Nadu; 6, multiple hood-stone-Kerala; 7, alignment (Series of menhirs)-Assam; 8, urn-burial-Tamil Nadu; 11, rock-cut cave-Kerala; 12, portholecist-Karnataka; 13, trancepted cist and 14, sarcophagus within a dolmenoid cist-TamilNadu. (Encyclopedia of Indian Archaeology. Fig.20-21)

Fig. 42 : Vikramkhol, Engravings.
(After S. Pradhan)

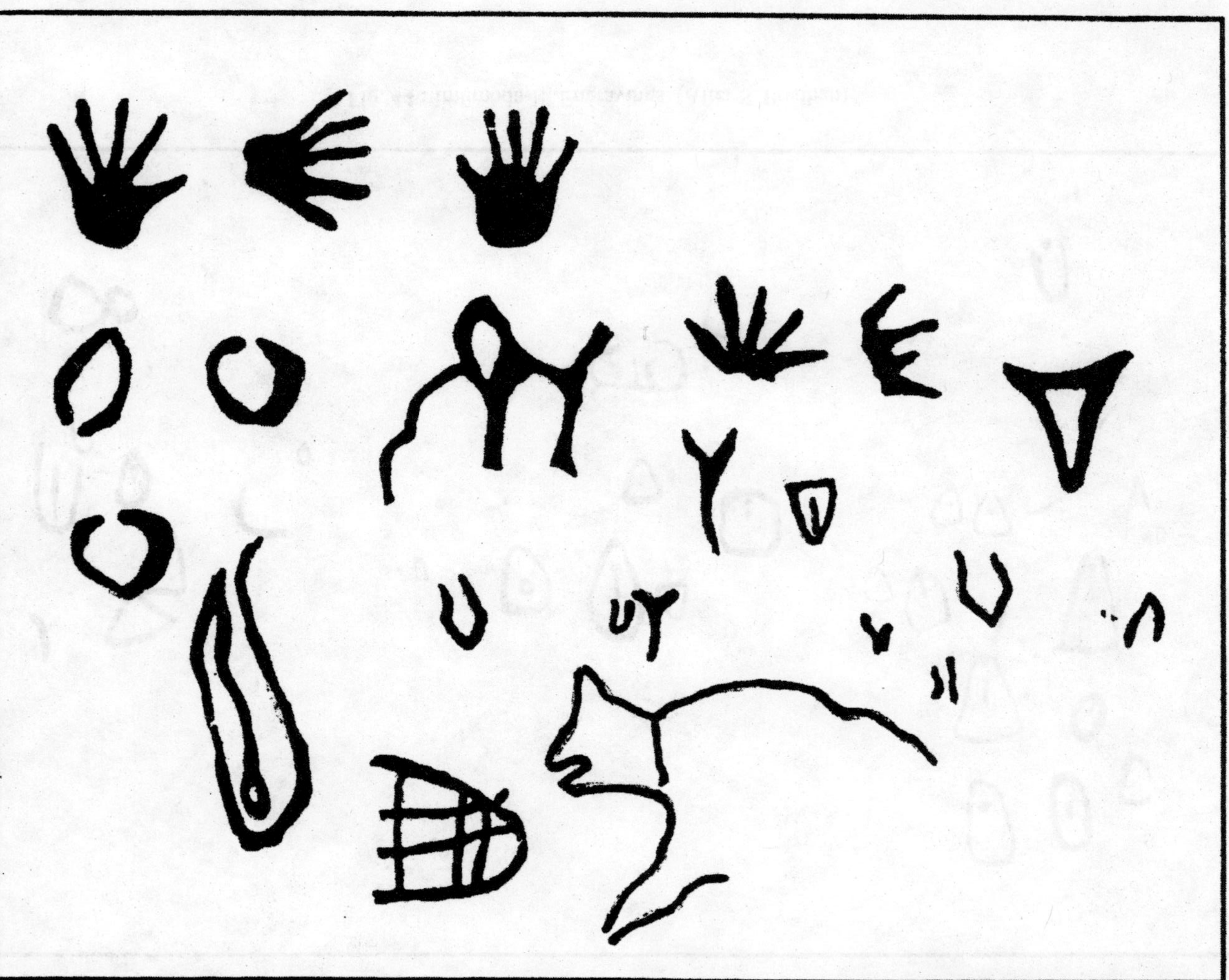

Fig. 43 : Ulapgarh Ushakuthi, Engravings. (After S. Pradhan)

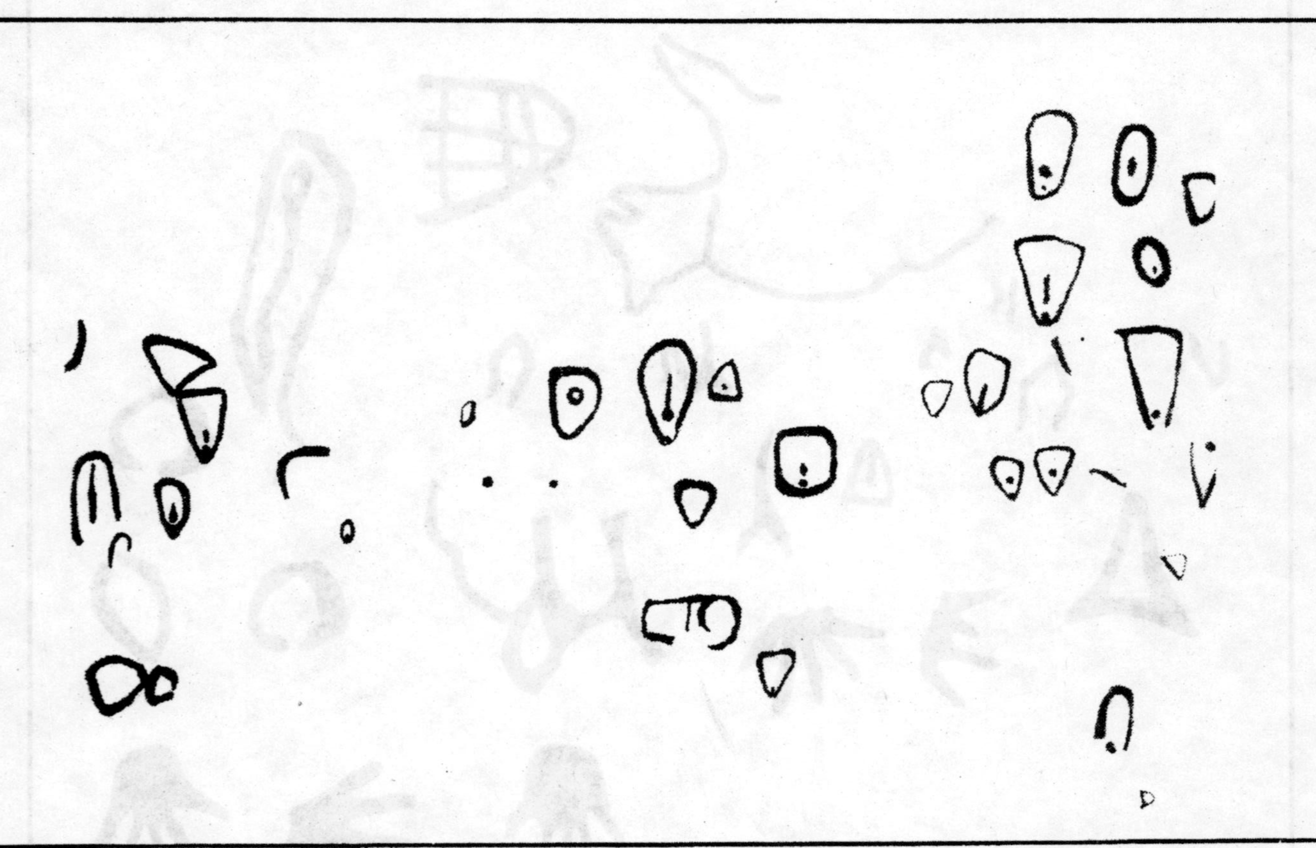

Fig. 44 : Imlimoda-II, Engravings. (After S. Pradhan)

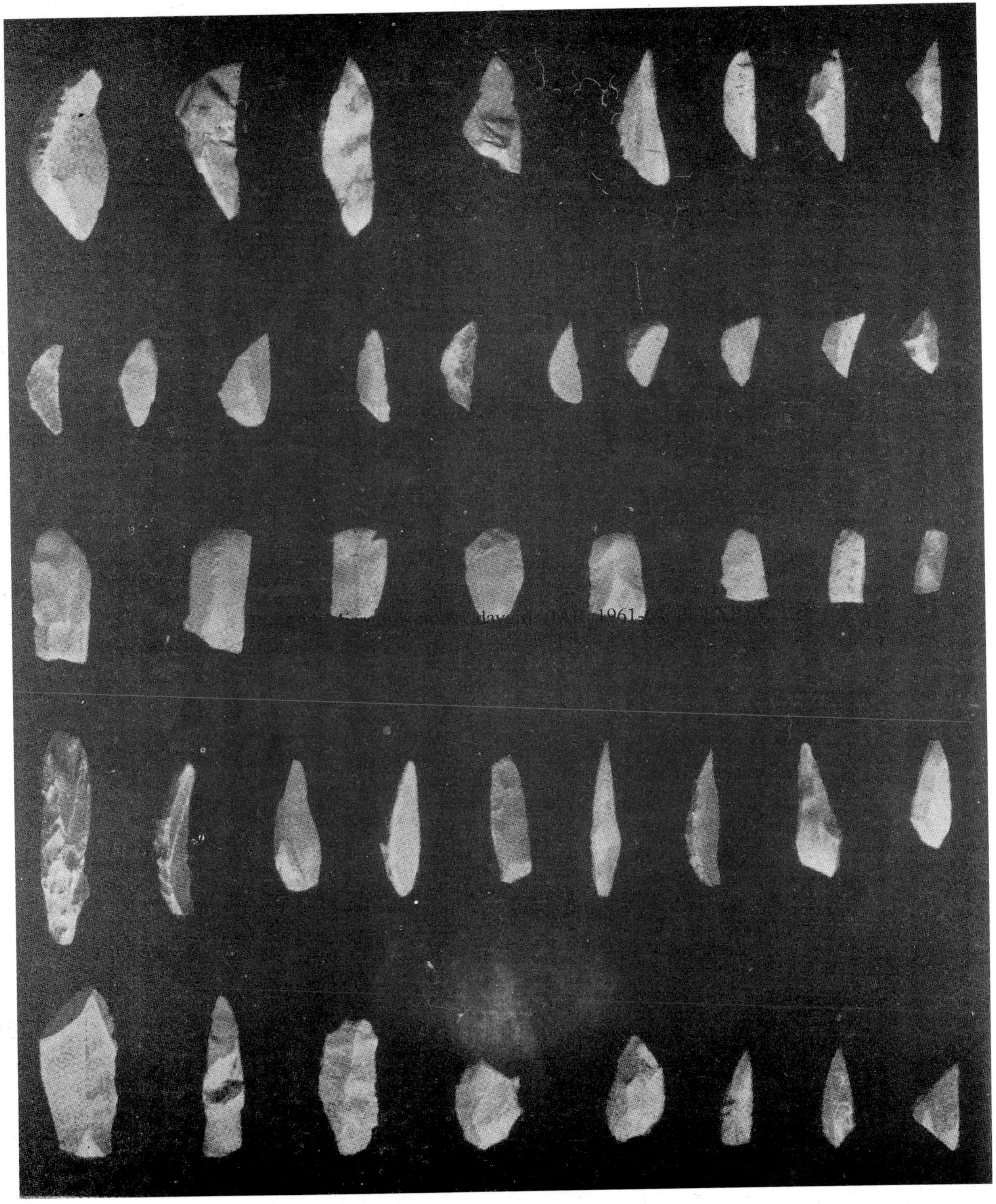

Plate 1 : Microliths from Udaygiri. (IAR: 1961-62, Pl. LXB)

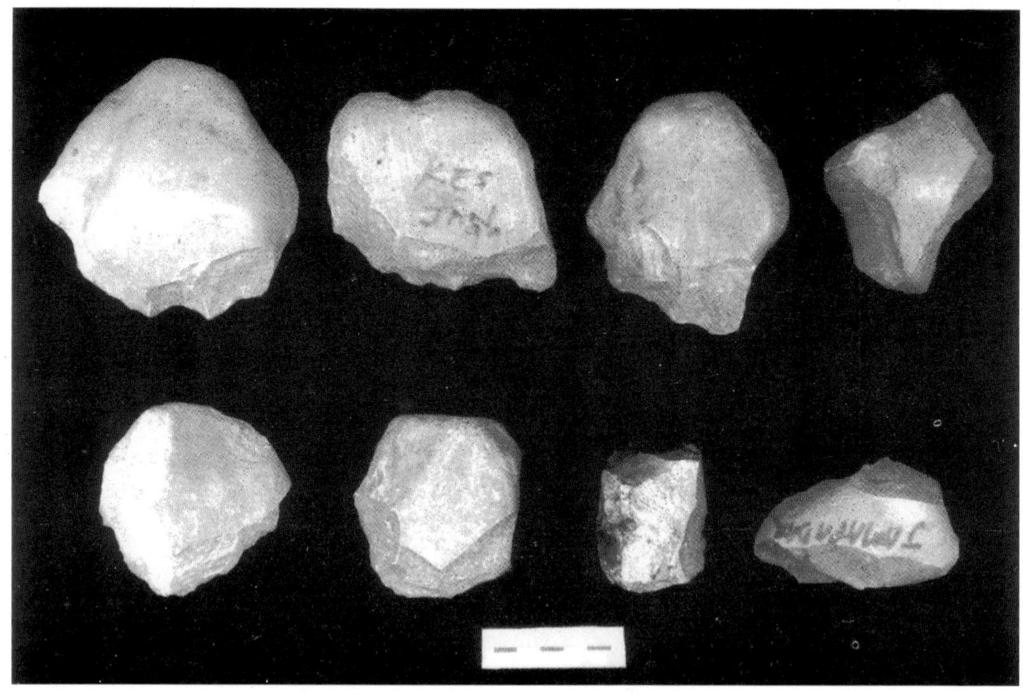

Plate 2 : Mesolithic Heavy Duty Tools.

Plate 3A : A Mesolithic site in Boudh District. (Curtsey B. Tripathy)

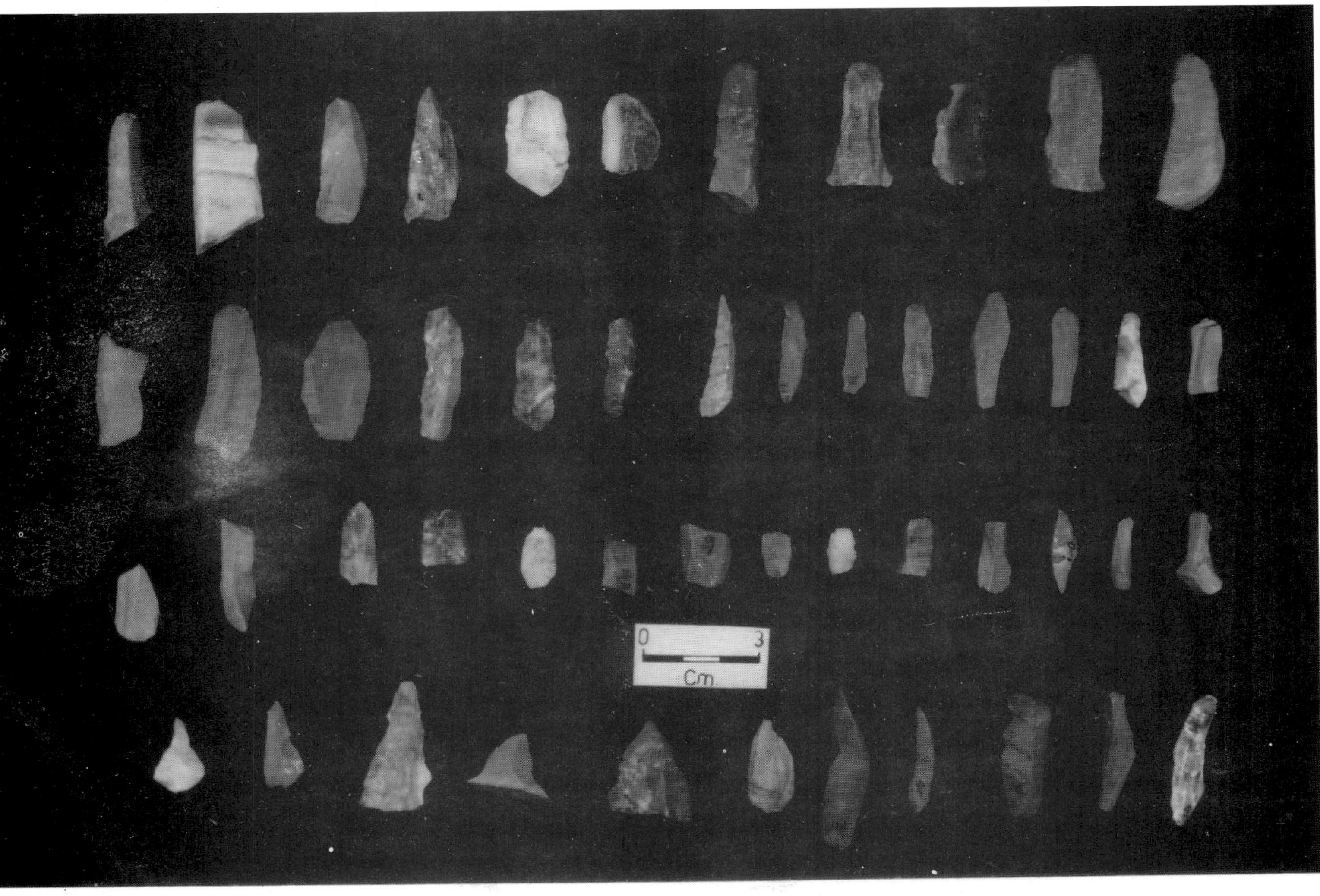

Plate 3B : Mesolithic Tools from Boudh. (Curtsey B.Tripathy)

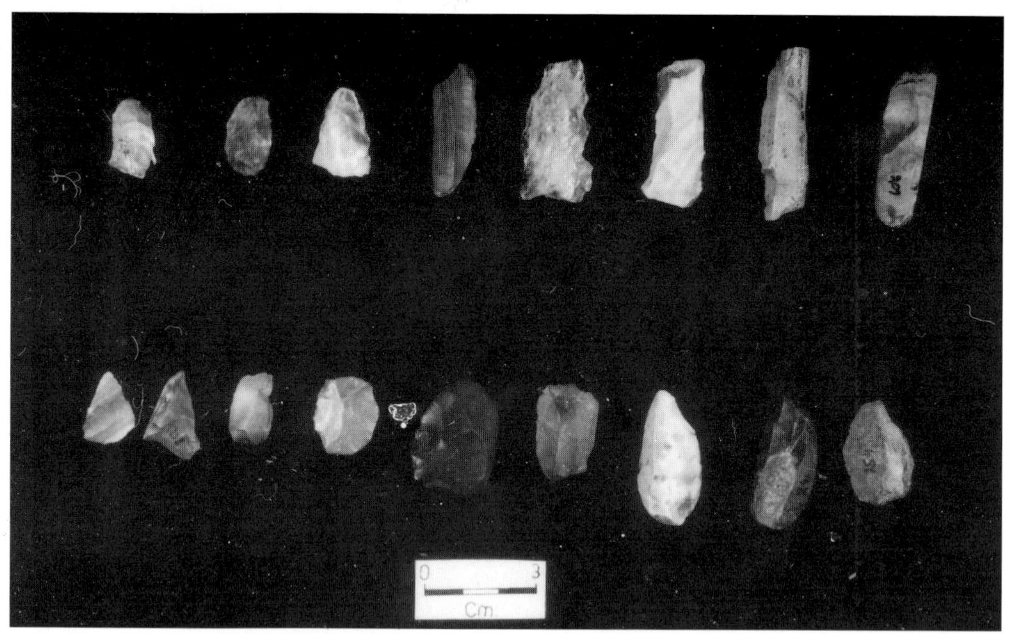

Plate 4 : Mesolithic Tools from Boudh. (Curtsey B.Tripathy)

Plate 5 : Golbai, Polished stone celts and adzes, Period-IIa. (After B. K. Sinha)

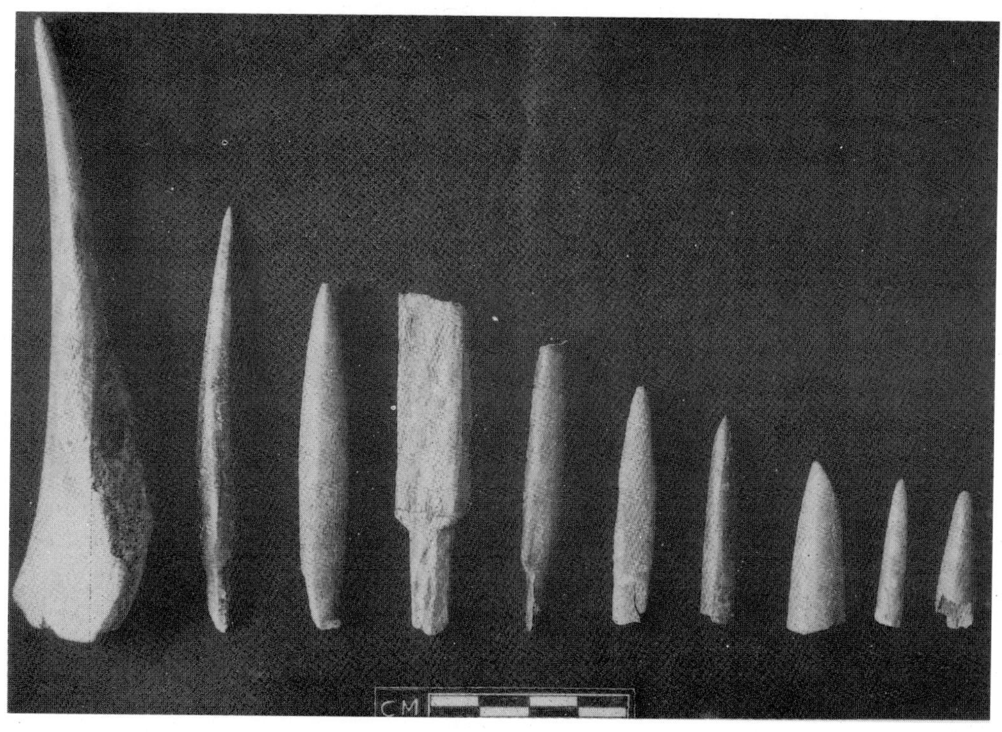

Plate 6 : Golbai, Bone arrowheads, Period-IIa. (After B. K. Sinha)

Plate 7 : Golbai, Spearhead, Period-IIa. (After B. K. Sinha)

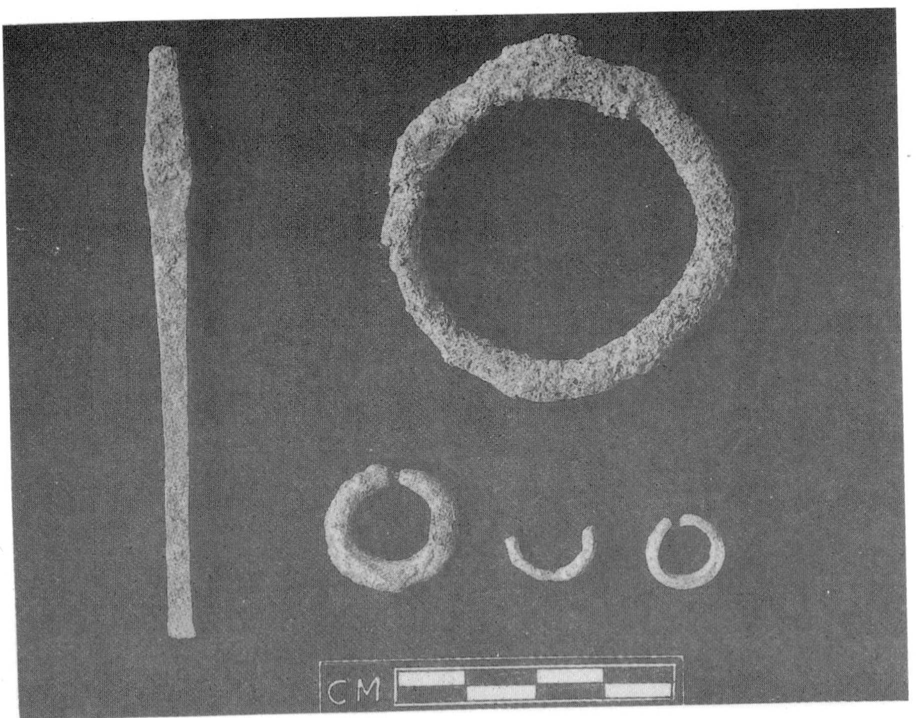

Plate 8 : Golbai, Copper objects, Period-IIa. (After B. K. Sinha)

Plate 9 : Golbai, Remains of a female child burial, Period-IIa.
(After B. K. Sinha)

Plate 10 : Golbai, Stone, iron and bone celts and adzes, Period-IIb. (After B. K. Sinha)

Plate 11 : Vikramkhol, Paintings and engravings. (After S. Pradhan)

Plate 12 : Ulapgarh Ushakuthi.Paintings. (After S. Pradhan)

Plate 13 : Rail Ushakuthi X, Engravings. (After S. Pradhan)

Plate 14 : Chormoda, Cupules. (After S. Pradhan)

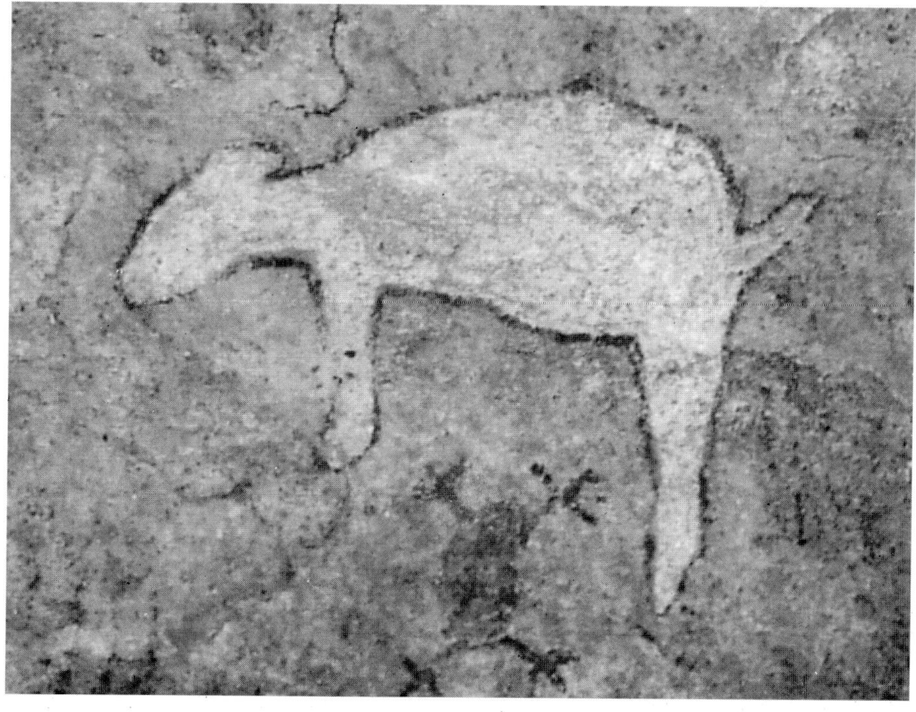

Plate 15 : Lekhamoda IV, Painting of Goat. (After S. Pradhan)

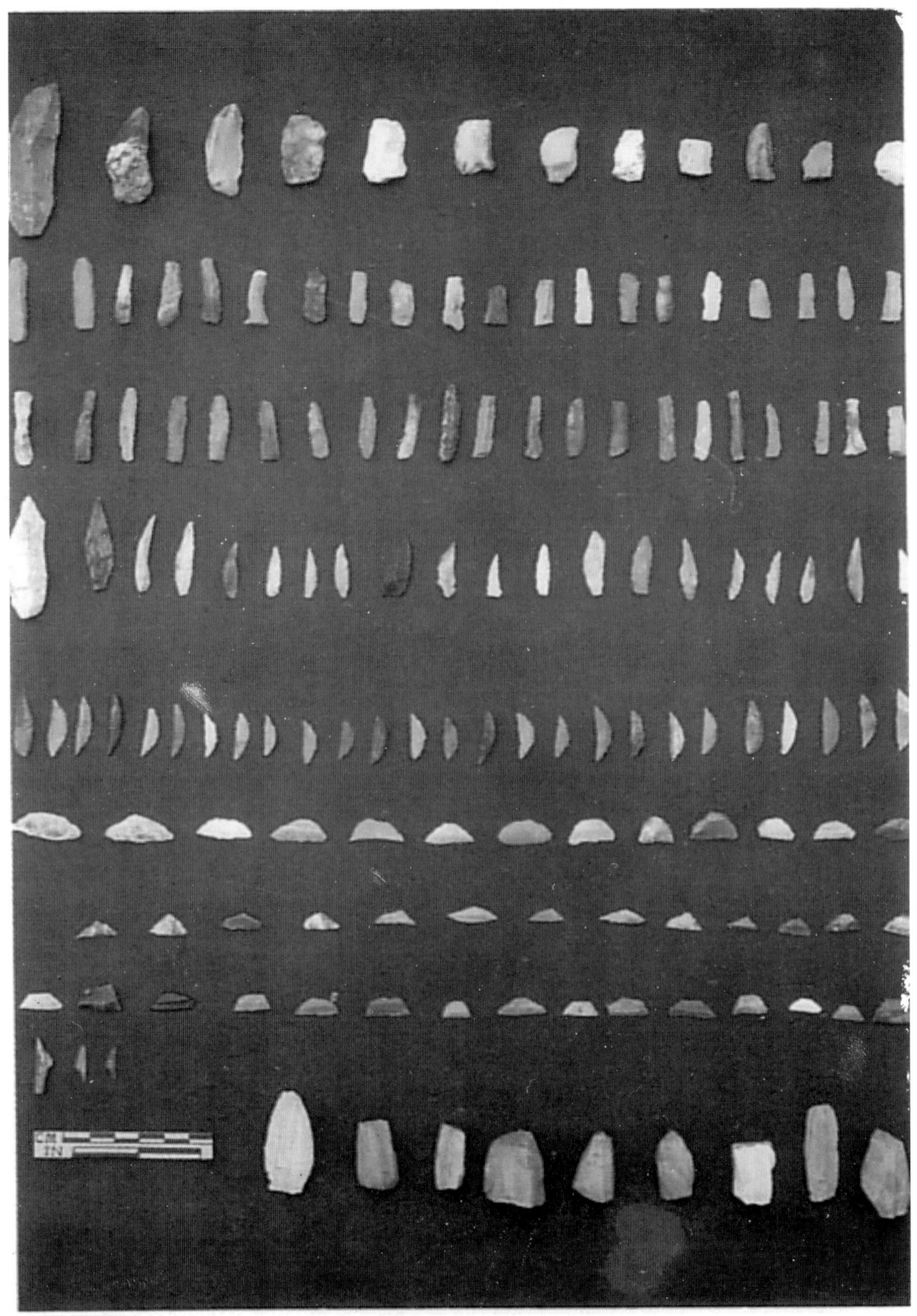

Plate 16 : Lekhamoda VI, Microliths. (S. Pradhan, 2001)

Plate 17 : Ushakuthi II, Broom pattern paintings. (After S. Pradhan)